Gerry Adams

The eldest of ten brothers and sisters, Gerry Adams was born in 1948 and grew up in the Catholic Falls Road area of West Belfast. He chronicles the history of that part of Belfast and details his early years in his book *Falls Memories: A Belfast Life* (Roberts Rinehart, 1994). After leaving school in the sixties, Adams joined Sinn Féin and went to work in a bar to support himself while he became more and more active in politics, leading several sit-ins, protests, and marches.

The introduction of internment by the British government in 1971 saw his father, an uncle, and two cousins imprisoned in Long Kesh without trial. In 1972, he himself was arrested and interned on the *Maidstone*, a prison ship anchored in Belfast Lough, a 'stinking, cramped, unhealthy, brutal and oppressive sardine can' as he described it in his book written at the time, *Cage Eleven* (Sheridan Square, 1993).

During internment, in common with several hundred other republican prisoners held without charge, he was made to endure endless interrogations, beatings and torture. To this day his health suffers from these episodes. He was released and subsequently re-interned, serving over four years in prison without trial. He spent those years studying and writing, and on release began to focus his energies on shaping Sinn Féin into a viable political force, and moving it into electoral politics.

Adams became president of Sinn Féin in 1983, and was elected to the British Parliament in the same year. Even though he refused to take his seat, since it required him to pledge allegiance to the Queen, he remained an MP until 1993, when 'tactical' voting by unionists in his constituency allowed the SDLP candidate to win his seat. With the Sinn Féin share of the vote amongst nationalists in Northern Ireland now exceeding forty percent, he is expected to regain the seat in the next election, if and when it is held.

Adams's ongoing dialogue with John Hume, the leader of the other major nationalist party in Northern Ireland, led to the 1993 Irish Peace Initiative, which lays the foundation for developing a peace process towards a united Ireland.

Granted a visa to visit the United States in February 1994 by President Clinton despite the objections of the British government, Adams appeared on several national television programs, including the Larry King Show, Pozner Donahue and the Charlie Rose Show.

This book is dedicated to the men, women and children who struggle for Irish freedom, and to freedom fighters everywhere.

FREE IRELAND

Towards a
Lasting Peace

GERRY ADAMS

President of Sinn Féin

Roberts Rinehart Publishers

Published by Roberts Rinehart Publishers,
Post Office Box 666, Niwot, Colorado 80544

Copyright © 1986, 1994 by Gerry Adams

Introduction © 1994 by Jack Van Zandt

Typesetting by Red Barn Publishing, Skeagh,
Skibbereen, Co. Cork, Republic of Ireland

Set in Garamond 11/13

ISBN 1–879373–95–3

Library of Congress catalog card number 94–66264

Verses from *The Rhythm of Time* reproduced
by permission of The Bobby Sands' Trust.

The electoral map of Northern Ireland reproduced
by permission of *The Irish Nation.*

First published in Ireland in 1986 by
Brandon Book Publishers Ltd.

Printed in the United States of America

Contents

There's an inner thing in every man,
Do you know this thing my friend?
It has withstood the blows of a million years,
And will do so to the end.

It is found in every light of hope,
It knows no bounds nor space,
It has risen in red and black and white,
It is there in every race.

It lights the dark of this prison cell,
It thunders forth its might,
It is 'the undauntable thought', my friend,
The thought that says 'I'm right!'

From 'The Rhythm of Time'
Bobby Sands, H-Block, Long Kesh Prison Camp

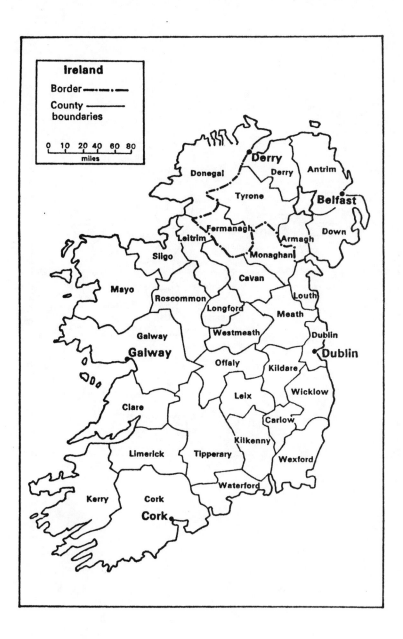

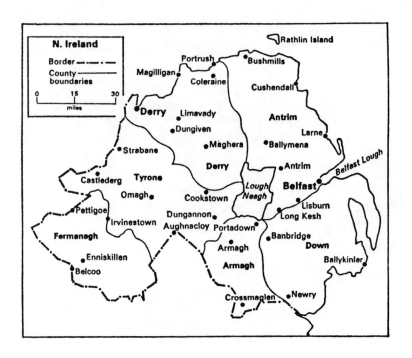

Introduction

Gerry Adams has a mouth, but he may not speak. Gerry Adams has a voice, yet he cannot be heard. Gerry Adams is subject to a system of justice which is based, like our own, on due process, yet in the past he has been tortured, beaten and imprisoned by the government without charge or trial. Gerry Adams is the democratically elected president of a legal political party, twice chosen to serve in a national parliament, but he is not allowed to travel to that nation's capital.

Censorship and internal exile have long been the fate of the critics of tyranny and unjust societies, and torture the tool of these states for extracting dictated 'confessions.' Therefore, you might be forgiven for assuming that Gerry Adams was a citizen of the old Soviet Union or a victim of the apartheid system in South Africa. Shockingly, this is not so, for Gerry Adams is an Irish citizen living in Ireland under the rule of Great Britain, a country considered to be one of the world's foremost democracies and one of our closest allies in the international community.

For Americans, with our rights to free speech and free expression protected by our Constitution, it is disturbing to discover that most of the rest of the world does not enjoy these 'inalienable' rights. We are used to hearing all and any views on issues expressed freely by those concerned, even if they happen to be crackpots or politically naive. We trust our fellow citizens to listen to all views, think for themselves, and make a decision that they feel is the correct one for them under the circumstances. This formation of public opinion is the foundation of our democracy.

Unfortunately, things aren't so simple in Britain, especially with respect to their 'colonial statelet' of the Six Counties of Northern Ireland. There is no absolute guarantee of rights in Britain as they have no Bill of Rights, only the precedent of common law, much of which is derived from the colonial era. Therefore, it is easy for Parliament to enact legislation for the purpose of the suspension of basic human rights. Successive British governments in recent years have used these powers to keep former civil servants from revealing embarrassing information about government activities, for instance, as well as using them to suspend civil rights in Northern Ireland.

This was recently evident in the Thatcher government's botched attempt to keep a book by a former spy (*Spycatcher*, by Peter Wright) from being published in Britain, while it was available in virtually every other country in the world. These powers also led to the suppression of an important and condemning official report on the British government's so called 'shoot-to-kill' policy in Northern Ireland (the Stalker report).

Outside of the censorship question, undoubtedly the most effective instrument for suspension of civil rights in Britain and Northern Ireland is the Prevention of Terrorism Act enacted by the British Parliament in 1973. This allows the police to detain and question suspects for seven days without charge, due process, or legal representation. As a result, there have been numerous instances of human rights abuses and cases of torture administered by the British police to extract confessions which are often in turn the only evidence used to convict alleged terrorists in court. This was recently highlighted in the popular film *In the Name of the Father*, but, according to Adams (backed up by Amnesty International Reports), these famous cases of miscarriages of justice are only the tip of the iceberg.

Another section of the Prevention of Terrorism Act provides for the implementation of an 'exclusion order' whereby named individuals can be banned from travelling to other parts of the United Kingdom if the British government so wishes. In what amounts to internal exile, victims of this provision are able to freely move about Northern Ireland, but are unable to go to England, Scotland or Wales. This is like banning a citizen of Utah from crossing the Rockies and visiting Kansas. The absurdity of this provision of the Act was recently evident to Americans when Gerry Adams had to travel to a 'foreign country' (the Republic of Ireland) to catch a flight to New York because he was banned from changing planes in London, the supposed capital of the statelet he lives in.

Gerry Adams and many other known republicans have been victims of the Prevention of Terrorism Act. However, many of the people detained under the Act have been ordinary Irish people picked at random. It is interesting to note that, out of the thousands that have been detained under the Act, only a very tiny number have ever been tried and even fewer convicted of anything at all.

Adams has also been the victim of 'internment.' This practice, currently not in force, is unique in Britain in its application to the Six Counties of Northern Ireland. What it amounts to is long-term imprisonment in 'concentration camps' without due process. In other words, anyone suspected of being involved in 'terrorist' activities (as opposed to ordinary run-of-the mill murderers, rapists, and the like) can be detained in prison indefinitely without charge, trial, or any other due process, and in the absence of any acceptable evidence whatsoever.

The British government tells the world that 'Gerry Adams is a terrorist.' Yet, except in the case of his attempt to escape from Long Kesh prison during one of his internments, Adams has never been tried or convicted of *any* offences, nor has any real evidence that connects him to 'terrorism' ever been produced. So while on the one hand the British government tells the American government that Gerry Adams is a dangerous terrorist and shouldn't be given a visa, he walks around the streets of the Six Counties a free man (albeit in 'internal exile') with no convictions or charges pending.

Internal exile, imprisonment without due process, torture, and censorship. Gerry Adams remains a victim of all these shameful practices. Adams has health problems from the physical abuse meted out to him by the British over the years. He was also critically wounded by loyalist gunmen who attacked him as he left a court in Belfast a few years ago, and his home has been bombed by loyalist paramilitaries. But these glaring injustices and hardships that Adams has suffered through his many years as an active republican would be easier to bear if he was allowed to freely put his own views with his own voice to his fellow citizens. As he puts it, 'the British have stolen my voice' through systematic censorship and suspension of his basic human right to free expression.

The absurdity of the method of censorship employed in the case of Adams (and other republicans) would be comical if it wasn't so tragic in its consequences. His face is allowed to be seen on television while his mouth moves, but his voice cannot be transmitted. This leads the British media to the unfortunate device of having an actor read his exact words as he mouths them. This absurdity transforms into a very important psychological event if you consider that the sound of the actor's voice can easily be manipulated to give Adams a menacing tone, or made shrill, high-pitched and inciteful. In fact, it is such a revelation when you do hear Adams's voice in person, that you wonder if this really is the same person whose face you have seen for so many years.

Another note of absurdity is that while Adams's fellow citizens are deprived of hearing him speak for himself, people in the rest of the world have heard him on many occasions. However, even this is less important then the fact that censorship has allowed the British and Adams's political opponents in Northern Ireland to turn him into whatever creature they like. It appears that, unlike America, British citizens aren't trusted to hear all voices and then make up their own mind freely. They are told what to think by their government, and aren't allowed to hear Adams's view, even if they want to.

As Adams rightly points out, most people in Britain never hear an Irish republican spokesperson because of censorship. So, how do people know what they stand for? There is clearly more to solving the problem than the simple removal of censorship—there are 'twenty-five years of British misinformation and disinformation' to deal with. But, as Adams also points out, at least by ending censorship, there is 'the possibility of having a real debate on the issues which takes in the views of the entire community in Northern Ireland.'

As an American living in Ireland for many years, I consider myself to be reasonably informed as to the situation and personalities involved in the conflict in Northern Ireland. I have my own views which I keep to myself and have never been outspoken on the issue. I do not actively support any one political party, and I am certainly against violence, whether perpetrated by the IRA, the UVF, or the British government. However, nothing in my experience of the situation prepared me for my first meeting with Gerry Adams in Belfast in preparation for the publication of this book.

As Americans who saw Adams on television during his visit to New York, in January 1994, will have seen for themselves, he is a polite, even-tempered, and soft-spoken man of very considerable intelligence. Despite the necessary constraints of his own security measures and the circumstances in which he is forced to live, he is surprisingly relaxed and his easygoing and hospitable manner immediately put me and my assistant editor at ease. Good humour was in abundance at our first meeting, and after a bit of 'slagging' back and forth (he teased me about the 'West Cork technology' of my little tape recorder), we could have quite naturally adjourned to a pub in the Falls Road for the rest of the day. Alas, loftier goals kept us from the few pints.

Over the course of my first meeting with Adams, I was able to dispel the myths and transform the image I had of him which had been established by years of listening to anti-Adams propaganda. However, the most arresting thing about him is his natural and prodigious intellectual ability. Armed with formidable analytical and rhetorical powers and a vast array of well reasoned ideas, Adams is nothing short of a philosopher. Born at another time or in another place, he might well be a professor of political philosophy in a major university, or perhaps a novelist exploring worlds of high ideals. Circumstances, however, have seen him become the formulater of modern Irish republican thought and therefore the intellectual descendant of Pearse and Connolly.

In *Free Ireland: Towards a Lasting Peace*, Gerry Adams weaves together strands of Irish history, and his own, as well as traditional, republican political and social philosophy, with current political considerations, into a powerful personal statement about modern Ireland. He concludes the book with his scenario for developing a viable peace process, and his vision for a future united Ireland. This is the most important statement about modern Irish republicanism since the partition of Ireland, and as it comes from the president of a political party with considerable support amongst the Irish nationalist community, it will have to be taken into account by anyone wishing to formulate an informed view of the Irish situation.

As the old saying goes, you never really know a person until you step inside their shoes and walk around for a while. Working with Gerry Adams to create an American edition of his book has afforded me the unique opportunity to do just that. And I can say unequivocally that Gerry Adams is a decent, sensitive and thoughtful human being who is passionate about achieving a lasting peace in Ireland and helping to create a better world for his fellow citizens. I am proud to know him as a friend and, in publishing his book in North America, equally proud to help him regain his voice.

I hope Americans will read this book and, along with the views of other parties involved in the conflict, take its contents into consideration when making up their own minds about how lasting peace should come to Ireland. Gerry Adams would wish for no more and hope for no less.

Jack Van Zandt, Publisher
March 17, 1994

1

Political Origins

> The development of democracy in Ireland
> has been smothered by the Union.
> *James Connolly*

IN 1961, THE last of the republicans interned during the
IRA's border campaign of the fifties were released. For most
of them it was a time for counting the cost and for adjusting
to life outside. There were no fanfares as they returned home:
imprisonment then, unlike today, evoked little active community
support or popularity. There were no coherent support organizations and the internees and their families were isolated.

I was thirteen years old and blissfully unaware of internment,
the IRA campaign and political matters in general. For me it was a
time of school exams—I had recently passed my 'Eleven Plus'—of
hurling matches and long summer holidays. My father had just
returned from working in England and he and my mother were
contemplating emigrating to Australia; uncles and aunts were
already scattered in Canada, Dublin and England.

A few of the released internees set about picking up the pieces of
a scattered and demoralized organization; in 1961 the total
strength of the Belfast IRA was twenty-four, their total armaments
were two short-arms. Republicanism had not died, but it had suffered a substantial defeat, and, amongst those who remained active,
a process of reassessment was begun while a low level of political
organization commenced.

Wolfe Tone committees were established by republicans
throughout Ireland to mark the 200th anniversary, in June 1963,

1

of Tone's birth. Theobald Wolfe Tone, the founder of Irish republicanism, was a Protestant barrister who, influenced by the
American and French revolutions, set up the Society of United
Irishmen in 1791 to unite 'Protestant, Catholic and Dissenter' in
the cause of Irish independence, and was secretary to the Catholic
Committee which campaigned for civil rights for Catholics. He
attempted to gain French military support for the fight for independence, but was captured in 1798 and sentenced to death. He
cheated his captors by killing himself before the sentence could be
carried out.

At the commemoration in Belfast, an internal controversy provoked a local leadership crisis in the republican movement. It was
the practice of republicans to carry the Irish tricolour on parades,
despite the fact that the flag, as the symbol of Irish nationalism,
was banned under the Flags and Emblems Act (1954). The failure
to carry it in June 1963 in defiance of the ban sparked off a period
of infighting, at the end of which a Belfast leadership supportive of
Cathal Goulding, Chief of Staff of the IRA since the previous year,
was firmly in control.

The tricolour played a role too in bringing me into politics.
During the Westminster elections in October 1964, rioting
occurred after a tricolour was displayed in the window of Sinn
Féin's election office in Divis Street in Belfast. Ian Paisley objected
loudly to the display of the flag and threatened to march on Divis
Street and remove it within two days if it hadn't been removed by
then. The next day a force of RUC men broke down the door of
the office and removed the flag. Two days of intense rioting followed and the republicans, accompanied by a large crowd of local
people, replaced the flag, only to have it removed again by RUC
men wielding pick-axes. Three hundred and fifty RUC men using
armoured cars and water-cannons and wearing military helmets
launched an attack on the Falls, and fifty civilians and twenty-one
RUC ended up in hospital. The government had responded to
pressure from Paisley and had provoked a violent reaction from the
Catholic working class. It was a stark reminder of where the balance of power lay in the Six Counties.

I was in school at the time, but the Divis Street events concentrated my mind on politics. I already possessed a vague sense of
discontent, and the naked display of state violence against the

people of the Falls made me feel I did not want merely to stand by looking on. I found myself spending a few evenings in the Felons Association rooms on the Falls Road folding election material for Liam McMillan, the Sinn Féin candidate. Despite, or maybe because of, all the republican candidates losing their election deposits, within a few months I joined Sinn Féin.

I suppose I was a member for about eighteen months before I realized what I was in at all. I had, after all, joined as a reaction to what had happened in Divis Street. This had had the effect of reawakening a sense of national consciousness which whetted my political appetite. I was eager to find out why things were as they were, and as I read those history books which were not on our school curriculum I became increasingly aware of the nature of the relationship between Ireland and Britain. Having reached the conclusion that this relationship was a colonial one, and having decided that it must be ended, I began with youthful innocence the task of ending it. My new-found knowledge dictated the logic that the British government had no right to govern any part of Ireland, that that right belonged to the Irish people and that we could surely govern ourselves in our own interests more efficiently than anyone else. All we had to do was to get rid of the British. With that I was, I felt, starting off on the right foot. I was to discover that I was a long way from fully understanding how we might get there.

I had a republican family background. My maternal grandfather, a prominent full-time trade union organizer on personal terms with both James Connolly and James Larkin, had worked for de Valera in the 1918 election; my paternal grandfather and his in-laws traced their republican involvement back to the Irish Republican Brotherhood (IRB). They reared republican sons and daughters who included my mother and my father who was shot and wounded by the RUC and imprisoned in the 1940s. In spite ' of all this, I was no more politically conscious than many of my contemporaries, but the everyday aspects of our situation were obvious enough: bad housing, poverty, political structures with which we could not identify and, above all, the endemic, structural unemployment. Many of my contemporaries left, complaining that the sectarian state where everything was rigged against them from the start was no place for a decent life; others reckoned they would stick it out and see if maybe they couldn't bring about some improvements.

I decided to stick it out. I was never in any doubt that I would. I loved the city of Belfast, its streets, its hills, its people; it was the world I knew and I had no intention of being forced out of my own place. I was also naive, like most of my generation, and thought that a few rational, sensible changes could easily be made which would improve the quality of life and bring about equal opportunities for all.

That sense of possibility was what lay behind my decision to become involved in political activism. The options were clear: you could emigrate; you could stay and adopt an attitude of passivity which would hopefully get you by; or you could get involved in trying to change things. Of course, I had absolutely no idea then where this would lead me or how events in the Six Counties would develop; none of us did. We were certain only of one thing: the injustice of the system could not go unchallenged. It was wrong. Irish national self-determination was the only solution.

Sinn Féin was a very small organization then. It was also illegal. You could almost describe it as an incestuous association, made up as it was of members of a few spinal republican families, some of whom could trace their involvement right back through the fifties, forties, thirties and twenties to the Fenians and the Irish Republican Brotherhood (IRB) and perhaps even beyond. There was a small number of young people—mostly from republican backgrounds like myself—a larger number of much older people, and a middle group of people who had been active in the 1950s; that is, people who had been imprisoned then.

The mid-sixties was a period of turmoil in the republican movement. Following the failure of the fifties campaign, there was a major rethink. The impetus for debate came from the leadership, but the need for reassessment was naturally apparent in the organization as a whole. In Belfast, we were picking up an outer ripple of a wave which was centered at national leadership level in Dublin. Accordingly, several developments were taking place more or less simultaneously both inside and outside the movement.

The Wolfe Tone Societies, formed in 1963, had become a meeting point for republicans and socialists, for Irish language enthusiasts and communists. They held occasional seminars and, while little actual work was done, the societies in Dublin, Cork and Belfast provided a platform for ideas and an important gathering point for anti-imperialist opinion makers.

This was set against a political background in the Six Counties which was characterized, on the nationalist side, by low-level social justice campaigning by individuals and small groups, most notably the Dungannon-based Campaign for Social Justice. The Dungannon people documented instances of discrimination and briefed the London-based Connolly Association, its *Irish Democrat* newspaper and a minority element in the British Labour Party, based around Kevin McNamara MP.

Despite this, the unionists ran the Six County state exactly as they wished. And as long as British interests were safeguarded there was no British interference. Apart from some of the more obvious features, 'Northern Ireland' was a police state similar to South Africa's apartheid system. It was a one-party state, 'a Protestant parliament for a Protestant people.' Efforts to change this by physical force activity, by publicizing the injustices or by the development of a party political alternative had failed. There were none of the usual manifestations of normal class politics; partition and sectarianism ensured that this was the case. Indeed, I came into politics just as the Northern Ireland Labour Party (NILP), which had enjoyed some popularity with electoral gains in 1958 and 1962, was poised to commit political suicide on the issue of whether swings in public parks should be chained up on Sundays.

Nationalist opinion was represented by the conservative Nationalist Party, though in Belfast and Derry there were more radical tendencies which were to come to the surface again in the years ahead. The Nationalist Party was occasionally abstentionist, totally ineffectual and politically amateur. It did not satisfy the needs of the emerging, better-educated, Catholic middle class, a section of whom were committed to working for social and economic reforms within the Six County state. After some attempts to ginger-up and democratize the Nationalist Party through a National Unity association which was established by a group of Catholic graduates, the rival National Democratic Party was formed. This development, and Dublin premier Sean Lemass's acceptance of an invitation by Terence O'Neill, the new

5

Prime Minister, to visit him at Stormont, led to the Nationalist Party entering the Stormont parliament and becoming the official opposition.

The Lemass/O'Neill meeting was probably the first step by Fianna Fáil towards recognizing the Six County state. It flowed naturally from the North–South collaboration against the 1950s IRA campaign. This, together with the acceptance by the Nationalist Party of the institutions of the state and the emergence of a politicized Catholic middle class in the National Democratic Party, pointed the direction for the possible rehabilitation of the Six Counties. Those who sought such a reformation took succour from O'Neill's apparent willingness to apply to the state the democratic veneer necessary for the demands of the twentieth century. But, even at that stage, it was too little too late. 'No Surrender' unionism would not be so easily brought to heel and already in the opposite camp, within the radical anti-unionist ranks, the disparate ingredients involved in the slow fermentation of agitation activity were coming together.

In 1965, the first Republican Club was set up in Belfast in an attempt to break the ban on Sinn Féin. In the same year, republicans attempted to set up 'one man, one vote' committees. However, largely because of their lack of political acumen, allied to the hostility of the NILP, that initiative floundered, but only temporarily. Within the Wolfe Tone Societies, the question of civil rights in the Six Counties had become a recurring theme. In August 1966, they hosted a conference on civil rights in Maghera, County Derry, and another in November in Belfast, where republicans were enjoying a rise in local support. In 1963 they had been badly fragmented over the question of whether to carry the tricolour or not, in 1964 the flag was seized and rioting resulted, but, in 1966, West Belfast saw a massive display of tricolours and banners in the parade to celebrate the fiftieth anniversary of the Easter Rising.

This Easter commemoration received very widespread support from nationalists and involved cultural associations, trade unionists and social groups, and there were organizations, almost street committees, for the making of flags, bunting and banners. There was a one-day pageant at Casement Park in Andersonstown and a week of events including concerts and the like, and for the parade itself about 20,000 people turned out.

In the unionist press there were scare stories about the IRA, and the 'B' Specials were put on stand-by. Two or three Belfast republicans received prison sentences for organizing the parade, which was illegal, and in Newry a local republican was charged under the Flags and Emblems Act. At this time also, a major influence in moulding the political character of my generation of republicans was the popularization of the writings of the leaders of the 1916 Rising, in particular the writings of James Connolly. The process of political education within the republican ranks was enhanced by the availability of a flood of publications, and we began to develop a view of the class nature of the struggle and of the relationship between its social and national dimensions.

The slight raising of the political temperature at this time led to a number of small but dangerous developments. In the months before Easter, there were petrol bomb attacks on Catholic homes, shops and schools. In May, a Protestant woman died in a petrol bomb attack on the Catholic-owned public house next door to her home.

The following month Paisley led a demonstration against the General Assembly of the Presbyterian Church. What is sometimes forgotten is that he marched to that demonstration through Cromac Square, a Catholic area. The residents who attempted to block the road were very brutally dispersed by the RUC who returned the following night and renewed the assault. The IRA played a small part in organizing people against these RUC incursions, and one local republican activist received a prison sentence. A few weeks later, Peter Ward was killed and two other Catholics were wounded outside the Malvern Arms public house on the Protestant Shankill Road. On the same night, a loyalist gang had attempted to enter the home of Leo Martin, a prominent republican. It was also discovered that a Catholic man, John Scullion, who died on 11 June, had been shot on 27 May in Clonard Street by a loyalist terror gang. On 23 July, Paisleyite marchers rioted in Belfast city centre, attacking the Catholic-owned International Hotel and attempting to burn down a bookmaker's in Sandy Row which employed Catholics.

These incidents offered examples of the politico-religious relationship within loyalism. The crisis of loyalism, as always, was finding its expression in attacks on Catholic property and in the assassination of Catholic people. At the trial of three UVF members for the murder of Peter Ward, the RUC stated that Hugh McClean, one of the defendants, had said when charged, 'I am terribly sorry I ever heard of that man Paisley or decided to follow him.'

In the midst of the growing tensions, republicans were trying to come to terms with the needs of the struggle, the needs of the people and the relevance of the struggle to the people and to the Ireland of the 1960s. There have always been three tendencies within the republican movement: a militaristic and fairly apolitical tendency, a revolutionary tendency, and a constitutional tendency. Throughout the history of the movement, one or other of these has been in the ascendancy. Since partition, however, there had been no dominant tendency capable of giving proper and relevant leadership to the mass of Irish people.

By the mid-sixties, the movement had shed most of its militaristic leanings and a small, politically conscious organization was developing and beginning to examine critically the role of republicanism and the task of finding a strategy towards the goal of an independent republic.

As part of a major review of strategy, the whole relationship between revolutionary struggle, armed struggle and mobilization of the masses—all of those now tired jargon phrases—was discussed at length. A very thorough and useful analysis was presented, which went right back to the days of agrarian struggle and the Fenians. Various questions were examined in a historical sense: why, for example, had Fintan Lalor failed, why had the Fenians failed, and so on. The republican movement had long been a conspiratorial movement which manifested itself almost exclusively in physical force actions. Since Connolly, Pearse and Mellows and the Republican Congress of the 1930s, there had been no real effort to put any meat on the ideas of what type of a republic was aimed at.

The impact of this major review was that Sinn Féin began to define its politics more, to the extent of talking about a 'workers' republic', 'a workers' and small farmers' republic' and a 'socialist republic' or a 'democratic socialist republic.' But what came most clearly from these discussions was a recognition that republicans needed to identify their philosophy as being relevant not to the vision of a future Ireland but to the actual Ireland of today, and that they needed to enlist mass support, or at least the maximum support possible, for the republican cause. As we immersed ourselves in the business of political education, that truth became of paramount importance. We could not free the Irish people. We could only, with their support, create conditions in which they would free themselves.

These kinds of conclusions resulted in people like myself becoming involved in housing action and the other agitation activities which the movement had begun to promote. In the Twenty six Counties, republicans became involved in the Waters Restoration Committee, a campaign for the restoration of inland waters to the Irish people. There were campaigns against absentee landlordism and against foreign investors; in one case, at least, this took the form of military action. An IRA volunteer from Cork was killed and Cathal Goulding was tried for incitement over his speech at the funeral.

There was a realization that one could not organize politically as an illegal organization; the party newspaper could not be sold, the Special Powers Act could be used against the organization and its members at the whim of an RUC inspector, and so on. So, that led to making a priority of the attempt to fight the ban on Sinn Féin, and this was a conscious decision to leave the back-room conspiracies and come out into the open.

The IRA in Belfast occasionally came into public prominence itself. Towards the end of 1966, a British army recruiting class at St Gabriel's School was broken up by Volunteers armed with hurling sticks and, in 1967, there were three attacks on British army training centres—two in Belfast and one in Lisburn. By this time there were five Republican Clubs in Belfast and I had graduated to being the PRO of the Andersonstown one. Contrary to its title, our small membership covered Ballymurphy, Turf Lodge and part of the Falls as well.

Our relatively low-level agitation in Belfast, the rising political temperature and the new openness of the republicans was bringing us into contact with various elements: members of the Communist Party, the NILP, the Republican Labour Party, Young Socialists and people who had long records of working against discrimination. We were meeting through the Wolfe Tone Society, through debates in St Malachy's Old Boys' Club, and through the beginning of the revival of Irish music. The sessions and *fleadh*s provided gathering points—in the docks, in the city centre, in the Falls—and, over a pint, people who might otherwise not have met were discussing the politics of the day. I worked in a pub, the Duke of York, at that time. It was close to the head office of the NILP and a number of trade union offices, as well as the *Newsletter*, and there you got a mingling of NILP and CP members, republicans, trade union officials and journalists discussing issues of the day.

The Vietnam war was one of those issues and I was one of many who went along to rallies against the war. Similarly, the black civil rights campaign in the United States not only had its obvious influence in terms of the anthem of 'We Shall Overcome' but also in terms of its affinity with what was happening in the Six Counties. Courtesy of television, we were able to see an example of the fact that you didn't just have to take it, you could fight back.

People did not live their lives in isolation from the changes going on in the world outside. They identified to a greater or lesser extent with the music, the politics, the whole undefined movement of ideas and changes of style. Bob Dylan, the Beatles and the Rolling Stones, long hair and beads, the 'alternative society', music and fashion were all markers put down by a new generation against the complacency of the previous one, and one of the most important messages to come across was that one *could* change the world. This was the promise of the sixties, that the world was changing anyway and the tide of change was with the young generation. This produced a sense of impatience with the status quo allied to a young, enthusiastic and euphoric confidence.

The public declaration of their existence by the Republican Clubs brought this mingling of elements into a new focus, and a great deal of attention became centered on the demand for the lifting of the ban which had been slapped on them almost immediately. There was a meeting in Chapel Lane at which republicans demanded that they be recognized and Liam Mulholland announced publicly that he was the Chairman of the Six County Executive of the Republican Clubs. Next day a newspaper had a huge photo of Liam and the headline: THIS MAN IS HEAD OF AN ILLEGAL ORGANIZATION. When the Republican Clubs were banned, students at Queen's University Belfast immediately announced themselves as a Republican Club, and from this small start young radicals like Michael Farrell, Tom McGurk, Bowes Egan and others came into a certain prominence and also came into contact with other political influences. Shortly after this, a colleague and myself were arrested for selling the *United Irishman* in what was a planned defiance of the ban on that newspaper. We were released, however, without being charged. While we were thus robbed of the opportunity of fighting a political case in the courts, one of the pickets who had retired patiently to a nearby pub while waiting for our arrest was so incensed and inebriated when the RUC eventually frogmarched us to the barracks that he found himself, contrary to instructions, attacking the arresting party and getting heavily assaulted and subsequently fined. We, of course, had to organize a collection to defray his court costs and pay the fine.

In Derry, Eamonn McCann (of the Derry Labour Party) and Finbar O'Doherty (of the local Republican Club) and others were busy exposing and opposing the appalling housing situation arising from the specific forms of discrimination there. In Dublin, Cork and Waterford, Housing Action Committees were also active and occasionally a number of us would travel to Dublin to attend housing marches and protests. The success of these activities led a few of us in Belfast to get together on the same issue, and we set up the West Belfast Housing Action Committee.

An example of the kind of activity we became involved in was a case when I was approached by people called Sherlock who were living off the Falls Road in Mary Street, which was a very small street of two-bedroomed houses in very bad condition indeed. We brought them along to the Housing Trust and tried to get them rehoused, and when no movement was forthcoming we simply took over a flat in what was then the beginning of the Divis Flats complex. In Derry and in Caledon similar squats had already taken place with some success. The Caledon instance, which had been organized by the local Republican Club, had received considerable media attention when Austin Currie, then a Nationalist MP, became involved.

The Sherlock case was the first instance in Belfast; it received some media attention and was successful in the end because the family was allocated a new house. And that experience and success provided us with a major impetus: it was proof that direct action could work and it was something that enjoyed popular support in the area. After the years and years of atrocious housing, here, at last, some break seemed to have been made. The Housing Action Committee was a very ad hoc creation, called into existence on the second day of the occupation. From this start we embarked on a campaign of occupying and picketing the Housing Trust's offices, and we found that other people came to us looking for help. Earlier we had attempted to agitate against the building of the Divis Flats complex, but without evoking popular support. Now we found we were able to organize in a much more coherent way, with much more support, and the residents of the Loney district marched against the tower blocks and in favour of the rebuilding of their own traditional houses.

There were only six or seven of us from the movement involved in the housing agitation and in the unemployment agitation which also developed, but when the Northern Ireland Civil Rights Association (NICRA) was formed, following an initiative by the Belfast Wolfe Tone Society with the assistance of the Campaign for Social Justice, the small groups active around such issues fitted naturally into the wider civil rights struggle. The meeting to establish NICRA was well attended and was packed by republicans, who wielded the biggest bloc vote.

Contrary to later claims by the unionists that republicans took over the civil rights movement, we were there from the very beginning. Republicans were actually central to the formation of NICRA and, far from using it as a front organization, those of us who attended the inaugural meeting were directed to elect only two of our membership to the executive. NICRA went through a low-key period of citizen advice activity at first. It held protest rallies in Newry and Armagh in 1968, after the banning of an Easter Commemoration parade in Armagh, but it turned down a republican proposal for a Belfast march.

The first NICRA march took place in August 1968, from Coalisland to Dungannon. It was barred from the centre of the town; a rally was held in front of an RUC blockade and the crowd dispersed following some confusion between the republicans and the others as to whether they should sing the Irish national anthem or the American black civil rights anthem. It was unimportant. The civil rights struggle had begun and the Coalisland–Dungannon march was the beginning of a broad-based, if uneasy and sporadic alliance between all the anti-unionist elements in the Six Counties. October 5 in Derry was to accelerate the process.

The organizers of this Derry march sought sponsorship from NICRA and from prominent people in the local community, including John Hume, who refused. NICRA very reluctantly and belatedly endorsed the march and Stormont banned it; the scene was set for confrontation. The republicans decided that, if there was going to be trouble, the people who should get hit should be the visiting MPs who had been invited to attend as observers. As the late Liam McMillan recalled in a pamphlet:

> The Belfast republicans had been instructed in the event of the parade being halted by police cordons to push leading nationalist politicians or any other dignitaries who were sure to be at the head of the parade into police ranks. This they did to such effect that one became the first casualty of the day of violence, receiving a busted head. In the ensuing clash the RUC spared no-one. A British MP, Mrs Anne Kerr, who had been invited over as an observer said the savagery that day was worse than anything else she had seen during the Chicago riots a short time previously. And the television coverage of the RUC brutality exposed the fascist nature of the orange–unionist domination and its ruthless denial of elementary democratic rights to a large section of its citizens.

A sizeable Belfast contingent went to the march. Unable to get yet another day off work, I watched the television coverage of the RUC smashing into the demonstrators who were only a few hundred strong. The following week a protest march against RUC brutality drew 15,000 people, and NICRA felt confident enough to state its demands clearly: universal franchise in local elections, an end to gerrymandered boundaries, the repeal of the Special Powers Act, an end to housing discrimination, disbandment of the 'B' Specials and the withdrawal of the Public Order Bill which the unionists were pushing through Stormont to outlaw civil rights demonstrations.

13

These demands also became a focus for the emerging differences between the republican leadership and some rank and file activists. The leadership felt that a democratization of the Six County statelet was necessary if republicans were to engage freely and legally in the social and economic struggle which affected both the unionist and anti-unionist working class. From involvement in these struggles would emerge, they argued, a united republican working class. For them the civil rights struggle was therefore a serious attempt to democratize the state. In the process the national question would be subordinated in order to allay unionist fears and, because the democratization was going to be a lengthy one, the movement was to be demilitarized. This theory had one serious defect: it underestimated the reactionary nature of the state itself and the reluctance of the Westminster government and its management at Stormont to introduce reforms.

The contrary position was dawning slowly upon those of us who were deeply involved in grassroots agitation. We were beginning to realize that the Six County statelet could not be reformed, that by its very nature it was irreformable and that the major effects of the civil rights struggle would be to show clearly the contradictions within the state, its colonial nature and the responsibility of the British government for this situation. This position only became clear as the civil rights struggle and the state's backlash intensified and as the leadership's position clarified.

The leadership maintained that, following the democratization of the state, there could be a coming together of Protestant and Catholic workers in support of progressive politics, and the way to achieve this was through a heavy involvement of republicans in the trade unions. Having accepted the desirability of finding common, neutral ground on which Catholic and Protestant could combine, the trade union movement was, on the British Communist Party model, identified as the organization in which we should be involved and which provided that mutual ground.

The strategy flew in the face of James Connolly's analysis of the loyalist workers as 'the aristocracy of labour.' It also flew in the face of reality, not least the reality of Catholic working class employment and unemployment. The members of the republican movement in the Six Counties who were supposed to implement this strategy were mostly Catholics who, if they had jobs, had mostly unskilled ones, and who had little or no meaningful access to trade unions. The vast majority of members were either unemployed or were building workers; there were no professional people involved at all, and the few skilled workers were bricklayers and joiners on building sites, occupations with a notoriously low level of union organization. With a ready labour market there was little motivation or opportunity to organize successfully.

Members of the Dublin leadership of the republican movement came to Belfast, and I was among those who went to the lectures they gave. I found them very interesting and instructive, but they failed to accord with my experience and opinions at that time. In my view, and to some degree with hindsight, the development of the 'stages' theory of progressive democratization was conditional in the first place on the state and its supporters being willing to redress the state's own injustices. This, it was rapidly becoming apparent, was hardly the case. In particular I felt that the analysis of the ways to unite the Protestant and Catholic working class ignored the very nature of the state and my own occasional personalized and parochial encounters with loyalism.

Where I lived in Ballymurphy, the relationship between Protestant and Catholic was devoid of any sectarian difficulties. Neighbouring Moyard and New Barnsley were Protestant estates and there was a good level of social intercourse between people of my age. A crowd of us used to go regularly to Moyard and meet with young people there. We would hang around the corners, talk and take our chances with the local talent. We never discussed politics or religion except in a joking or bantering fashion. Then I became involved in a small campaign which involved both Catholics and Protestants.

On the Springfield Road, a child from New Barnsley had been knocked down at the junction with the Whiterock Road, and I went to New Barnsley and saw the parents and then went to Ballymurphy, which even in those days had a fairly energetic and well organized tenants association. We organized a small campaign to have safety rails put up at the corner and also to have a pedestrian crossing nearby. The campaign was successful and we were delighted. Not only was it a gain, albeit small, but it was Catholics and Protestants coming together—in a very parochial sense but nonetheless coming together—and agitating. News of this percolated upwards into the unionist establishment, and one of Paisley's people arrived on the scene, and for the first time, I heard serious talk about 'papists' and 'pope-heads' and 'fenians' and 'taigs.' The Protestants in New Barnsley who had previously been involved with us just stopped their involvement like that.

What we were saying to the Dublin visitors was, 'Look, you can talk about all this coming together of Protestant and Catholic working class, but here's yet another instance where the sectarian card was played and the people who had been united were effectively separated. Your notions just don't square with reality.' If the state would not allow Catholics and Protestants to get a pedestrian crossing built together, it would hardly sit back and watch them organize the revolution together.

They also saw the trade unions as an important means of pursuing politics. But again my experience gave me doubts. I was working as a barman and was sacked for demanding the trade union rate for the Twelfth of July holiday, which was double time and a day off in lieu. I went to the trade union of which I was a member and wanted them to fight it, but they wouldn't. Although there were no sectarian overtones, it was characteristic of the fact that apprentices were a dime a dozen and in this context, even when one tried to look for something very simple through the trade unions, they just didn't respond.

My own experience was that the sectarian card could be invoked effectively and that there was little basis for making any progress on the national question through the trade union movement. And both of these experiences flew in the face of what the republican leadership was proposing.

The nature of the civil rights struggle added to these contradictions. For example, the directive to Belfast republicans to push visiting notables into the front line at Duke Street, on 5 October in Derry, was really a common sense instruction. But it also accepted that while attempting to democratize the state there was a need for dramatic confrontations in order to expose what was wrong. And these confrontations flatly contradicted the leadership's position of being non-provocative. Furthermore, the people who were making the running on the ground were developing their own thinking on the issues which confronted us. We were not at the centre of the policy-making process, but we were in the centre of what was happening on the ground, so that, for example, in January 1969, following the loyalist and RUC attacks on the Burntollet marchers, it was republican stewards who took the initiative, discarded their armbands, and turned with gusto on the RUC at a banned march in Newry.

The other important development was, of course, the emergence of People's Democracy after the 5 October march. They were to have the most unified approach of all the elements involved in the civil rights campaign. It was they, by their Burntollet march in January 1969, who showed that the reforms promised by O'Neill, in November 1968, and the public relations exercise which followed his 'Ulster at the Crossroads' television appeal in December of that year were meaningless.

The Burntollet march showed that nothing had changed. The British state of Northern Ireland had certainly not made reforms gratuitously. It would never, of its own accord, have even moved towards a situation of doing away with some of the things which were disfiguring the state. In fact these things were quite consciously maintained and, once there was any movement towards removing them, the very foundations of the state became insecure. In hindsight it was inevitable, as we approached 1969, that we were headed for a major confrontation. Something had to give and it wasn't going to be us. At the moment that the RUC smashed their way into the crowd in Duke Street, it was as if all the small things that had been happening suddenly came together in a more coherent and a more ominous shape. The civil rights movement, the creation of the republican leadership, was out of their control. There would be no turning back. What had started as a campaign for civil rights was developing into the age-old struggle for national rights.

2

From Reform to Revolution

An té nach bhfuil láidir ní foláir dhó bheith glic.
(If you are not strong you had best be cunning).

AS PART OF the 'United Kingdom of Great Britain and Northern Ireland,' the Six County state was part of 'British democracy,' enjoying some of the fruits of progressive British social legislation, and it was an administrative sub-section of one of the most prominent states in developed, modern, capitalist Europe. Such was the appearance and, to an extent, the reality. Yet a profound contradiction existed: this was an apartheid state in which a very substantial minority of the citizens were disenfranchised and denied social, economic, political and civil equality. It was a state fashioned by sectarian power and privilege, a state which practised wholesale suppression and discrimination.

Confronted by the civil rights movement, the contradiction exploded in the face of the British government and the state rapidly began to come apart at the seams. A generation of people stood up, cried 'enough' and found the means to build a popular and implacable resistance to inequality and oppression. Previous generations had attempted to develop resistance, had opposed the state and its powers of suppression; republican activists had devoted lifetimes to the struggle and some had lost their lives in the fight. But their struggle had been isolated; carried out by small numbers of dedicated individuals, it had never been based on a broad sector of the population determined not only that change should come about but that it could and must come about. Catholics in the Six

Counties had been as substantially opposed to the state before but, abandoned under the terms of the Partition Act, few had believed that they could achieve any significant change in the situation.

Some date the watershed to 5 October 1968, others to January 1969; the precise date is unimportant. What was exposed was that in the late twentieth century in the developed, modern European world, an utterly outdated, undemocratic regime was engaged in the violent suppression of those who were seeking the elementary demands of western democracy.

Whatever outward trappings of statehood the Six Counties have ever possessed, they have always been completely subservient to the British government at Westminster. The position is summed up in Article 75 of the Government of Ireland Act (1920):

> Notwithstanding the establishment of the Parliament of Northern Ireland, or anything contained in this Act, the supreme authority of the Parliament of the United Kingdom shall remain unaffected and undiminished over all persons, matters and things in Northern Ireland and every part thereof.

It is a position which is expressed with admirable clarity and which has often been restated.

In recent years, the British government has attempted to suggest to international public opinion that Northern Ireland is attached to the United Kingdom by nothing more durable or binding than the will of the majority of its inhabitants. Nothing could be further from the truth: all relevant Acts exclude any right to secession, and the Northern Ireland Constitution Act (1973) states that 'It is hereby declared that Northern Ireland remains part of Her Majesty's Dominions of the United Kingdom.'

The British attitude to the Northern state was prefigured in the approach of leading British politicians prior to its establishment. In July 1912, Bonar Law, leader of the Conservative Party, declared, 'I can imagine no lengths of resistance to which Ulster will go in which I will not be ready to support them.' Lloyd George, in May 1916, wrote to Edward Carson, 'We must make sure that Ulster does not, whether she wills it or not, merge with the rest of Ireland.'

19

In instituting the statelet and in imposing partition, the British government also instituted the full apparatus of sectarianism. The armed wing of Protestant unionism was institutionalized in the form of the 'A', 'B' and 'C' Specials, which were armed, uniformed, organized and paid for by the British government. In the process of consolidating the British state in the Six Counties, 475 Irish people were killed and 1,766 injured in two years. In Belfast, 11,000 of the city's Catholics were put out of their jobs and 23,000 were driven from their homes; republicans were executed by RUC murder gangs and internment was widely used.

In the 1960s, people of my generation, even those who, like me, came from republican backgrounds, were aware only in the vaguest terms of how the state had been established. When Ian Paisley began his anti-Catholic crusade, when Catholic areas were attacked by the RUC and Peter Ward was killed, we heard some of the old people say that this kind of thing had happened before. But we were young and like most young people I suppose we believed that the lessons of the past were of little enough relevance to the immediacy of the present. We understood very little about the workings and dynamics of the state and of unionism. Nevertheless, it was clear even to us that the Six Counties was a puppet state, subservient to the British government, that nothing went on without the underlying and express approval of the British.

The Stormont parliament was in reality a menial regime and was debarred from legislating in relation to:

> The Crown, peace and war, the armed forces, treaties with foreign states, treason, naturalization, trade with any place outside Northern Ireland, radio, air navigation, lighthouses, coinage, weights and measures, copyrights and patents.

All the appurtenances, in other words, of statehood were denied to the Stormont 'government' and were retained by Westminster. It was also denied control of the Post Office, savings banks and about ninety percent of its own taxation. What powers it did possess—over justice, policing, land purchase, agriculture and housing—could be withdrawn at any time.

The role of the Stormont government was to maintain the status quo, to carry out on the ground the logic of the partition that had ensured a permanent majority for the unionists by ceding three of Ulster's nine counties to the Dublin government. One-party rule was established and was guaranteed almost immediately by a system of ward-rigging and voting qualifications; proportional representation was abolished, business votes were established and franchise was limited at local government level to ratepayers and their wives. Unionists were placed in control of the entire political system. As part of the control of votes, Catholics were denied equal access to housing, and as part of the control of population—and thus of votes—Catholics were denied equal access to employment.

When the British government introduced universal suffrage, abolishing the restricted franchise for local government in 1945, the Stormont government secured the exclusion of the Six Counties from the provisions of the legislation. They also went beyond that by introducing, in 1946, their own Representation of the People Bill which restricted the franchise even more by taking the vote away from lodgers who were not ratepayers and retained company voting whereby up to six votes were allocated to the directors of limited companies. The thinking behind this legislation was eloquently expressed by Major L. E. Curran, the government Chief Whip: 'The best way to prevent the overthrow of the government by people who had no stake in the country and had not the welfare of the people of Ulster at heart was to disenfranchise them.'

To keep the lid on a blatantly oppressive system, coercive legislation was introduced, with the full approval, of course, of the British government. Under the Civil Authorities (Special Powers) Act, the Civil Authority (the Minister for Home Affairs) and the RUC were empowered to:

1. Arrest without warrant.

2. Imprison without charge or trial and deny recourse to a court of law or to *Habeas Corpus*.

3. Enter and search homes without warrant and with force, any time of the day or night.

4. Declare a curfew and prohibit meetings, assemblies, fairs,

markets and processions.

5. Permit flogging as punishment.

6. Deny claim to trial by jury.

7. Arrest persons it is desired to examine as witness, forcibly detain them and compel them to answer questions, under penalties, even if answers may incriminate them. Such a person is guilty of an offence if he refuses to be sworn or answer a question; this applies even when no offence is known, provided a police officer has reason to believe that one 'is about to be committed.'

8. Do any act involving interference with the rights of private property.

9. Prevent access of relatives or legal advisors to a person imprisoned without trial.

10. Prohibit the holding of an inquest after a prisoner's death.

11. Arrest a person 'who by word of mouth' spreads false reports or makes false statements.

12. Prohibit the circulation of any newspaper.

13. Prohibit the possession of any film or gramophone record.

14. Forbid the erection of any monument or other memorial.

15. Enter the premises of any bank, examine accounts, and order the transfer of money, property, vouchers or documents to the Civil Authority. If the bank fails to comply an offence is committed.

16. Arrest a person who does anything 'calculated to be prejudicial to the preservation of peace or maintenance of order in Northern Ireland and not specifically provided for in the regulations.'

The Civil Authority was the Stormont Minister of Home Affairs, and he was empowered to delegate the powers granted him under the Act to any RUC man he wished, and he was also authorized to make new regulations and new laws without consulting parliament. The Special Powers Act, as it became known, was renewed every year from its inception in 1922 until 1928 when it was renewed every five years; it eventually became permanent in 1933 and was superseded in 1973 by the Northern Ireland (Emergency Provisions) Act. Such powers, fully sanctioned by the British government, were no mere passive presence in the background; they were the active means by which the existence of the state was maintained and all opposition was suppressed. Organizations, meetings and newspapers were banned. Curfews were imposed, whole (Catholic) areas were searched, and internment without trial was used in 1920–1, 1922–4, 1938–45, 1956–61, 1969 and 1971–5.

It is hardly surprising to learn that Mr Vorster, who was then South African Minister for Justice, remarked in 1963 that he 'would be willing to exchange all the legislation of that sort [Coercion Acts] for one clause of the Northern Ireland Special Powers Act.'

People such as myself knew little about the precise provisions of the law; we simply absorbed a general awareness that if they wanted to get you they could, that power in all situations rested with them—with the state, the RUC, the law courts. We were not of a class that understood terms such as habeas corpus and, while we were aware that the Campaign for Social Justice and others were complaining about the state of affairs, we had no real understanding of how the unionist system worked.

Blatant discrimination in access to jobs and housing allocation was something one took for granted, almost like part of the landscape. In 1969, out of 109 people employed in the technical and professional grades of the civil service only thirteen were Catholics; of the 319 employed in the higher administrative grades only twenty-three were Catholics. Of the 115 people nominated by the government to serve on nine public boards only sixteen were Catholics. Yet I registered the fact that the conditions I knew in the Falls were similar to those I saw in the Shankill Road and the Old Lodge Road, both Protestant areas; the conditions in Catholic Ballymurphy were similar to those in Protestant Moyard. The fact was that conditions in the Six Counties for working class people were pitiable, irrespective of whether they were Protestant or Catholic.

As I absorbed all of this I came to understand the centrality of partition in the whole dreadful scheme. I also realized that without a proper understanding of the reason and consequences of partition there could be no understanding of the problem, and thus no solution. Partition was, and remains, the main means by which equality is denied us and the principal method by which self-determination is withheld from us. Partition aborted a national independence struggle in the 1920s and secured Britain a toehold in a part of Ireland from which she could influence all of Ireland; it divided the Irish people into two states, and within one state it established a unionist monopoly which divided us once more.

The break-up of monolithic unionism in the late 1950s began as a result of moves initiated by unionism in its own self-interest. When the linen and ship-building industries were in their heydays, which coincided largely with the two World Wars, there had been an industrial base in the north-east of Ulster which was integrated into British and British Empire markets. This provided the economic foundation of the narrow concept of unionist self-interest which was expressed in the notion of Stormont as 'a Protestant parliament for a Protestant people.' The Unionist Party was then the property of the landed gentry, people who probably would have felt more at home in the British House of Lords and who were in many instances related to the British aristocracy.

When Terence O'Neill took over as Prime Minister from Lord Brookeborough in March 1963, the basis for the old narrow self-interest had already been succeeded by a new dynamic. The linen and ship-building industries were in steep decline and O'Neill, a former Minister of Finance, perceived the need to attract multinational capital. The evidently antiquated social relations which characterized the Six County state did not appeal to the British, European and US companies he sought to attract in the build-up to EEC membership and in the wake of the decline of the British Empire, and so he tried to modernize the style of government and to project an image of the state which was more in tune with the twentieth century.

The process required at least an appearance of some kind of partnership, both in relation to the other state on the island, the Twenty-six Counties, and in relation to the minority which had been so systematically excluded from having an equal role in the society of the Six Counties. The most obvious grievances of the nationalist population and the crudest facets of unionism gave the Dublin government a problem. The Prime Minister of the Twenty-six Counties, Sean Lemass, could not afford to be seen to deal with people who were blatantly mistreating a sizeable section of the population. And this led to a new era of unionism characterized by certain liberal noises which were expressed not just by Terence O'Neill but also by publications such as the *Belfast Telegraph*, which had previously expressed a traditional Protestant ascendancy perspective.

All political ideology is based on either the self-interest of those who support it or on what they *perceive* to be their self-interest. The self-interest of unionism was to keep the 'papists' down. This playing of the Orange card, this exploitation of the perceived self-interest of working-class unionists, was an essential element in keeping unionism intact and united; and despite social contradictions between elements of its support it still remained a monolith, firmly set on the foundation of supremacist ideology.

When O'Neill tried to alter the appearance of the state, he ran into major difficulties. There were two reasons for this: firstly, those who saw their self-interest as being sectarian, narrow and anti-papist rose up against any such liberalization, even when its value was explained to them in the most schoolmasterly language. It was at that point that one found Ian Paisley throwing snowballs outside Stormont at Sean Lemass's cavalcade. The second reason for O'Neill's difficulties, which was totally coincidental in relation to this development in unionism, was the rise of the civil rights movement.

O'Neill has largely escaped criticism and has in a quite unrealistic manner been portrayed as a liberal who, if only he had been given a chance, would have achieved social progress. A rather parochial answer to that view is provided by what a man said to me one day several years ago in the Falls Road. 'I don't mind a bigot,' he said, 'because a bigot doesn't know any better. I don't mind a bigot, but I can't stand an educated bigot.' Terence O'Neill was an educated bigot. He was just sophisticated enough to know that the self-interest of unionism could no longer be sustained by the crude methods of the past, but the Orange monster which unionism and the British colonial ethos had created could not take the change. At the same time, the demand for ordinary civil rights could not be dealt with, as it had been previously, by straightforward coercion.

An important factor in the difficulties which unionism faced with the civil rights movement was television. For example, in the early sixties Brian Faulkner had been engaged in aggressive provocations in the Longstone Road, but they were not covered by television. The RUC action on 5 October 1968 was not the first action of its kind by any means, but it was the first time that such brutality had been enacted in front of television cameras. Years later, the killing of John Downes was by no means unique: other people had been killed by plastic bullets; thousands of rounds had been fired; numerous people had been injured. The killing of John Downes was different because it was seen by the media. The fact was that in the electronic age, unionism and later the British, could not cover up all that was happening.

O'Neill's attempt to modernize the appearance of the state, combined with the rise of the civil rights movement, began the break-up of the unionist monolith as the cover-all philosophy which had been able to unite all kinds of different strands and strata. When it had suffered small cracks in the past—when the NILP had been able to win Protestant votes, for example—it had cemented itself again with the glue of sectarianism. It could do this easily when it did not have to make any gestures of goodwill towards its non-citizens, the Catholics. These days were now gone, and the divisions within unionism widened as a result.

O'Neill attacked the Burntollet march as 'a foolhardy and irresponsible undertaking' and civil rights marchers as 'mere hooligans.' He ignored the violence inflicted upon peaceful demonstrators by the sticks and stones of loyalists, ignored the fact that about one hundred of the ambushers were members of the 'B' Specials, and ignored the assault by drunken RUC men on the Bogside in Derry. Instead, he warned that he would mobilize the 'B' Specials. Yet, despite O'Neill's vitriol against the civil rights marchers, he found himself under attack from the extreme right. In an attempt to bolster his position, he called an election for 24 February 1969, hoping to emerge with an increased number of his supporters in Stormont. It was an election which saw the Nationalist Party lose ground to civil rights candidates, but, more importantly in terms of unionism, the election exacerbated the tensions within the Unionist Party between pro- and anti-O'Neill factions and heralded the emergence of the fledgling Paisleyite party. The fundamentalist branch of unionism had begun to achieve new prominence.

The Unionist Party had always enjoyed the support of the disparate elements in the Protestant community because it had been able to ward off any threat to Protestant privilege. For centuries the Protestants had been told that they were the chosen people and that the Catholics were scum. 'I wouldn't have one about the place,' said Prime Minister Brookeborough. Religious demagogues pumped out their message of hatred against 'the purple whore' and the 'fenians breeding like rats.' The reactionary nature of unionism grows from the fact that they have to defend the indefensible. When one cannot defend one's position in an honest and rational way, one naturally adopts a kind of laager mentality and forgets about trying to convert world opinion. In this sense the unionists have the same problem as the old white regime in South Africa used to have.

Terence O'Neill (later the great white hope of Dublin middle-class opinion as represented by *The Irish Times*) expressed his own difficulties in terms which achieved a typical combination of condescension and prejudice:

> It is frightfully hard to explain to Protestants that if you give Roman Catholics a good job and a good house they will live like Protestants, because they will see their neighbours with cars and television sets.
>
> They will refuse to have eighteen children, but if a Roman Catholic is jobless and lives in the most ghastly hovel, he will rear eighteen children on National Assistance...
>
> If you treat Roman Catholics with due consideration and kindness they will live like Protestants, in spite of the authoritative nature of their Church.

Little wonder that O'Neill failed to convince anyone, not least his fellow unionists. Not only did they successfully depose him but, in classic *coup d'état* style, they blasted electricity installations and the Silent Valley reservoir in the process. The IRA, which was blamed for these operations, during this time had to content itself with petrol bombing a number of Belfast post offices in retaliation for the beating to death of Samuel Devenny by the RUC in Derry.

The unionists appeared to have everything, including bigger bombs. Nevertheless I, for one, did not have a clear understanding then of what unionism was and certainly did not identify any of the ordinary Protestants I met daily as having anything to do with the open sectarianism and coercion of the state.

In rural areas it was different. There the folk memory of the perceived superiority of political Protestantism over Catholics remains very strong to this day. People can show you the land that was taken from their family three or four hundred years ago, and they will name the families that took it. In fact, this is not unique to the Six Counties; one finds it all over Ireland. The indigenous population were dispossessed of their land by planters, and from time to time these planters had to fight tooth and nail to retain that land by means of various forms of coercion, including the Penal Laws. These laws effectively created an apartheid system, with the Catholics placed in basically the same situation as the blacks in South Africa. In terms of the land, the oldest male child of a family could only inherit land if he converted to Protestantism; otherwise the land passed to all the male heirs. This quickly reduced the size and viability of Catholic-owned farms.

In modern times, this apartheid system was supported at every turn by the assurances of senior British political figures or the British government itself. The institutionalized form which their assurances took was the loyalist veto. Unionists refused, and refuse still, to deal with their Catholic neighbours as equals because they didn't need to. Unlike their black counterparts in South Africa, however, the Irish Catholic labour force, both rural and urban, wasn't necessary for the well-being of the state. Deserted by Dublin, displaced persons in their own country, they had no political or economic muscle with which to gain equality. And the refusal of the unionists, though I didn't understand it then, was, in the circumstances, understandable from their point of view. They had been told by the British government that their privileged position as an ascendancy would remain for as long as the union with Britain remained, and that would be for as long as they desired it. As if to underline this, in April 1969, five hundred extra British troops were flown in from England to guard installations against further IRA attacks. The attacks, of course, had been the work of the UVF.

In the beginning I was puzzled by all this, and by the state's reaction to even the most passive form of dissent. Why should we be forbidden to sell our newspaper, to wear an Easter lily commemorating the Easter rebellion of 1916, to fly a tricolour flag? Why couldn't jobs be provided and what was so rebellious about asking this? What was so treasonable about demanding a decent home? Where was the subversion in the demand for equal voting rights?

I did not have a very clear understanding of the Northern Ireland state, of what it was. Our housing agitation was as much aimed against the old nationalist politicians and their failure; they seemed to be involved in a very sterile, do-a-favour-for-a-constituent type of politics. Our approach was that the people have a right to a house so let's get them a house. Being young and enthusiastic we didn't see why we should have to wait, when you could go into the Housing Trust and do a sit-in and get results. It wasn't clear to me in the beginning that the housing problem had anything to do with the state as such, or even with voting.

At that time there was cross-community communication, which I don't want to exaggerate, but it was there. I knew a lot of Protestants, I worked in a Protestant area; there were differences, but they seemed only to come to the surface around the Twelfth. But, even then, I watched Twelfth of July parades and bonfires and I enjoyed them. The nasty side of sectarianism hadn't manifested itself yet.

It was only as I started to meet reactions that I started to ask why: why did small things lead to over-reaction? Over the Sherlock squat a number of us got something like fifty-seven summonses; at that time we laughed about it, but in retrospect it was a gross over-reaction. The RUC activity of landrovers patrolling the Loney area of West Belfast was a similar over-reaction. When I started to go to debates and listen to people who obviously had well-documented proof of discrimination, I began to go through a process of politicization, and that, combined with my experience of the reaction of the RUC, pushed me to clarify my views of the situation. I began to realize that Catholics were being denied houses because that meant that they could be denied votes. I discovered that gerrymandering in Derry was a conscious practice carried out to maintain one-party control. In a very parochial sense, I began to realize that this kind of sectarianism wasn't just a blind hatred of Catholics but was something which was being used tactically for unionist political advantage.

I was, as mentioned before, about eighteen months in Sinn Féin before I realized what I was in. Then, as I started to examine the situation, I began to see that we were not dealing with just a unionist hatred of 'papists' but that it was actually in the state's interest to stop, for example, the sale of republican papers, to stop the ideas of republicanism being promoted.

When William Craig reacted immediately by banning the Republican Clubs, I realized that the unionist government was opposed to the organization of political opinion which was radically different from theirs. Through that process I began to get an understanding of the state. The British government claimed ulti-mate responsibility over the Six Counties area. It was thus responsible for the situation, but it had deluded public opinion at home and abroad into believing that responsibility rested with the Stormont regime. This regime was refusing to introduce the mini-mum reforms demanded by the civil rights agitation, and the British government was unwilling to force such reforms upon its puppet government. The republican leadership's strategy of pro-gressive democratization could not succeed in the face of such intransigence. But neither could the British continue to disguise their role. Increasingly they were being forced, by the contradictions inherent within their statelet, into taking a more dominant role. Many of us saw this as a useful development, with the potential for ridding us of the barrier administration at Stormont and placing the responsibility clearly where it belonged—with the colonial power in London.

In 1963 I hadn't even been sure what the border was. Going to the Donegal *Gaeltacht*, I looked out to see where the border was and what it looked like. I didn't know in 1960 or 1961 what the IRA was. I remember myself and a friend in school trying to work it out and deciding it was the Irish Rebel Army. There was a certain bravado in singing a rebel song, in shouting something at the RUC. There was the famous case of a fellow known as 'Throw-the-Brick.' He was working on a building site and when the British Queen came to Belfast on a visit he threw a brick at her. Everybody wanted to meet him, and when he came out of prison you'd be delighted if you saw him on the street because he was famous, but you didn't really understand what it was all about. It was enough to know that it wasn't our Queen he'd thrown the brick at. The only face of unionist power that I really encountered was the RUC; in rural areas, harassment by the 'B' Specials was a constant fact of life, but in Belfast they were not a particularly significant feature.

Most working-class Catholics were overwhelmingly fatalistic and apathetic. One older man, a veteran of the IRA's 1930s campaign, was unaffected by my youthful zeal and probably spoke for most of his generation when one day he told me wearily: 'Never bother yourself. It'll be all the same in a thousand years.' People weren't politicized, most were finding it hard to make ends meet and there was a high level of emigration. But the feeling of isolation, of alienation from the state, was not confined to the Catholic working class, who were mostly resigned to their fate. The professional class were also affected.

A new generation of young Catholics with expectations of being able to rise socially, having fulfilled the educational requirements, found it difficult to accept the status quo which denied them their place in the sun. The student radicals, the most prominent of whom was Bernadette Devlin, were articulate and defiant; they weren't going to be chased back into the ghettos and they were well able to state their case on television. This new element combined with others to act as a catalyst for the mobilization of the non-unionist population.

The state at any time could have undermined the civil rights agitation by moving swiftly on what were normal democratic demands; and perhaps in the global sense if wider issues had occurred earlier the natural consequence of EEC membership would have been to modernize the state. But movement came too late. In fact, whatever civil rights reforms were granted were only granted after the holocaust, after the whole thing was up in the air.

By 1969, well before the pogroms, I sensed that we were playing with something extraordinarily dangerous. I had numerous arguments with Liam McMillan because I didn't think that the Belfast or Dublin leaderships understood what was happening. They appeared unable to give proper direction in the face of the

31

small riot situations which were beginning to develop in Ardoyne and Unity Flats. Elsewhere throughout the Six Counties, tensions were also rising. The RUC, the 'B' Specials and loyalist counter-demonstrators were clashing frequently with Catholic civilians. In July, renewed attacks by the RUC in the Bogside area of Derry lasted three days, and in Dungiven they batoned a Catholic man to death.

Our agitation around Divis Flats was becoming a series of ever more frequent skirmishes with the RUC, whose ferocity was a revelation. The particularly frightening aspect of it was that we, the small group of republican activists, had been identified by this stage as leading the local agitations, so that—and I've had this experience many times since—we found ourselves, as we ran like hell, looking over our shoulders at the baton chargers passing other protestors and obviously heading for the republicans, heading for us.

I felt, in the eye of the storm, that we were moving rapidly towards catastrophe, and I was absolutely frustrated that the people who were in the leadership of the republican movement did not appear to understand what was happening. Maybe they did. Maybe I was too young and too dogmatic.

I remember on one occasion at Hastings Street barracks, where there was frequent rioting, there was a baton charge and people turned to face it and the RUC fled back into the barracks. We then proceeded to the barracks door and, armed with a telegraph pole, about fifty of us started to use the pole as a battering ram against the door and then, through a series of shouts, another fellow and myself were accepted in as a delegation. There was a feeling of recklessness, that we had them, and we relished that feeling. I saw the same thing later, in 1971 in Ballymurphy, where young people went into the barracks there and drove out the British army landrovers.

Being nineteen or twenty years old and not having any responsibilities; being fit enough to go and spend three, four or five nights in succession sitting in a squat, going to Unity Flats, to Hooker Street, and in between times off for a weekend in Dublin or to a *fleadh*, an Irish music or dance festival. There was a sense of freedom, a youthful, naive and mistaken feeling that the revolution was happening all around us and that the world was beginning to respond. By July we were actively involved in trying to get people in Ardoyne and Unity Flats organized to defend themselves against further RUC and loyalist attacks during the Orange parades. In the meantime, the republican leadership was in no way prepared for any sort of military defence, never mind an offensive. It was, instead, engaged in semantics.

By August the balloon was up. There were days of heavy rioting in Ardoyne and in Unity Flats. Patrick Corry, a Catholic, was beaten to death in an RUC barracks. The first Catholic families were being intimidated out of the Crumlin Road area by loyalist gangs. In Derry, a Bogside Defence Association had been established by republicans in preparation for expected loyalist and RUC attacks during the annual loyalist parade on 12 August.

On 8 August, Prime Minister Chichester Clarke, his Home Affairs Minister and James Callaghan the British Prime Minister met in London to discuss the situation. British troops were put on stand-by in Derry and Belfast in support of the unionist regime. The highly provocative loyalist march was going ahead and the 'croppies' were expected to lie down once again. But they didn't. Instead, the battle of the Bogside began.

RUC armoured cars attacked the Bogside barricades and, for the first time, CS gas was used. Defenders hurled stones, bricks, broken paving slabs and petrol bombs, and the tricolour flew from a tower block alongside the flag of James Connolly's Irish Citizen Army, the Starry Plough. The siege continued day and night, but even with a force of 700 at their command, with armoured cars, batons and CS gas, the RUC could not subdue the Bogside.

On the second day, at an emotional meeting of NICRA in Belfast, we heard a tape-recorded plea from the Bogside for help. A proposal to draw the RUC out of Derry, or at least to prevent reinforcements being sent in, was enthusiastically endorsed. Rallies were to be organized throughout the Six Counties. On behalf of the West Belfast Housing Action Committee, I informed the meeting that we would hold a protest march and meeting on the Falls Road. A NICRA delegation was later to go to Stormont to plead for the withdrawal of the RUC from the Bogside. We left the meeting to make petrol bombs. The NICRA request was refused and the Six Counties erupted.

At 5 p.m. on 14 August 1969, British troops entered Derry and took up positions. The RUC and 'B' Specials were pulled back and the troops remained outside the Bogside. In Belfast, barricades had been erected on the Falls Road. Loyalist mobs, in many instances led by 'B' Specials, attacked and burned Catholic houses. The RUC, with Shorland armoured cars and Browning heavy machine guns, fired into Divis Flats, and in Ardoyne they opened up with sub-machine guns. Seven people were killed in loyalist and RUC attacks, including John Gallagher, who was shot dead in Armagh by the 'B' Specials. The IRA had virtually no guns with which to resist the attacks, but a small number of weapons was mustered and played a role in driving the loyalists and Specials out of the Falls Road.

Arms were rushed up from the Twenty-six Counties and barricades were strengthened to meet the continuing loyalist attacks. British troops took up positions on the Falls Road; they did not intervene to take down barricades, but neither did they intervene when loyalists burned down the whole of Catholic Bombay Street and a young Fianna boy, Gerard McCauley, was killed trying to defend the street. As the RUC and loyalists attacked Ardoyne, another Catholic street, Brookfield Street, was burned down. In all, 1,820 families left their homes in Belfast, 1,505 of them Catholics, during July, August and September.

The situation had developed rapidly. The demands of the civil rights movement had been demands for rights which were taken for granted in western Europe, and they were demands for rights which existed in the rest of the so-called United Kingdom. In retrospect they were, in themselves, unremarkable, simple and moderate demands. Yet they had evoked a ferocious response from the state and its supporters, and the consequence of that response had left the authority and stability of the state in tatters. When I had first become involved in political action I had asked myself what was so rebellious about asking for jobs, what was so treasonable about demanding a decent home, so subversive about seeking equal voting rights. I had received my answer, as had we all.

The civil rights movement had been looking for democratization of the state, but the state had made abundantly clear the fact that it would not and could not implement democratic reforms. The movement had placed its demands on the state; it had not demanded the abolition of the state, nor a United Ireland. Now, however, with the reaction of the state and the intervention of the British army, the constitutional question had come to the fore and the whole existence of the Six County state stood in question.

The republican strategy of organizing politically to achieve democracy within the state, which had involved a turning away from the physical force tradition and a dumping of arms, had run headlong into the reality of the irreformable sectarian state. That the republican movement now turned to armed resistance had nothing to do with any ingrained militarism, but had everything to do with the stark realities of the situation.

The republican movement of the 1960s had proved incapable of responding adequately to events as they evolved in the Six Counties. The spontaneous popular uprising of August 1969—uncoordinated, locally organized, lacking any general plan—and the subsequent effects in the Twenty-six Counties found the movement ill-prepared and unable to cope with the needs and potential of that period.

Failure and inadequacy did not relate solely to the question of defence for beleaguered nationalist areas. Indeed, lack of guns was not a primary problem as it was made up quite rapidly. The primary problem was lack of politics, a shortcoming which was to remain even after guns had become plentiful.

This lack of politics, affecting all tendencies in the then disunited republican movement, arose from an inability to understand what was happening on the ground, its causes, effects and possible consequences. Many of those who warned, quite correctly, of the need for armed defence contingencies, many of those who were strident in their condemnation of the republican leadership's failure to provide such necessities, did not understand the political requirements of that time. But the leadership was clearly lacking in political understanding and this led to their failure to prepare properly on all fronts, not least on the question of defence.

Understandably in the circumstances, their failure was seen simply in terms of military preparedness, and this view, allied to a suspicion amongst the older republicans of the politicization process in which the movement was engaged, led to the split in 1970, a major set-back for the republican cause. It also ensured that the reinvigorated republican struggle which emerged then was an inadequate one, because the only republican organization which arose from the ashes was a military one: it had little or no proper educational process, no formal politicization courses, and there was scant regard paid by the leadership to such needs.

Everyone connected with the movement at that time was, of course, responsible for such shortcomings, and perhaps the situation could not have been otherwise. As in the case of any radical movement, republicans have had to grapple not only with the movement's historical shortcomings but with the whole question of finding a strategy for moving towards the independent republic. This is an on-going task requiring continuous analysis, co-education, good internal and external communications, re-assessments, flexibility and, most of all, agreement on the final objective. At some stage in the late sixties, the republican leadership lost sight of most, if not all, of these requirements, and the lessons of that period are as important today as ever. Any leadership which ignores these lessons will, like the Goulding leadership, do so at a terrible cost to itself and the people it seeks to serve.

3

The IRA/Óglaigh na hÉireann

Irishmen and Irishwomen: In the name of God and of
the dead generations from which she receives her old
tradition of nationhood, Ireland, through us, summons
her children to the flag and strikes for her freedom.

1916 Proclamation

T HE CLASSIC PERIOD of republican struggle, the
period which is impressed upon one's mind as the
definitive image of the IRA, is the Tan War, with its flying
columns taking on the Black and Tans. At its height, it was a
military campaign with a background of incipient forms of
alternative government apparatus functioning through the
republican courts in certain parts of the country. The flying
columns moved about as fairly self-contained units; they were fed
and accommodated in sympathetic households or sometimes they
commandeered unionist houses and lived off the occupants.

In the 1930s and 1940s, the IRA enjoyed no such background
in the country, and its military actions took place in England, in
the Twenty-six Counties and only in one or two places in the Six
Counties. The 1950s campaign was restricted to the border counties—there was literally no activity in Belfast—and a lot of the IRA
people involved came from the Twenty-six Counties and presumably worked around the border counties or maintained small flying
columns based in Fermanagh, Tyrone and South Armagh. By the
end, this campaign, like those before it, consisted of just five or six
active republicans skipping between five or six houses.

The current phase of armed struggle is different from any other, apart perhaps from a resemblance to the situation in the Black and Tan War in those areas that enjoyed some kind of governmental status. In the 1970s, the struggle developed into a broad political and armed campaign, but even the military aspect developed its own politics of physical force.

What particularly characterized this phase is that the IRA fought within the occupied area and existed cheek by jowl with the British forces, which had at their command a massive array of technological resources. The IRA is one of the few guerilla forces in the world which has operated in and from within the occupied area, and, despite the long duration of this phase of struggle, the IRA has continued to enjoy unsurpassed community support.

I wish that physical force had never been part of the political struggle in my lifetime in Ireland. But a statelet which was born in violence has maintained itself throughout its seventy years of existence by violence and has been supported in so doing by the British army and government. The conflict which has resulted in the deaths of over 3,300 people began, in 1966, with the UVF campaign of assassinations of Catholics; it continued in its early stages with attacks by loyalists and RUC on civil rights marchers and graduated to the joint loyalist/RUC attacks on Catholic streets in Derry and Belfast, and the first member of the RUC to be killed at this time was shot by loyalists on the Shankill Road. The IRA's armed struggle in this period originated as a defensive response to the combined attacks of the RUC, loyalists and the British army, and it has always been massively outgunned. There are in the Six Counties today something like 123,000 legally held guns, and these are not in the possession of the IRA. There are approximately 30,000 members of the British forces, between British soldiers, the UDR, the RUC and the RUC Reserve. They are armed with sophisticated weapons, with armoured cars, a massive battery of electronic surveillance equipment, with cameras trained on many streets of West Belfast and Derry, and they are backed by the law which, in Brigadier Frank Kitson's phrase, is 'just another weapon in the government's arsenal...little more than a propaganda cover for the disposal of unwanted members of the public.'

From defensive origins the IRA campaign developed into an offensive against the state, and there is no denying the fact that innocent bystanders were killed and injured as a consequence of IRA actions. Death by violence is always a sickening tragedy and no talk of 'the inevitable casualties of guerrilla warfare' can do anything to alter the fact. I deeply regret all the deaths and injuries which occur in the course of this struggle and, although I have never tried to justify civilian casualties or fatalities of IRA actions, I am challenged constantly by some journalists and television inter-viewers, imitating the attitudes of their political masters, with having placed myself and the whole republican movement outside the bounds of political debate by refusing to condemn the IRA, and the IRA is commented upon in an unreal way as if its motiva-tion were the pursuit of violence for its own sake. It is commented upon in a way which ignores and diverts attention away from the circumstances which account both for its origins and for the con-tinuation of its armed activity.

Óglaigh na hÉireann takes its historical and organizational ori-gins from the forces which engaged in the Easter Rising of 1916, though one can trace its ancestry much further back if one wishes. But the circumstances which shaped the recent support for the IRA are, above all, the experience of the barricade days from 1969–72. Those days are of continuing importance not just in terms of the IRA but because they saw the development of tremendous commu-nity solidarity, more than a memory of which remains today.

In response to joint RUC and loyalist attacks, nationalist Derry was barricaded from August 1969, until July 1972; in Belfast, for a much shorter period, there were barricades in up to twenty-six Catholic enclaves, with the major concentration in West Belfast. Massive shifts in population caused by the loyalist pogroms—the biggest forced movement of population in Europe since the Second World War—led people to open up their homes behind the barri-cades to refugees. Everyone had to develop self-reliance and mutual solidarity in order to cope with the situation. Working people took control of aspects of their own lives, organized their own districts, in a way which deeply antagonized and traumatized the Catholic middle class, and particularly the Catholic Church hierarchy. It was an experience of community oneness, of unselfishness at every hand. And, when more than barricades were required for defence from the armed forces of the RUC, loyalists and, soon, the British army, this generation of the IRA emerged.

39

The IRA was, in August 1969, disorganized, almost completely unarmed, and unable to play the role it had played in previous pogroms, in the 1920s and 1930s, of defending the areas under attack. In one or two instances, firearms were produced by individual republicans in attempts to hold off attacks, but the IRA was in no shape to offer any organized response. Yet, by March 1972, the IRA had not only created a defensive force of unprecedented effectiveness, they had also carried out a massive offensive which had succeeded in its aim of bringing down the Stormont government.

In the days, weeks and months after the August 1969 pogroms, republicans worked with frantic energy to raise money, to procure arms and to reorganize the IRA to meet the demands of a situation of armed siege. In a remarkably short time, a people's army took shape; closely knit with the nationalist community, it was made up of the sons and daughters of ordinary people, its members indistinguishable to any outside observer from the rest of the community. Whether people in the nationalist areas agreed or disagreed with the IRA and all its actions, they recognized it as their army, knew for the most part which of their neighbours were members, and referred to it simply as the 'ra.'

Streets, houses, people and even churches were under attack, and IRA volunteers—most of whom were very young—put their lives on the line to protect them. At first, sticks and stones, petrol bombs and unsophisticated guns were used against the forces of the state, which were equipped with the most up-to-date weaponry. And, in the midst of days of rioting and skirmishes, the IRA was screening, training and attempting to instil discipline into large numbers of new recruits. Much had to be done under intense pressure and at breakneck speed; but, before long, the IRA had adopted clear structures for its operations and had acquired explosives and guns that stood a chance of generating an effective counter to the firepower being directed against the nationalist areas.

When the barricades were up there was a great sense of euphoria; this was perhaps naive, but it was nonetheless real. When the IRA campaign began, the civil rights campaign was still going on, albeit on a smaller scale than previously, and the honeymoon period immediately after the arrival of the British troops was over. For the first time in the Six Counties one had the combination of armed struggle and mass, popular struggle. Most of the Catholics had withdrawn from the institutions of state and, when internment came, they all withdrew. The armed struggle began to be waged with great intensity and with major support and tolerance. There was also the feeling that things were happening in Dublin, as reflected in the Arms Trial crisis in Fianna Fáil, and that tended to give Northern Catholics succour.

When Prime Minister of the Six Counties Faulkner said things like 'We have them on the run' and the IRA came back the next day with a devastating series of operations, the effect that had in lifting people's morale was enormous. The free run for republicans in the barricaded areas meant that the areas were almost entirely free of petty crime, and this had more to do with an identification with the struggle than with any policing methods of republicans.

The ambassadors for the British government on a daily basis were the British soldiers. They were 'welcomed' initially because they were seen as relieving a siege, whether in the Falls Road or in Derry, but it was an uneasy welcome. They got tea in only a few households. People did not know whether to cheer or what to do. Even in the past when Catholics had joined the British army for lack of available jobs, their families had been inclined to feel a bit guilty about it. At the very least, there was a consciousness that these were British soldiers and that, in one sense or another, we were Irish. Another factor which came quickly into play was the racist attitude of many British army regiments. They antagonized whole communities by their behaviour and especially by their attitude to womenfolk. So, while there were initially mixed feelings about the British army, once it became apparent what their role was, all ambiguity went out of the window. Within a very short space of time, people were shouting insults at the soldiers and people were suddenly talking about memories of the Black and Tans.

Bombay Street, and, two months later, Coates Street, were burned down by loyalist gangs and the RUC after the British troops had arrived and after the larger scale burnings had already taken place. Whole streets of houses were burned out, people were killed and about a hundred injured during the two-day attack on this Catholic area in the Lower Falls. The fact that the British army did not intervene taught nationalists an important lesson.

The Falls Road curfew, in July 1970, made popular opposition to the British army absolute in Belfast. Three thousand British troops invaded the Falls Road and, from helicopters, voices over PA systems announced that the area was under curfew and that anyone on the streets was liable to be shot. Five civilians were killed, more were injured, and 300 were arrested. The invasion and curfew lasted for two days, during which 1,600 canisters of CS gas were fired. Troops smashed down the doors of houses, pulled up floors, wrecked people's homes. The siege was broken, at great risk to themselves, by hundreds of women who massed together and simply marched past all the 'squaddies,' who did not know how to cope with this direct expression of popular feeling. After that, recruitment to the IRA was massive. IRA organization and capability increased so dramatically that, by June and July of 1971, they were able to carry out as many as 125 bombings in those two months—an average of more than two per day. The Stormont government and the British army were not succeeding in their attempts to crush the resistance.

The shooting dead, in Derry, of Seamus Cusack and Desmond Beattie marked a critical turning point. Prime Minister Faulkner had, in May, given the British army *carte blanche* to fire on anyone acting 'suspiciously'; on 8 July 1971, they obliged, and two unarmed Catholics were killed. The struggle for civil rights had continued, despite the RUC beating people to death, despite loyalist attacks, despite the Battle of the Bogside, the upheavals of August, and the shootings of people in the Falls Road. But the shootings of Cusack and Beattie marked a change, and this change was cemented by the use of the British army forces as the implement of repression. Before that it had been primarily a battle between beleaguered nationalists and the Stormont administration for equal rights; then it became a battle between beleaguered nationalists and the British establishment.

The British government could have defused the situation, could have prevented it reaching the stage of open armed conflict. If they had understood and taken note of what the Campaign for Social Justice was saying in 1965, they could have moved then to introduce the norms of democracy at a time when republicanism was virtually dead. In such circumstances it would have been impossible for the IRA to survive. If in London the will had existed to make even limited changes, the long-sighted agitators would have pointed out how small the changes were and how unsatisfactory, but the British government would have succeeded in undercutting support for republicanism.

Instead of defusing the situation, the British government copper-fastened popular support for the IRA. In Ballymurphy in West Belfast, for example, there were six semi-active republicans and ten supporters in 1969; today Sinn Féin draws its biggest vote from that area. The crucial transformation came about when a British army regiment came into Ballymurphy and attempted to beat its people into submission. If they had come in with kid gloves they would still have been unwelcome, but they would not have generated the same phenomenon of implacable republican resistance.

Internment, introduced on 9 August 1971, had a major effect in making people conscious participants in the struggle. Those who were already politicized were not surprised by the introduction of internment, but there were many Catholics who did not believe that such a thing could happen, and to them internment came as a crucial indication that the road to reform was blocked off. Brutal confirmation came with the shooting dead of unarmed demonstrators in Derry on Bloody Sunday, 30 January 1972. Óglaigh na hÉireann was inundated with new recruits.

When Stormont fell in March 1972, it was a time of complete and utter jubilation. I remember talking to a middle-aged man in Ballymurphy in the midst of a colossal gun battle. (Although many people might not realize this, a lot of those big gun battles fought to defend an area from attack—in this case attack by the British army—had as many as two hundred people standing and watching what was happening.) This man, who had lived through the imposition of partition and the setting up of Stormont, kept saying, almost as if he was drunk, 'Jesus, you'd never think you'd see the day!' He represented a feeling that, so quickly after the events of 1968–9, something that was hated, something that was symbolic of all that was wrong in the state, had been removed. And probably most people who were anti-unionist felt, quite rightly, that they had played a part in the removal of Stormont. The IRA was clearly seen as acting on their behalf.

The fall of Stormont was very decidedly a watershed. The feeling was that 'we'll never go back to that again.'

The impact of the fall of Stormont on the unionists, as well as the disarming and disbanding of the 'B' Specials, must obviously have been catastrophic. Having said that, the actual impact may have been exaggerated by commentators. Just after the fall of Stormont, I found myself committed to the *Maidstone* prison ship, which was anchored in Belfast Lough in the hinterland of loyalist East Belfast, and we felt very vulnerable to attack by an Orange mob enraged at the abolition of their Protestant parliament. The Vanguard Party was in its heyday, with its parades and rallies featuring fascist salutes. Unionist leaders were making threatening noises, and, if there was going to be a real Orange backlash, that was the moment at which it should have occurred. But it didn't, and, in assessing the dangers of a future loyalist backlash, one must take this into account. They said they would not accept the fall of Stormont, but they did; they said they would fight to the last man, but they didn't.

What loyalist response there was came in a form which has been seen on many other occasions since. Although their fight over the proroguing of Stormont was with the British, they engaged in a spiralling campaign of killings of Catholics. There was not the major backlash that had been threatened, but there were the phenomena of mutilated bodies and 'romper room' torture, and it was a very frightening period for many Catholics, marked also by the growth to quite massive numbers of the UDA, which paraded in paramilitary gear and masks. There was also a major confrontation between the UDA and the British army in Woodvale in Belfast. The British army climbed down.

Unionism had depended for so long on its leadership that, when that leadership failed to deliver, unionism was for a period lost—not only because its leadership had proved inadequate, but also because the British government on which it depended, to which it pledged allegiance, to which it felt bound and of which it was a subject, took away Stormont. Their disarray became exacerbated when the British, under direct rule, took more and more of the everyday decisions and there was no real role for unionist politicians. They had no power.

On the nationalist side, Óglaigh na hÉireann enjoyed credibility and popular support, but the republican movement failed to intervene politically, and effectively handed over the role of political representatives of the nationalist people to the SDLP. Many Catholics adopted a pragmatic attitude then of support for the IRA's military struggle and voting for the SDLP. Some elements claiming to be 'republican' or 'nationalist' made attacks on Protestants. These attacks were quite wrong and, like 'feuding' between republican and other groups, did not serve any anti-unionist interest.

Support for the IRA amongst the nationalist population of the Six Counties has been, as the tacticians of guerrilla warfare such as Mao and Che put it, the sea in which the people's army has swum and, like the sea, it has its tides, its ebbs and flows, but it is always there. The nationalist people had withdrawn their consent to being governed by Stormont; they and the IRA had brought Stormont down and proceeded, in succeeding years, to make the Six Counties ungovernable, even in an environment of British military saturation of nationalist areas. However, a situation of deadlock in which Óglaigh na hÉireann were able to block the imposition of a British solution, but were unable to force the British to withdraw, produced a sense of war-weariness. The IRA had succeeded in bringing down Stormont and they had promised victory in the form of British withdrawal. But victory had not come and the troops were still on the streets, still kicking down doors in the night, wrecking nationalists' houses, dragging people off for interrogation, torture and internment. British army patrols were sometimes truculent, sometimes terrified, but they were always there; whether you were going shopping or to work, to the pub or just around the corner to a relative or friend, they were always there. And that operated in many ways: it made people determined to resist, and it made people weary. British soldiers harassed children leaving schools; mothers went down to the schools to bring their children home and prevent them responding to the provocations of the soldiers with stones; mothers saw sons graduating from stones to petrol bombs to membership of the IRA, to Long Kesh internment camp. Hardly a family was untouched by death, internment or imprisonment. Heroically they kept their households going, often holding down a job while their husband and perhaps a son as well were in prison, coping on the barest level of subsistence, visiting Long Kesh regularly. Some became political activists in the Relatives Action Committee or in Sinn Féin; they marched and demonstrated and came to be the heart and soul of popular resistance.

Chapter Three

In the face of the suffering of the war of resistance in the nationalist ghettos, it was inevitable that a war-weary opposition to the IRA would surface on occasions. It may well be, as other observers and authors have suggested, that some of these movements of opposition received encouragement and finance from the British government, including British army sources. The appalling disruption of everyday life, the incessant assault on nerves by the tension of wondering whether a son, daughter, wife, husband, brother or sister was going to be lifted, beaten up in interrogation, interned or killed, the frequent dangers of loyalist assassination campaigns—all the strains of the situation inevitably raised the question in people's minds as to whether it was all worth it. No one wanted to go back to the 'normality' of rule by Stormont, but with no immediate prospect of a British withdrawal, support for the struggle of the IRA was bound to waver. In particular, the British government exploited every opportunity to increase the sense of war-weariness; and, especially when Óglaigh na hÉireann killed or injured civilians, the British were always, in classical counter-insurgency fashion, cynically prepared to exploit these mistakes or to create the conditions in which they might occur.

There always has been and there always will be a yearning for peace among Irish people. The so-called 'Peace People' are the best-known example of an organized movement against the IRA campaign, but there have been other organizations through the years, such as 'Women Together' and 'Protestant and Catholic Encounter,' and there have been occasions when people in nationalist areas have protested against IRA actions without actually forming any organization. But whenever this understandable and undoubtedly genuine desire for peace manifests itself, it is open to exploitation for one political purpose or another. It is easy to suggest that peace is somehow not political and that peace marches are not political, and then sincere people can be swept along behind a vague and emotional demand.

I have very strong personal feelings about the 'Peace People' campaign of 1976. The IRA man, Danny Lennon, who was shot dead in the incident which gave rise to the campaign, had been a particular friend of mine since we had met in Cage 11 in Long Kesh. It was tragic enough that he and the Maguire children had been killed, but, when the British lie about his death was picked up by the media and gained general acceptance, I found it a great deal more difficult to deal with.

The facts of the incident were that Danny Lennon was shot dead at the wheel of the car he was driving by British soldiers firing from an armour-plated landrover and the car ploughed into the Maguire family at the side of the road. Mrs Maguire was seriously injured and three of her children, the oldest of whom was eight years and the youngest only six weeks, were killed. It was never clear whether they were killed by the car or by bullets fired by British soldiers; unusually, the results of the autopsies and inquest were never published.

No attention was focused on the fact that the British troops had opened fire on a car without regard for the lives of civilians on the street. Instead, the headlines shouted their message that an IRA car had killed three children. And, on BBC TV News that night, Mrs Maguire's sister, Mairead Corrigan, broke down crying and understandably affected millions of viewers deeply.

Danny Lennon had been shot dead, yet he was being held solely responsible for the deaths of the Maguire children. It was bad enough that innocent children had been killed. That was awful. But Danny Lennon, now dead and unable to defend himself, was being blamed. That concern may appear ridiculous to people who have an image of IRA volunteers as terrorists, but the reality is that members of Óglaigh na hÉireann are just ordinary citizens who are forced through difficult circumstances into resistance, and Danny Lennon was an ordinary nationalist youth, a member of a large family in Andersonstown, who had become involved in resistance. The tragedy of the deaths of the children rankled, and, in particular, the way in which the British escaped any responsibility at all, by exploitating the children's deaths, and because of the cynical way in which the incident was manipulated.

The 'Peace People' lost credibility in nationalist areas very quickly. In fact, what credibility it had consisted basically of sympathy for the Maguires and, indeed, for the Lennons. Only four days after the deaths of the Maguire children, a twelve-year-old girl, Majella O'Hare, was shot and killed by British soldiers in South Armagh; the 'Peace People' offered no criticism of the British army. Two months later, fourteen-year-old Brian Stewart was shot dead by British soldiers in West Belfast; again, the 'Peace

People' were silent, and when they went to a meeting in Turf Lodge they had to be escorted from the hall because of the fury of local people at the one-sidedness of their condemnation of violence. If that was not enough to seal their fate in Catholic areas, they put the cap on it when they characterized the RUC, UDR and British army as 'the only legitimate upholders of the rule of law' and played down what they called 'the occasional instances when members of the security forces may have stepped beyond the rule of law.'

The movement showed that there is always a hope among people that there can be peace, an element of war-weariness that grabs at straws. The people who marched and prayed and engaged in rallies were expressing perfectly reasonable emotions, but these emotions were exploited. The 'Peace People' were not even calling for real and general peace: what they were calling for was an end to the armed struggle of the IRA. And that was at best a partial kind of peace, in both meanings of partial—prejudiced against only one element in a violent conflict and incomplete in that it did not base itself on the elements of social justice without which peace simply cannot grow. It was an attempt to move people away from republican physical force politics, and it failed because it did not even seek to remedy the reasons why people felt compelled to have recourse to physical force.

As soon as they tried to examine what peace was and how it could be attained, the leadership of the 'Peace People' began to collapse. The media, perhaps because of their nature, represented the failure as lying in the falling out between Mairead Corrigan, Betty Williams and Ciaran McKeown as they disputed who should get what money. But the real reason was far larger than this merely symptomatic disintegration. Peace rallies and prayer may give succour to people, but they cannot of their own volition bring peace. Peace is a political question and cannot be successfully approached without a commitment to political change.

For a short period, the 'Peace People' succeeded in diverting public—and particularly international—attention from the real problem of the political situation in the Six Counties. In the end, it brought into question the credibility not only of its own leaders but also of the Nobel Peace Prize, Joan Baez, and others who associated themselves with it.

The episode—for that is what it was—of the 'Peace People' deserves to be regarded as a particularly sad one, because it represented a perversion of what is a very important demand. In practice, people have been demanding peace since long before the IRA became active. In my own area of Ballymurphy, community groups have long demanded employment, decent housing, play centres, facilities for the aged, the handicapped and the young. They have sought freedom from heavy rents on homes they will never own, freedom from the dole queues and freedom from the Assistance Office. At the time of the 'Peace People,' the facilities of the area were a public house, a row of shops, and a bookmaker's office. One hundred of the six hundred families had more than ten people living in cramped, ill-repaired, misplanned, jerry-built houses. Forty-seven percent of the residents were unemployed. Sixty percent of the population were children and teenagers faced with a future which offered them nothing. Those demands for the kind of peace which is based on justice and equality were made year after year, and year after year they were refused.

We cannot have justice and peace in Ireland, because we do not have a society capable of upholding them. Instead, we have a system based on coercion, violence, sectarianism and exploitation. By its very nature, British rule cannot be just or peaceful and, while this is so, revolutionary struggle will continue to strive to overthrow it in pursuit of true justice, peace and happiness. Violence in Ireland has its roots in the conquest of Ireland by Britain. This conquest has lasted through several stages for many centuries and, whether economic, political, territorial or cultural, it has used violence, coercion, sectarianism and terrorism as its methods and has had power as its objective. While the armed struggle has traditionally dominated republican strategy, in this phase it has involved and depended upon a considerable degree of political support. IRA members do not go to people who provide support without being receptive to their thoughts. They do not constantly ask people to do things for them without being responsive to their needs, being careful about how they deal with them, and taking on board some of the criticisms they might have of aspects of the armed struggle. Not only is that receptiveness and responsiveness correct in political terms, it is also a practical necessity in everyday circumstances. If a person providing support is

49

offended by the actions of Óglaigh na hÉireann, then that person will withdraw their support and it will not be possible to continue with the armed activity as before.

Aspects of the nature of the armed struggle can be explored by comparing the British soldier and the IRA volunteer. The British soldier is brought to Ireland; he has all his equipment handed to him, he is put into a garrison, given his transport and pointed at whatever task it is that he has to perform. IRA volunteers first of all have to obtain weapons; these may be given to them by higher command or they may have to procure them themselves. They then have to arrange to be able to dump those weapons, and to do this they have to enlist someone's support. If they are on the run, they have to arrange billets for themselves, they have to go and ask someone if they can stay in their house. They have no meal tickets: someone has to agree to feed them. And if they want to get from A to B, they have to get someone to agree to provide transport.

To get through a normal day, an active IRA volunteer is involved in politics all the time, continually enlisting support, going to people and asking them to do this and that for him or her. Even if one could describe the armed struggle of Óglaigh na hÉireann as militaristic, it bears little resemblance to what may be called militarism in terms of a standing army. Despite all the British propaganda stories, it is obvious that the IRA exists and operates with the active consent of a sufficient number of people to finance, arm, clothe, feed, accommodate and transport IRA volunteers and in every way build up around them a voluntary political infrastructure.

The armed struggle requires the development of reflex physical force politics. Even if there were no unarmed political struggle, the armed struggle itself has a significant political dimension to it and involves a significant political relationship with the community. As volunteers develop their politics, their vision of the goal they are aiming for, as they come to understand the politics of their opponents and the way the struggle needs to develop, then comes an understanding that armed struggle itself is a tactic and that one cannot shoot or bomb an independent Ireland into existence. You may be able to bomb and shoot a British connection out of existence, given many other necessary political conditions, but you will not bring anything into existence.

The tactic of armed struggle is of primary importance because it provides a vital cutting edge. Without it, the issue of Ireland would not even be an issue. So, in effect, the armed struggle becomes armed propaganda. There has not been, at least not yet, a classic development from guerrilla action to mass military action registering territorial gains; instead, armed struggle has become an agent of bringing about change. That reality is understood even by middle-class professional people, people who have a stake in the Six Counties. Very many people who disagree absolutely with the IRA nevertheless see it as a very important part of the political equation. They might deplore it, dislike it, have moral objections to it, but still have the feeling that if it did not exist there would be no hope of getting change. At the same time, there is a realization in republican circles that armed struggle on its own is inadequate and that non-armed forms of political struggle are at least as important. As a means of struggle against the British presence in the Six Counties in pursuance of national independence, armed action represents a necessary form of struggle; it has, however, no role to play in the Twenty-six Counties. The struggle there must be non-armed, complimentary to the struggle in the Six Counties and aimed also at securing national independence.

There are considerable moral problems in relation to armed struggle. I cannot conceive of any thinking person who would not have scruples about inflicting any form of hurt on another living being. The republican carrying out an armed action might be very ruthless, determined and callous, but intellectually and emotionally he or she would have difficulty. That difficulty would rarely lie in any sense of religious morality, but would have to do with the type of struggle involved, because it is close-up and it is nothing like joining a 'regular' army with a whole ethos about being trained to kill. IRA volunteers are actually civilians, political people who decide, for short periods in their lives, to take part in armed action. That is different from somebody who wants to join a 'regular' army, who wants to be a good shot, who wants a military career. The reality is of people who have consciously decided that armed struggle is a political necessity and that they will, in a fairly haphazard way, train themselves in the rudiments of military capability. There are no careerists in the IRA. Republican volunteers face futures of suffering, imprisonment and death.

Chapter Three

What gives many people a problem is the length of the struggle. Even ordinary people who feel reservations might not have the same reservations if they felt it was going to be over in a short space of time—a two- or three-year war after which you start building right away. And it is worth pointing out what has happened in other, analogous situations, that the revolutionaries become the best builders; apart from their political commitment, perhaps because of their previous involvement in the destruction of other human beings.

The morality of the establishment does not concern me at all. It is a case—to borrow a phrase from Seamus Deane's *Civilians and Barbarians*—of a 'political code disguised as a moral code.' I once heard the then Taoiseach Garret FitzGerald saying that he would not talk to those who would not renounce violence, and then he went to meet Margaret Thatcher, who was up to her neck in the use of armed force in Ireland and other parts of the world. No republican would have the brass neck to express such blatant double standards.

Obviously, I would prefer a situation where armed struggle was unnecessary or even where armed struggle could be limited completely to what one could awkwardly call 'clean' operations, where you had Óglaigh na hÉireann and the British army shooting it out. I do not mean 'shooting it out' in some kind of heroic sense. The odds are stacked against the IRA volunteers and they operate at great personal risk against forces which are numerically and technologically superior and much better equipped. I admire the tenacity, determination and self-sacrifice of IRA volunteers, but I do not think that any war should be glamorized. In the Six Counties, armed struggle is a terrible but necessary form of resistance which is engaged in as a means towards an independent Ireland. The assessment in November 1978, by Brigadier J.M. Glover of British army intelligence, concluded that, while the British army remained in Ireland, the IRA would remain in existence to fight them. Most impartial observers and many opponents of republicanism recognize that the British presence is the catalyst for the armed struggle.

There are no material benefits for volunteers. Even a *Sunday Tribune* investigation had to conclude that they could find no evidence of republicans making material gains from their involvement. If the life of an IRA volunteer was a career, one might be able to talk about people who wanted to keep the war going rather than lose their livelihoods, but there is not even that mercenary element. War is a very draining process and, at some time, we are going to have to get on with our own lives and pursue our own private ambitions. After all the years of struggle, I look at the city of Belfast which I admire so much and I feel sick about the way in which it has been turned upside-down and I regret that people throughout the course of this war have suffered so much in so many different ways.

A repeated assertion by past Dublin governments and some other elements opposed to us is that, because republicans are engaged in armed action now, they would continue to use armed action in an independent Ireland. What I think they are really saying is that an independent Ireland poses a threat to them, that getting rid of partition means opening a Pandora's box. They are threatened by the spectre of the working people, Protestant and Catholic, no longer divided by partition or sectarian privilege and as a majority galvanizing their political position. They are threatened by the notion of normal class politics developing in an independent Ireland, invigorated and encouraged by an immense feeling of euphoria after the settlement of this long war. And the only people who are threatened by that are those who have a vested interest in maintaining the status quo. These, then, are the people who are loudest in their condemnation of the armed struggle and who nowadays hold up the prospect that the republicans are going to come over the border and visit violence upon the Twenty-six Counties. This is not going to happen.

I meet members of the public constantly in the Twenty-six Counties. I cannot be anywhere in a public place or even walk down the street without people coming over and telling me what they think. Their main concern in relation to the IRA is that the war is going on so long. Some have a particular political attitude, in that they would like to see the British out, some are concerned about the loyalists and the difficulty posed by the strength of loyalism. But, in all my fairly widespread travels in the Twenty-six Counties, the worry about the IRA being habituated to violence has not been expressed.

Even if one looks at the matter from a purely tactical point of view, the ingredients for armed struggle are inherent in the Six County state. But, following the restoration of Irish national independence, there would be no popular support for armed struggle. The handful of people who make up Óglaigh na hÉireann could not hope to win anything by pursuing armed struggle without popular support. In its origins and in its continuing role, the modern IRA is an almost entirely working-class organization of political militants which enjoys popular support amongst nationalists in the cities, towns and countryside of the Six Counties and a degree of passive support in the Twenty-six Counties. British army Brigadier J.M. Glover was forced to conclude that:

> Our evidence of the calibre of rank and file terrorists (sic) does not support the view that they are merely mindless hooligans drawn from the unemployed and unemployable.

A study of lawyers of defendants appearing before the Diplock (non-jury) courts charged with 'scheduled' offences produces another outsiders' view of IRA volunteers (though by no means all those charged before the courts were IRA members or even republican activists):

> We are satisfied that the data establishes beyond reasonable doubt that the bulk of the republican offenders are young men and women without criminal records in the ordinary sense, though some have been involved in public disorders of the kind that frequently took place in the areas in which they lived. Both in this respect and in other records of employment and unemployment, they are reasonably representative of the working-class community of which they form a substantial part ... They do not fit the stereotype of criminality which the authorities have from time to time attempted to attach to them.

It seems strange to reproduce such sociological comment upon my comrades of the republican movement, but I am aware that there may be readers of this book who are habitual consumers of the British press, the Six Counties press or the Twenty-six Counties press and who are habitual listeners to or viewers of British or Irish television and radio. Given the constant stream of lies which have spewed out over the years, not just from the British and Dublin governments but also from the media, it may be useful to show that even lawyers and a senior figure in British military intelligence are forced to recognize that the IRA are neither hooligans nor criminals.

I find it ridiculous to have to make these points because they have nothing to do with reality; they have instead to do with a crude propaganda war. The very people who originate the propaganda lines that wind up as press headlines know perfectly well that the IRA is not a matter of 'godfathers of crime,' of 'pathological killers,' of 'mad bombers,' of 'mindless hooligans;' they know that, in dealing with the IRA, they are dealing with determined political opponents who are using the only means at their disposal to bring home their message in terms that will be understood and taken seriously enough to result in action and movement.

An example today of how far the British government is prepared to go to break republican resistance can be found in their efforts to dehumanize women republican prisoners by the brutal means of forced strip-searching. It is an indication of the courage and resilience of these women that after years of being subjected, sometimes on a daily basis, to this brutal, degrading and inhuman treatment, the women remain unbowed and unbroken. Similarly, there is the plight of long-term prisoners, especially the young prisoners, serving unprecedented sentences at the whim of a British judge or a British government minister. Many of these prisoners started their sentences as juveniles and are now in their thirties. Others were young married men and are now grandfathers. This experience has obviously traumatized their families, and it is a miracle of human endurance and a credit especially to the wives and mothers that their families have survived. It is also remarkable that so many released prisoners return to the struggle, and it is an indication of the durability of resistance that there is still an active struggle to embrace them after ten, twelve or thirteen years of imprisonment.

The IRA is ordinary people facing up against the monster of imperial power. It is part of the long tradition of physical force in Irish politics created by British militarism in Ireland

Our fervent hope is that today's IRA volunteers will be the last of that long line of fighters for Irish freedom. By removing the causes of conflict in our country we will speed that day.

4

Political Status

If you strike at, imprison or kill us,
Out of our prisons or graves.
We will still evoke a spirit that will thwart you,
And, mayhap, raise a force that will destroy you.
We defy you! Do your worst.
James Connolly, December 1914

T HE MOST SUSTAINED British propaganda campaign
against the IRA was organized against the background of a
protracted cessation of IRA activity around the attempt to
portray IRA members as 'common criminals.' Abolishing political
status for prisoners charged with 'scheduled' (i.e. war-related)
offences, the British engaged in an intense and energetic campaign
of psychological warfare, or 'psy-ops.' Press releases, speeches and
statements from the administration referred consistently to republican leaders as 'godfathers' and suchlike. Stories of corruption and
gangsterism in the republican movement were invented and judi-
ciously placed in Fleet Street. The advent of the 'Peace People' in
August of the same year, 1976, was well-timed to add substantially
to the British propaganda effort.

In the nationalist ghettos, popular mobilizations were at an
all-time low and the prevailing atmosphere was one of war-weariness. Sinn Féin, its ability to organize constantly undermined by
arrest, harassment and imprisonment, was a small protest organization and support group for the IRA and was only experiencing the
first stirrings of a feeling that it needed to develop itself as a political
organization capable of intervening and mobilizing on a range of

issues. The Relatives Action Committee, comprising almost exclusively women from the ghettos of nationalist West Belfast, stood outside the republican movement and had only a limited capacity to mobilize support for the prisoners. The policy of 'criminalization' struck at the heart of the republican struggle, and it did so at a time when it was politically weak. The resilience of nationalist resistance and the central question of support for the IRA were to be tested over the six years from 1976 to 1981 as never before.

The republican insistence on the importance of political prisoner status has nothing to do with any contempt for the 'ordinary criminals' who are so often the victims of social inequality and injustice. From Thomas Ashe to Bobby Sands, the concern has always been to assert the political nature of the struggle in which the IRA has been engaged. In September 1917, eighty-four republican prisoners went on hunger strike for political status; one of them, Thomas Ashe, leader of the Irish Republican Brotherhood, died after force feeding; political status was granted then by the British authorities and Ashe's death proved a turning-point in rallying mass support behind the demand for independence. British governments have from time to time granted and withdrawn political status. In June 1972, a hunger strike in Crumlin Road prison in Belfast led by Billy McKee resulted in the recognition of political status. Republicans were asserting the political nature of their struggle and contradicting the British attempt to suggest to the world that the political crisis in the Six Counties was not a political crisis at all, but was merely a problem with criminal elements.

The contradictions in the British position were enormous but their access to world media and the resources they could bring to bear in the propaganda war meant that they could achieve considerable success in presenting the struggle in the Six Counties as a species of 'Mafia terrorism.' When the contradictions threatened to emerge, they used various means in their continuing psy-ops war to obscure the reality of the situation. And the reality was that special laws had been enacted to counter the armed struggle of the IRA; the law was being used, to repeat Brigadier Kitson's phrase, as 'just another weapon in the government's arsenal...a propaganda cover.' Special courts had been established, known as the Diplock courts, to deprive those accused of 'special category' or 'scheduled' offences of trial by jury. Special concentration camps had been constructed to house those convicted of special category offences, as well as those interned without trial. To turn around then and deny that these were special category prisoners was to fly in the face of logic and reality.

An essential element in Britain's criminalization strategy was the conveyor-belt system of—to use Kitson's phrase again—'disposal of unwanted members of the public.' Juryless courts were not sufficient to secure guaranteed convictions of republicans, but the systematic use of torture, primarily carried out in the purpose-built interrogation centre of Castlereagh in Belfast, ensured that detainees could be forced to sign incriminating statements. Once anyone had signed a statement, it was only a matter of passing them on to the next stage of the conveyor-belt where British judges did the job they were paid for and processed them on to the final stage, the H-Blocks of Long Kesh or the Women's Prison in Armagh.

Republicans faced an uphill battle in trying to reverse the tide of British government propaganda. Even when the facts indicated to any competent journalist that wholesale torture was producing litanies of dubious confessions, the media were determined to avoid reporting anything which might seem to support the republican position. However, when, in June 1978, Amnesty International called for a public inquiry into the 'maltreatment' practised at Castlereagh RUC station, the media were at last prepared to admit that something was going on and the first chink appeared in Britain's propaganda war. Giving just seventy-eight cases of maltreatment of suspects, and estimating that between seventy percent and ninety percent of Diplock court convictions were achieved on the sole or main basis of self-incriminating statements, the Amnesty report was far from comprehensive and failed to document the extent and intensity of the torture policy.

However, weak as it was, the Amnesty report posed enough of a threat to Britain's psy-ops for the Independent Broadcasting Authority (IBA) to step in and ban a television programme on it. Later in the same year, Fr Raymond Murray and Fr Denis Faul published a far more extensive report on Castlereagh. Fr Faul was in the habit of making vitriolic attacks on republicans and received considerable media attention for these attacks; on the other hand, his and Fr Murray's collations of British brutality, such as their file on Castlereagh, were either ignored or received with hostility by the media.

However, the success of this British strategy began to falter when a police surgeon, Dr Robert Irwin, came forward to state that he had personal knowledge of at least 150 people who had been seriously injured in RUC custody at Castlereagh. Even Independent Television News could not ignore such authoritative evidence, and the British government were faced with a problem. The busy beavers of the British army intelligence psy-ops department quickly spread rumours designed to destroy the doctor's credibility, alleging that he was seeking revenge for his wife's rape by a British soldier. The government also rushed out a report, the Bennett Report, which offered the mildest of rebukes to those engaged in the torture in Castlereagh. However, the British had suffered a setback in their propaganda war, and it was probably at this time that they began to lay plans for the use of paid informers to secure convictions.

Attention switched to the H-Blocks of Long Kesh, where republican prisoners developed their own opposition to British policy. Prisoners required under the new conditions, after 1 March 1976, to a wear prison uniform, rejected this badge of criminalization and, not permitted to wear their own clothing, wore blankets instead. The republican attitude was well captured in Francie Brolly's song:

> I'll wear no convict's uniform
> Nor meekly serve my time
> That England might
> Brand Ireland's fight
> 800 years of crime.

Kieran Nugent, the first person to be sentenced for a 'scheduled offence' after the arbitrarily chosen date, was first to refuse, on 14 September 1976, to wear prison clothing. 'If they want me to wear a convict's uniform,' he said, 'they'll have to nail it to my back.'

Parallel with their withdrawal of political status, the British government stepped up their propaganda campaign to portray the IRA as 'godfathers of terrorism' manipulating naive teenagers into committing robberies so that these same 'godfathers' could live in luxury houses and drive luxury cars. In particular, they successfully promoted to sections of the British media the image of Maire Drumm, Vice-President of Sinn Féin, as a 'godmother of terrorism' and 'grandmother of hate.' She was shot dead in bed at the Mater Hospital in Belfast where she was being treated for cataracts.

Prison warders subjected the 'blanket men' to constant harassment. In 1978, they attacked prisoners as they went to and from the latrines, kicked over chamber pots in cells and threw the contents of pots onto beds. The prisoners were forced to respond by escalating the 'blanket' protest to a 'no wash' stage; they refused to shave, wash or empty chamber pots. Conditions rapidly became appalling.

Cardinal Tomás Ó Fiaich visited the H-Blocks in August 1978 and gave the following description:

> One could hardly allow an animal to remain in such conditions, let alone a human being. The nearest approach to it that I have ever seen was the spectacle of hundreds of homeless people living in the sewer pipes of the slums of Calcutta. The stench and the filth in some of the cells with the remains of rotten food and human excreta scattered around the walls was almost unbearable.

At the time, the prison authorities, the government and the media portrayed the 'no wash' protest as arising simply from a conscious decision by the prisoners. However, I was brought to Long Kesh, held on remand on a charge of IRA membership, and discovered for myself how the provocation by the prison officers had brought the situation about.

Relatives—almost all women—of prisoners had, in late April 1976, set up the Relatives Action Committee to campaign for the restoration of political status. However, within Sinn Féin we lacked a structured national political response to the prison crisis. This began to change after the 1978 Sinn Féin Ard Fheis, at which Ruairi Ó Brádaigh, then President of Sinn Féin, drew attention to the true nature of the situation and signposted it as a priority for the movement. From that point on, we attempted to build support on the outside for the protest of the prisoners.

The Relatives Action Committee, which was campaigning energetically, was a Belfast-based organization and, while we related to
it locally, we were unable to take a national approach to it. But,
recognizing our considerable shortcomings in dealing with the question, we held a national conference on the prison issue in 1979, a
conference which involved the whole membership in detailed consideration. It was the first time that Sinn Féin had actually sat
down and looked at a single issue, analyzed it, discussed it and then
embarked on spreading the knowledge shared and the conclusions
come to, and it marked an important development for us.

We set about creating a proper POW department, which until
then had been simply a service for the prisoners, and we began to
look at the issue in terms of a political campaign. We produced
pamphlets and leaflets and we began to seek ways to broaden out
the campaign to involve other forces apart from our own members.

The creation of the H-Block/Armagh Committee as a united
front was a very important element of the hunger strike. In 1978,
we made a mistake in our approach to a conference called to discuss
the building of a broad anti-unionist front. Lack of experience and
lack of preparation on our part resulted in this Coalisland conference becoming a lost opportunity to build unity, because the price
our representatives asked for that unity was that all within the front
should express support for the armed struggle of the IRA. It was a
price that many of those who wished to unite in anti-unionist
action were not prepared to pay. One of the problems we suffered
from at that time was that we were still emerging from a basically
conspiratorial type of organization. Also, we suffered from the
effects of a high rate of attrition: members who had been involved
in earlier united action with the Political Hostages Release
Committee (1973-4) may well have learned lessons from it, but
many or most of them were in jail or for other reasons were not
involved in our intervention in the Coalisland conference.

Sinn Féin was a protest movement and a movement of support
for the IRA; it was, at that time, only just beginning to discuss
strategy and tactics, to assess what our attitudes should be in any
given circumstances. Part of the impact of our conspiratorial background was that we were temperamentally and organizationally
disinclined to engage in any form of action with elements outside
the movement itself. The movement had its origins in armed

61

struggle, which had dominated to the extent of even being considered the only form of struggle; in such circumstances conspiratorial methods were, of course, essential. But what we were slowly and unevenly realizing was that one could not build a political intervention on the basis of conspiratorial methods and approaches.

The IRA was constantly being denounced from all quarters and all standpoints. It was understandable that members of the movement had considerable difficulty in accepting the right of people with whom they were involved in joint action to attack the IRA. Members were increasingly coming into contact with organizations that expressed a position of 'critical support' for the IRA, and any republican was bound to feel that one either supported the IRA or one did not; 'critical support' seemed a contradiction in terms and a dishonest one at that. It took a maturing process on the part of republicans to appreciate that a position of critical support was better than one of not supporting at all.

By October 1979, our attitude to united action had changed dramatically and we had dropped the insistence on support for the armed struggle. At a conference in the Green Briar Hotel in Andersonstown, organized by the Relatives Action Committee, the organizations which set up the H-Block/Armagh Committee included Sinn Féin, the Irish Republican Socialist Party (IRSP), People's Democracy (PD), the Trade Union Campaign Against Repression (TUCAR) and Women Against Imperialism (WAI). There were even representatives present from the 'Peace People.'

While we were making attempts to organize the political campaign, the protest was continuing inside the prisons, and the IRA, for its part, was carrying out a campaign of shooting prison officers, nine being killed in 1979. To the prisoners themselves it seemed that little headway was being made, and they began to suggest that they should instigate a hunger strike. Brendan Hughes and others wrote from Long Kesh pointing out that the protest had been going on for three years and suggested that, while the older prisoners could take it, the length of the protest placed an intolerable burden on the young prisoners coming into the blocks. Eighteen- and nineteen-year-olds faced the prospect of spending ten years on the blanket and no wash protest. There was an almost parental concern on the part of the older prisoners. And they felt that the onus was on them to achieve a short-term resolution of the prison conflict.

This they proposed to pursue by means of a hunger strike. We advised strongly against hunger strike and promised—perhaps somewhat rashly and naively—to achieve movement on the issue by intensifying our efforts on the outside.

Meanwhile, the crisis in the prisons intensified. In February 1980, male guards wrecked the cells of republican women prisoners at Armagh jail and beat up several of the women. Prisoners were allowed to wear their own clothes at Armagh and so there had been no 'blanket' protest, but now the women responded to the attacks on them and joined the struggle of their male comrades by embarking on the 'no wash' protest. In March, the British government extended the denial of political status to those prisoners who had been sentenced before 1 March 1976; there was no sign that the government was willing to take significant steps to defuse the crisis.

The H-Block/Armagh Committee worked hard to raise public consciousness and bring pressure to bear on the British government. Allied to this campaigning, we engaged in intense lobbying. But the H-Block/Armagh campaign was unable to force the British government into movement on the issue, and, in October 1980, the prisoners decided to go on hunger strike. In Sinn Féin we felt we were in no position to stop them, as a year previously we had said that we would sort it out and now they were saying to us, in the nicest possible way, that we had failed. So, we were under an obligation to support the hunger strike—we had tried our means, now the prisoners were going to try theirs.

In late October, seven H-Block prisoners started a hunger strike; in late November, they were joined by three women prisoners in Armagh and, in December, thirty more H-Block prisoners went on hunger strike. One of the seven weakened physically more rapidly than the rest: he was losing his sight and was on the verge of lapsing into a coma. The British government, despite taking a hard line of 'no concessions' in public, indicated that a compromise could be reached and that a document setting out details of a settlement would be presented to the prisoners if they came off hunger strike. The hunger strikers considered the condition of Sean McKenna, who was fast approaching death, and considered the indications of movement by the government. Sean McKenna was too ill to take part in their deliberations. On the fifty-third day of the strike, 18 December, they called off the protest. Later

63

that day, the British presented a document to the prisoners, but, meanwhile, they were presenting the world news with a story of surrender, without giving details of any compromise package. The women in Armagh refused to come off hunger strike until they were assured by us that the men had actually ended their fast.

The document did not represent the kind of settlement that the prisoners would have accepted after negotiations, but Sinn Féin tried very hard, with Bobby Sands who was OC of the IRA in Long Kesh at the time, to work positively within the confines of this very ambiguous and undefined set of proposals. Had they possessed the political will, the British government could creditably, within the terms of their own document, have found a basis for a step-by-step implementation of the prisoners' demands, but I presume that, when they saw the decline in morale which followed the end of the hunger strike, they decided to obstruct any form of movement within the prisons. Twenty prisoners tested the willingness of the government to implement changes by coming off the 'no wash' and blanket protest, and relatives brought clothes to Long Kesh, but, on 20 January 1981, the prison authorities refused to distribute the clothes to the men. The prisoners drew their conclusions and, one week later, a group of them smashed up their cells. Preparation began immediately for a second hunger strike.

Through Bobby Sands, the prisoners conveyed to the republican movement outside the prisons their absolute determination to embark on another hunger strike. In calm, reasoned correspondence, they showed that coldly and clinically they had worked out in great detail exactly how it would proceed. From the outside, we continued to advise the prisoners that their deaths would not necessarily achieve the improvements they sought. They could be dead without any advantages accruing, either in terms of prison conditions or of the overall struggle. Also, we felt that the movement could not stand another defeated hunger strike. I wrote to Bobby Sands: 'Bobby, we are tactically, strategically, physically and morally opposed to a hunger strike.' But, by the time we had gone through all the arguments in our correspondence, I knew that Bobby Sands was going to die.

The prison conditions could have operated as a safety valve: a sophisticated British government could have defused the situation quite easily and avoided a confrontation between itself, as

unyielding colonial power, and a group of defenceless political prisoners, which is how it largely came to be seen internationally. The
first hunger strike having ended, they would not have been acting
under duress if they had allowed for some new arrangements on
the specifics of prison conditions. But, as the prisoners pressed for
a second hunger strike, they knew that this time not only would
some of them have to die but also that they were engaging in a
fight with the British government which now went beyond the
issue of prison conditions; they were pitching themselves, with the
only weapons at their command, against the imperial power. As
they faced the prospect of death, they felt that the spectacle of their
deaths in prison was going to be politically productive for the
republican cause to which they were committed.

Hunger-strike is unlike any other form of struggle. An IRA volunteer does not go out to get killed; if he or she gets killed it is
because he or she makes a mistake or some other circumstance arises.
But a hunger striker embarks on a process which, from day one, is
designed to end in his or her death. However, when people con-
template their own deaths, there can be no guarantee that all will
go according to plan, no guarantee that they will go through with
it to the end. It takes a very particular kind of person to go all the
way, to resist the voices in one's own head, the concern of friends
and family, not to mention the pressures of the authorities, and it is
extremely difficult to know, until one is staring death right in the
face, whether one is that particular kind of person.

Our opposition in Sinn Féin to the hunger strike had to do
partly with that difficulty, partly with the fact that close personal
relationships existed between the prisoners themselves and between
prisoners and republicans on the outside, and we all knew that we
were entering a period of intense anguish. But, primarily, we
opposed it because we did not believe that it would succeed in
moving the British government. It must also be said that, in terms
of the political priorities of the movement, we did not want the
hunger strike. We were just beginning our attempts to remedy the
political underdevelopment of the movement, trying to develop the
organization, engaging in a gradual build-up of new forms of
struggle and, in particular, we were working out our strategy in
relation to elections. We were well aware that a hunger strike such
as was proposed would demand exclusive attention, would, in

effect, hijack the struggle, and this conflicted with our sense of the political priorities of the moment.

Bobby Sands started his hunger strike on 1 March 1981, the fifth anniversary of the phasing out of political status. A large demonstration marched down the Falls Road in support of Bobby Sands and the five demands of the prisoners:

1. The right to wear their own clothing at all times.
2. Exemption from all forms of penal labour.
3. Free association with each other at all hours.
4. The right to organize their own recreational and educational programmes.
5. Full restoration of remission.

Francis Hughes joined Bobby on hunger strike on 15 March, Ray McCreesh and Patsy O'Hara a week later.

After the initial march in Belfast, the campaign of support developed slowly. It was difficult to mobilize people after the demoralizing effect of the first hunger strike, and we struggled to organize even small-scale actions such as pickets. However, the calling of a by-election in Fermanagh/South Tyrone, where sitting MP Frank Maguire, an independent nationalist, had died suddenly, provided an immediate and dynamic focus for the campaign.

Young and not so young Sinn Féin members had no experience of organizing an electoral campaign, but they had plenty of energy and commitment and they combined well with independent republicans in the constituency, with Bernadette MacAliskey (formerly Devlin) and with big Joe Keohane—up from Kerry to canvass support. On 9 April, Bobby Sands was elected Member of the Westminster Parliament with 30,492 votes. His victory exposed the lie that the hunger strikers—and by extension the IRA and the whole republican movement—had no popular support. The British campaign of 'criminalization,' which motivated their removal of political status, had sought to portray republicans as 'godfathers' operating by intimidation and as isolated fanatics. Their propaganda had now been dramatically refuted and the election of Bobby Sands resounded internationally. For many in the British Labour movement, it was their road to Damascus. It had a particular impact on British MPs simply because of the status that the parliament at Westminster enjoys: a man had been elected on a massive popular vote who was, according to their lights, a terrorist and a criminal who was offering the people nothing.

The election victory intensified international interest in the hunger strike and uplifted absolutely the confidence and morale of republicans. There was a feeling amongst some of our members and supporters that surely the British government must yield sufficiently to bring about an end to the hunger strike. We had been challenged for years to submit ourselves to the ballot box and now we had done so. We had demonstrated massive popular support in votes; the hunger strikers had shown immense and awesome determination; we had mobilized mass demonstrations. Yet, whether we played by their rules or not, the British government, as we had feared from the outset, showed no willingness to make concessions.

However, we began to receive a stream of envoys from the Dublin government whose message was that the British would concede. Charles J. Haughey, who had recently succeeded Jack Lynch as Taoiseach and leader of Fianna Fáil, wanted to hold a general election in the Twenty-six Counties, but the hunger strike brought a degree of instability, or at least of unpredictability, which he was at pains to avoid. The envoys were well-known people in public life and they conveyed a uniform conviction that Charles Haughey was about to secure a means of resolving the hunger strike. One of the phrases used more than once was 'You're pushing at an open door'—a phrase which seems almost to be his motto, since he is said to have used it in several discussions and in negotiations. All the time, the message was that the British government were about to concede the five demands. Our approach, in consultation with the prisoners, was to say, 'Alright, we'll believe you, but could we have that in writing, please?' And it seemed that, as soon as we said that, all agreement collapsed, and to this day I do not know how genuinely those envoys believed in the message they brought to us.

In the midst of everything, some light relief was afforded by a spokesperson for the Dublin government. He was on the phone to Owen Carron in our Belfast office, conveying the same line that Haughey's envoys had been repeating one after the other, only more so. I and a number of others were in the office at the time listening to the conversation, and we were saying to Owen to ask him this and ask him that. Eventually the government spokesperson outlined what he said was a very definite offer from the British government, and Owen asked him if he would stand over that.

'No,' replied the caller, 'as far as I am concerned, I never had this conversation with you.' 'Well,' said Owen, 'you're trying to get this hunger strike stopped. There has to be something more substantial than that.' 'Tell him,' I said to Owen, 'that you have the conversation taped.'

Well, Owen did just that and the government spokesperson erupted with the most amazing tirade of bad language in which the politest epithet was 'fucking bastard'!

There was something perversely funny, too, about the on-off story of the elections in the Twenty-six Counties. Every time an overture was being made to us, the Dublin media were reporting that an election was almost certain to be announced within days. And, as the overtures faded into thin air, the speculations and predictions about election dates were suddenly being dismissed in the media. The Fianna Fáil leadership understood, of course, the possible effect of the hunger strike, and they were trying to get it defused in order to have a clear run in an electoral contest.

In the course of their efforts they placed great emphasis on the International Red Cross, an organization that had already expressed its opposition to political status. Members of Bobby Sands's family were sent for with great urgency; as they travelled south they were met at Swords in north County Dublin by a garda escort and rushed in the early hours, in fairly dramatic circumstances, to see the Taoiseach. Enormous pressure was put on them: if the prisoners, it was said, would only see the Red Cross, then the British would give in and Bobby Sands's life would be saved. After such intense pressure, and with great misgivings, Marcella Sands agreed that the Red Cross should see Bobby. But there was never any real substance to the Red Cross intervention, and they were certainly not a vehicle by means of which the five demands were going to be granted.

Margaret Thatcher maintained her inflexible approach and, despite all the earnest assurances of their envoys, the Dublin government did nothing to shift her from it.

Bobby Sands died on 5 May 1981, the sixty-sixth day of his hunger strike.

This book is not the place to record my personal feelings about the death of this friend and comrade, nor about the deaths of the other hunger strikers. Even if I was able to express those feelings adequately, I am probably still too close to them to be able to reflect upon them in tranquillity. I would not like to live through the awful experience of the hunger strike again. Scarcely a day goes by in which I do not think of the lads who died.

One hundred thousand people followed the funeral procession of Bobby Sands through West Belfast. It was an overwhelming outpouring of public grief and of identification with Bobby Sands and the IRA. Masked volunteers fired a ceremonial volley of shots over the coffin.

Francis Hughes died on 12 May.

On 19 May, the IRA killed five British soldiers with a land mine in South Armagh.

Patsy O'Hara and Ray McCreesh died on 21 May.

On 23 May, local elections took place in the Six Counties. Sinn Féin did not participate, but two IRSP and two PD members stood and were elected to Belfast city council, in the process unceremoniously dumping Gerry Fitt from the seat he had occupied for twenty-three years. Fitt had publicly called on Thatcher not to concede the five demands; now the Conservative Party's favourite Irishman, his political life in Ireland was over.

The Dublin government called a general election for 11 June; the hunger strike continued. The National H-Block/Armagh Committee put up nine republican prisoners—four of them hunger strikers—as candidates.

The media were unanimous in writing off the chances of the prisoner candidates. Political correspondents and editors were so strongly prejudiced against the republican movement that they deserted whatever professional skills, experience and standards they may have possessed and indulged instead in an exercise in wishful thinking. They dismissed the prisoners' campaign as being insignificant and proceeded to ignore it.

So, with no media coverage apart from curt dismissals and condemnations, the campaign had its problems, but we had always received hostile media attention and we knew that there was a layer of potential support which was not dependent for its views on the media mandarins. What posed a more substantial obstacle was the fact that the dominant concerns of voters were economic and social; it was only to be expected that they would cast their ballots according to which parties and candidates seemed to offer the best policies in terms of the matters that affected their everyday lives. Our campaign offered nothing, but asked simply for support for the five demands of the prisoners in the Six Counties. The prisoners were in no position to be able to serve their constituents, so anyone voting for them would have to be content with the notion of not being represented in Leinster House—a consideration of particular significance in a state where politics was so dominated by clientilist concerns and approaches. The National H-Block/Armagh Committee had no base of constituency workers such as provided the foundation for the electoral campaigns of the political parties; in two weeks and without prior constituency work towards an election, campaigns had to be built up and carried out in nine constituencies.

In the event, two prisoner candidates—Paddy Agnew and Kieran Doherty—were elected; a third, Joe McDonnell, was within 300 votes of being elected, and the nine together ran up a very respectable tally of 40,000 votes. It was a triumphant expression of popular support for the prisoners.

Despite the message of the elections, the new government headed by Garret FitzGerald refused, as had Haughey's government, to take the steps proposed by the National H-Block/Armagh Committee: to recall their ambassador from London; to expel the British ambassador from Dublin; end army and garda collaboration with the RUC and British army. The intransigence of Margaret Thatcher was criticized, but no measure was taken which might have caused her to modify her stance.

In late June, the British parliament changed the rules of its own 'democracy' by passing what became known as the 'Sands Bill,' which prevented convicted felons from standing for Westminster elections. They had long demanded that we submit to the ballot box. We had done so and had been spectacularly successful. Their response was to ignore the results, refuse to recognize the MP and the movement he represented, and to change the rules to prevent a similar candidate being elected again.

Our response was to stand Owen Carron, who had been Bobby's election agent, for the new by-election in Fermanagh/South Tyrone.

Joe McDonnell died on hunger strike on 8 July.

Martin Hurson died on 13 July.

Kevin Lynch died on 1 August.

Kieran Doherty, who had been elected to Leinster House, died on 2 August.

Tom McElwee died on 8 August.

Micky Devine died on 20 August.

On the same day, Owen Carron was elected as MP for Fermanagh/South Tyrone, exceeding Bobby Sands's vote by 800.

On 3 October, the six remaining hunger strikers ended their protest. In the meantime, some of the hunger strikers had taken individual decisions to end their hunger strikes. Ten men had sacrificed their lives and massive popular support for their stand had been shown in demonstrations, funerals and elections. Things would never be the same again.

No republican will ever attach the slightest shadow of blame to those hunger strikers who individually ended their fasts. What the ten who died had done was so extraordinary that one almost needs another language in order to convey it in all its awful reality. Catholic clergy intervened with the relatives of hunger strikers to encourage them to bring about an end to the fasts by requesting medical help. But, even without their intervention, it was inevitable that some hunger strikers would eventually pull back in the face of death. I have no regrets whatsoever that some came off their hunger strikes; my regrets are reserved for those who died. My anger is reserved for the government that could quite easily have reached an honourable compromise in the face of the ultimate in selfless dedication to a cause.

Following the end of the hunger strike, adjustments in the prison regime along the lines of the five demands began to be implemented. In an unprecedented way, the prisoners had insisted on being recognized as prisoners in a war of national liberation, and their identity as such had been accepted throughout the world. Britain had been seen internationally as an intransigent force clinging to its last remnant of colonial control. The political and moral standing of Irish republicanism had never been higher.

As the hunger strikers had died and as the H-Block/Armagh campaign had its impact, a process of republicanization took place. Republicans who had done their time in prison and had subsequently dropped out of the movement—people with valuable experience and maturity—recognized that the hunger strikers were undergoing something far harder than anything they had had to suffer, and they came back to the movement. The hunger strike did away with spectator politics. When the only form of struggle being waged was armed struggle, it only needed a small number of people to engage in it. But, with the hunger strike, people could play an active role which could be as limited or as important as billposting, writing letters, or taking part in numerous forms of protest.

The IRA eased back on operations during the hunger strike. But, by the time a number of hunger strikers had died, there was a considerable popular demand for the IRA to take punitive action. Toleration of the IRA increased very significantly, as did identification with it, and this had some strange consequences. There were occasions when IRA volunteers came out on the Falls to engage in armed action, only to have to withdraw because people were crowding around, applauding and patting them on the back.

Prior to the hunger strike we had been planning a slow build-up of electoral intervention, but we were impelled very rapidly into an instant, ill-prepared electoral strategy. The stunning initial success, with the election of Bobby Sands, the election of two prisoners in the Twenty-six Counties and the increased vote in Owen Carron's election, gave many of our members the impression that elections were all about winning. It was not until our second intervention in the Twenty-six Counties, when we tried to follow up the success of our prisoner candidates, that our members began to gain some kind of perspective.

The hunger strike, and the electoral successes associated with it, changed the course of the relationship between the republican movement and British strategy, and set in train a process which continued through to the Hillsborough treaty. The perceived threat posed by republicanism since the hunger strike had led to the new, open relationship between Dublin and London, whereby the two governments now explicitly engaged in collaboration on a joint policy, the overriding aim of which was to deal with the republican threat.

In 1976, the British government tried to criminalize the republican prisoners. In 1981, the republican prisoners criminalized the British government.

5

British Strategy

'For the British to calumniate Republicans and belittle their cause by besmirching them is one thing, but for the Free State to do it is another, and different and worse thing. Because the British will not use British arguments to cloak their actions but Irish ones 'out of our own mouths.'

Liam Mellows, 1922

'Ruling by fooling is a great British art—with great Irish fools to practise on.'

James Connolly, 1914

'The Prime Minister of Ireland...has accepted for all practical purposes and into perpetuity, that there will not be a united Ireland.'

Tom King, 1986

WOLFE TONE DESCRIBED the connection with England as 'the never failing source of all our political evils.' History has confirmed his view, for as long as Britain has sustained its intervention in Ireland it has prevented us from coming to grips with developing on our own terms, as people of all religious denominations and none, an Irish democracy.

The British government and army have no right to Ireland and no right to be in Ireland. Yet today they retain complete authority over the affairs of the people of the Six Counties and dominate the affairs of the people of the Twenty-six. They have never brought peace; rather, in pursuit of their own interests they have created and fostered bitter divisions.

Ireland is historically, culturally and geographically one single unit. The partition of Ireland, established by the British 'Government of Ireland Act' and subsequent British Acts, divides Ireland into two artificial statelets, the boundaries of which were determined by a sectarian head-count and can be maintained only by continuing sectarianism. As the English writer, C.P. Scott, wrote of partition in 1920, it was done 'to entrench the Six Counties against Nationalist Ireland. Its effect will not be to make a solution of the Irish question easier but harder by creating a fresh and powerful obstacle.'

The British connection has lasted through several stages for many centuries and, whether economic, political, territorial or cultural in substance, it has used violence, coercion, sectarianism and terrorism as its principle methods of wielding power and exercising control. It has produced governments which have terrorized to maintain the status quo, organizations which fight to maintain their own privileged positions within it and organizations which fight in opposition to it. It has established partition, fear, distrust, sectarian privilege and poverty, disunity and faction fighting. It has brought death to many Irish people, to its own British soldiers and to English civilians.

The British connection denies civil and human rights to the Irish people and is maintained by concentration camps, summary executions, torture, paid perjurers and kangaroo courts. By its very nature, the British presence is not and never has been a just or peaceful presence, and because of this relationships between the Irish and British peoples have been poisoned. When the root cause of violence in Ireland is removed, then and only then will the violence cease. Then the people of Ireland and Britain will find common cause to move forward into an era of mutual respect and solidarity that has been denied them by successive British governments.

The system established by Britain in the Six Counties created and constitutes the prop on which sectarianism depends. Its essential basis is the holding by a 'pro-British' national minority of a position of privilege over a dispossessed majority. It is important to recognize the often-ignored truth that this utterly undemocratic system was established, is controlled by and is the responsibility of the British government. The 'pro-British' elements will face up to the reality of the situation only when the British prop, and the system which uses them as its tools and its stormtroopers, is removed.

The British presence is not a matter only of the army and governmental institutions. It is also a matter of the domination of the economy. As James Connolly wrote:

> The subjection of one nation to another, as of Ireland to the authority of the British Crown, is a barrier to the free political and economic development of the subjected nation, and can only serve the interests of the exploiting classes of both nations.

Partition has divided the Irish economy into two parts which were forced to lean separately on Britain. The Six Counties is a dependent enclave within the UK economy, without any powers of economic development or initiative of its own. It has no power to control capital movements, to set up state industries of its own or to vary the exchange rate so as to promote economic and employment growth. The population of the Six Counties amounts to only two and a half percent of the population of the 'United Kingdom.' It is a tiny minority in an area on the fringe of British economic development.

Within an independent Ireland, the political and economic weight of the North's population would be greater in relation to a national government than it is now in relation to the London parliament. While the British retain control, the Six Counties will suffer further de-industrialization and greater dependency on politically motivated hand-outs from Britain. Despite such hand-outs, there has been an enormous decline in employment, at rates of between fifty-five and eighty percent from 1952 to 1984, in agriculture, shipbuilding and textiles.

Foreign ownership of the North's manufacturing industry is now forty percent of the total. Gross earnings have always been lower and unemployment figures higher than in the rest of the 'UK.' The official British reports have identified the reasons for all this as being the narrow industrial structure in the Six Counties, a narrowness deriving from the role of the Six Counties as a peripheral area within the 'UK' and also from the fact of its separation from its natural hinterland, the Twenty-six Counties. This problem is most acutely seen in the special social and economic problems affecting the border areas because of partition. These areas have been turned into peripheral areas within the Six and Twenty-six County states, with their natural economic links severed by decades of partition. In the Six Counties this problem was increased by discrimination by the Stormont regime against towns like Strabane, Newry and Derry.

As a regional economy on the periphery of the 'UK,' it suffers also from the wholesale export of capital. For example, according to the Hall Report, it is estimated that the amount of 'Northern Ireland capital held outside Northern Ireland exceeded the amount of external capital held in Northern Ireland.' The consequences have been higher rates of poverty, unemployment, bad housing, demoralization and ill-health.

The economy of the Twenty-six Counties has been similarly distorted by partition, which separated the larger part of the island from its northern industrial base and reduced the size of the home market. The neo-colonial character of the Twenty-six Counties was clear from the start; Lord Birkenhead, in defending the signing of the Treaty in the British House of Commons, described it as a matter of protecting British interests on the island with an economy of British lives. Thus they developed a neo-colonial relationship in which it was possible to protect their economic and strategic interests without the nuisance of having to occupy, garrison and administer the Twenty-six Counties.

The economy of the Twenty-six Counties is dominated by foreign capital; massive proportions of the profits generated by Irish industry are exported, in particular to Britain. The resources of the state are controlled and exploited by foreign interests, and even the ruling class is not based principally on native capitalism but is an 'agent' class, acting as agents for foreign capital. This ruling class, put into power by the British, appreciates that its interests lie in the maintenance of partition and feels its interests threatened by popular political struggle; economic dependence on Britain translates in terms of political interest.

While the existence of a degree of political autonomy in the Twenty-six Counties, under the 1921 arrangement, enabled some economic progress to be made, this was at great social cost and on the basis of new kinds of neo-colonial dependence upon Britain. The loss of twenty-nine percent of the population and forty percent of the taxable capacity of the country, as well as the main industrial area and the largest city, Belfast—a port through which passed one third of the national trade before partition—meant that any attempt to build a viable economy would be doomed to failure. The loss of the industrial area around Belfast was particularly important. Metal goods had to be imported from Britain and paid for in goods Britain would accept. These were agricultural, mainly cattle. So dependent did the Twenty-six Counties become on this trade that, in the 1950s, the population was decreased to its lowest numbers while the state carried the highest number of cattle in its history. Indeed, since the Free State was established, half of its population has had to emigrate.

A whole network of small farming communities was broken up and economically exiled as more and more land was gobbled up by big ranchers. The disparity in prices between the beef exports and the industrial imports affected the process of capital formation. It strengthened the power of mercantile as opposed to industrial interest and it encouraged capital to migrate. The deficiency arising from the adverse balance of trade—due to the failure of the cattle trade to earn enough to pay for industrial imports—increased the reliance on foreign capital as the principal motor of economic development. This accelerated from 1958 and led to the absorption of the Twenty-six Counties into the EEC on Britain's coat-tails.

Ireland is now a small, divided and powerless part of a new kind of collective imperialism in Europe, an economic arm of NATO and part of a common front of ex-colonial powers against the Developing World. The treaty on European Union (the Single European Act), which came into effect in January 1992, committed the Dublin government to supporting a NATO view of international affairs and abandoned absolutely any remaining vestige of 'neutrality' or of Irish independence in foreign affairs. The Maastricht Treaty, which had been ratified by all EC member states by 1993, has as its ultimate aim a European federation which will further entrench Ireland's dependency. While EU (formerly EC) membership has seen the further erosion of Irish sovereignty and control of natural resources, the dependency of the Twenty-six Counties on Britain is seen in its foreign trade, which is still fifty percent with Britain. And despite the increase in American, German, French and Japanese investors, British investors still run the largest bloc of its manufacturing industry.

The small size of the domestic market and its excessively 'open' character is perhaps the most extreme in the developed world. This was caused directly by partition and worsened by the EU. Before EU membership, because of the dependency on foreign imports and the influence these had on shaping the capital formation, it would have been difficult for even a radical Dublin government to foster output and employment throughout the state. Now, EU membership makes it 'illegal' to take the normal steps to control capital movement or to initiate state intervention by means of quotas, tariffs or aids to Irish industry.

Not only has partition and British domination of the economy distorted the economic potential of the country but it has also stunted the development of class politics. The trade union movement has been subjected to this general distortion. Any Dublin-based movement immediately evokes a hostile reaction from the loyalist work force in the Six Counties and any London-based movement has a tendency to become at least benignly imperialistic. The Stormont government refused to deal with the Irish Congress of Trade Unions (ICTU) until it established a separate northern committee, thus ensuring loyalist domination of trade union affairs in the Six Counties and a major influence in British trade unions' attitudes to Ireland. The trade union movement failed to develop policies against discrimination and lost altogether the socialist republican legacy of James Connolly. The same problems that beset the trade union movement applied in the case of building a class-based socialist party.

Ordinary people throughout Ireland have absorbed the reality of their powerlessness under British domination, whether in colonial or neo-colonial form. The resources of the country lie far beyond their reach and all the decisive elements of the economy, even of society in general, are outside their control. When it comes to an industrial dispute, very often the workers cannot even get to grips with their real opponents, the foreign owners and the central decision makers of the multinationals. The government and other political and religious elements step in and warn about job losses;

they complain that, if the workers continue with their action, the foreign company that employs them will leave the country and that Ireland's image as a place for investment will be tarnished, with the result that other foreign companies will not invest and other jobs will not be created.

Multinationals are presented by the government with the people's money and the people's labour and then they take away the profit that is created by the people. Even within the terms of capitalism, it is an absurd situation. Successive Dublin governments have claimed to base themselves upon the Proclamation of 1916, yet, far from the ownership of Ireland belonging to the people of Ireland, it is clear that the economy is planned in the interests of a very small clique. The Proclamation talks about 'cherishing all the children of the nation equally,' but the reality expressed in constant emigration is that the children of the nation not only could not be cherished equally but they were forced to leave and continue to be forced to leave.

Partition subverts the aim of an economy which can fulfil the domestic needs of the Irish people. The Twenty-six Counties has proportionally the highest youth population in western Europe and the highest elderly population, and these people need a whole infrastructure of schools, houses, factories and roads, yet in all these respects the economy and the state are unable to deliver. We have an agricultural country which is given over to big ranching interests exporting beef; our horticultural imports undermine attempts to build up home-based industries.

A pre-condition for creating an economy which is able to deliver on the promise of the Proclamation, which is able even just to provide a living for its citizens in their own country, is independence. At present the Six Counties is administered directly in the British interest and the Twenty-six Counties is administered by Dublin governments whose economic planning is determined by British and other outside interests. The only way forward is to create an economy based on the needs of the Irish people.

In the Six Counties, British control involves the maintenance of structural discrimination. For a long time, discrimination in employment has been a feature of life, and, furthermore, those Catholics fortunate enough to get work suffer from discrimination in the type of job open to them. These are mostly in seasonal or unskilled occupations, and, in white collar and public sector jobs, Catholics find their promotional opportunities severely restricted, rarely rising to executive or managerial level.

Some unionists maintain, despite the evidence, that there was never any discrimination. Of those who reluctantly accept its existence, most maintain that it has now been eliminated. This is not the case. Since direct rule, a more sophisticated approach in terms of presentation regarding discrimination has been adopted, and, in 1976, discrimination was declared illegal, yet no meaningful measures were undertaken to reverse the structural inequality. Legal platitudes or rhetoric cannot change reality, nor are they intended to; they are only meant to disguise it. Even the British government's own Department of Economic Development had to conclude, in its 1986 report entitled *Equality of Opportunity in Employment in Northern Ireland,* that 'the message of equality of opportunity in employment does not appear to be making a significant impact in relation to any dimension.' One of the main features of discrimination lies in the actual structure of the economy which, broadly speaking, is based on those areas with a Protestant majority. Thus we have a disparity between the mainly Catholic rural west and the mainly Protestant industrial east, and, even within these regions unemployment figures are much higher in areas with a Catholic majority.

The facts of discrimination under the old Stormont regime are well documented elsewhere. The facts of discrimination under direct British rule are revealed with great regularity by the British government's own Fair Employment Agency, and there is no evidence of any real change. For example, less than five percent of the work force in Short's Aircraft is Catholic, and this despite assurances from British Ministers that there would be equality in employment and equality in opportunity of employment. The very few large-scale British government-sponsored investment incentives have been aimed directly at undermining support for republicanism—a foolish and spurious reason for investment. None have made any impact on redressing the balance of employment on a regional basis. During the economic boom, the opportunity to do this was not taken and, in the post-oil crisis situation of recession, the introduction of Thatcherite monetarist policies made matters worse.

Structural inequalities have been reiterated and reinforced since the introduction of direct rule, while the overall situation of the peripheral economy has declined, with more closures and massive redundancies. The policy of cut-backs has meant an increase in unemployment across the board, with structural discrimination remaining as much a feature as ever.

Britain's economic interests in Ireland and their consequences represent, however, only one thread on the loom of colonial control and intervention. The strategic reasons behind the initial English conquest remain to some extent centuries later, and I do not believe that the British government has at any time in the last thirty years seriously considered leaving Ireland. Not because Ireland has failed to feature as a priority, but because they accept the situation as it is. Many commentators suggest that a problem with the British government is that they are always concerned with other priorities. I do not believe that that is a real problem; the fact of the matter is that they just accept that the Six Counties are part of their set-up, their 'United Kingdom.'

In spite of the technology of modern warfare, Ireland represents a strategic area of some importance. Economically, Ireland is at the very least a considerable marketplace and its industrial base is dominated from Britain. Politically, it has been argued that for Britain to unwind its relationship with Ireland would be to unwind the whole nature of the British state. Any radicalization of Irish society becomes a threat to the British establishment, to the extent that it offers encouragement to people in Britain and has a radicalizing effect in specifically British political terms.

It is not, however, out of the question that in certain circumstances the British government would find a united Ireland completely acceptable. Their attitude has consistently been towards all of Ireland. Even the basis on which the Six and Twenty-six County states were established provided for a council of Ireland, and one can argue that partition was seen only as a temporary necessity to consolidate in a territorial sense British control over part of Ireland as the bridgehead of its influence over the whole island. Territorial unity of the Six and Twenty-six Counties would not necessarily threaten British interests; indeed, the Dublin government has acted as a junior partner in relation to

London, expressing the thread of common interest that has always existed between the Irish and British ruling classes.

What threatens British government interests is not the simple joining together of two partitioned statelets into their one geographical unit. The prospect that threatens them is national self-determination: a united nation defining and implementing independent policies both internally and externally, acting in the interests of the Irish people as a whole. Such an independent Ireland would pass out of Britain's combined colonial and neo-colonial control.

The right-wing Tory Monday Club has warned of the danger of Ireland becoming a Cuba on Britain's doorstep. I do not believe that there is any real basis for that scenario, but it is nevertheless understandable that NATO and the Western Alliance are implacably opposed to an independent Ireland which would not be aligned with them. Under the present arrangement, because of Britain's membership of NATO, this military alliance has a foothold in Ireland with the Six Counties incorporated directly into NATO.

National self-determination would mean the Irish people defining their foreign policy in their own interests and fraternally in the interests of those with whom we could identify in a general sense. It would mean alignment with emerging small nations, with ex-colonies, with people struggling for self-determination and equality, instead of the big power blocs.

Irish foreign policy would be based on positive neutrality, not the mediocre notion which is sometimes pontificated upon by Dublin politicians but an active, positive policy of neutrality opposed to militarization, nuclear weapons and working for the internationalism of, as Connolly put it, 'a free federation of free peoples.' An independent Ireland would develop relationships with other countries to their mutual advantage and to the general benefit of humankind. The suggestion that Irish neutrality should be swapped for Irish unity and independence is a contradiction in terms, for neutrality and independence must be two sides of the one coin.

In its foreign policy, an independent Ireland could play a positive role as a catalyst, but we should not have an inflated sense of our own importance. Some people have the rather chauvinist idea that Ireland would take its place at the head of small nations; such a notion is unrealistic, but in various small ways there is no doubt that Ireland could intervene against the domination of the power blocs which still threatens the world with nuclear catastrophe. To take one appropriately small example, the various appeals for money and other aid in the Developing World have obviously caught the imagination of all kinds of people in Ireland who have been very generous with donating money. What an Irish government should be doing at the same time is using its influence to demand change of those countries that monopolize and destroy food products on a regular basis. An independent Irish foreign policy would seek to intervene to subvert the stranglehold of a world economic order which squeezes large parts of Africa dry and promotes the most reactionary and oppressive regimes world wide.

The strategic concerns of British policy towards Ireland have obviously undergone many changes of emphasis over the centuries. In recent decades, its strategic interest has been one shared, by and large, by the western European and US governments: for the maintenance of stability and social order in capitalist Europe. Britain, in the post-colonial era, does not act alone in the grand manner of its imperial heyday. Indeed, it has been reduced on occasions to acting simply as the US government's largest aircraft-carrier. But the traditional British claim to the territory of Ireland is buttressed by the US and European concern to maintain the status quo, and, in pursuit of this kind of 'stability,' the British government has employed a wide variety of techniques of oppression.

Between 1800 and 1921, the British government enacted 105 separate coercion acts dealing with Ireland. *Habeas corpus* was frequently suspended and the jails of Ireland and the penal colonies in Australia were regularly populated by Irish political prisoners. Since partition, this policy of coercion, modernized and updated, has continued.

From the establishment of the Northern Ireland state, Britain has armed and financed a sectarian apparatus of repression. By 1922 it had organized, armed and was paying for a combined force of over 45,000 loyalists in the Six Counties, made up of 'A,' 'B' and 'C' Specials whose memberships were based upon the loyalist paramilitary organization, the Ulster Volunteer Force (UVF), and the RUC. These so-called 'security forces' were employed in an openly partisan political manner to suppress nationalist opposition and were backed up by an array of repressive laws. Internment was provided for and was used to suppress anti-unionists. Judges were almost all openly associated with the ruling unionist Party.

Britain began by 'arming the Protestants,' to use the phrase that provides the title for Michael Farrell's study of the formation of the Specials and the RUC, and by establishing the 'Protestant parliament for a Protestant people' together with an administration and judiciary which were overwhelmingly loyalist. Having achieved this, their strategy consisted simply of supporting the Stormont government as the basis of social and political stability.

From 1969, however, Britain has exercised a greater degree of direct control, replacing the 'B' Specials with the Ulster Defence Regiment (UDR). The UDR (recently renamed the Royal Irish Regiment) while almost identical in composition to the 'B' Specials, was, and is, under the control of the British army. Britain initially placed British army regiments in the front line of confrontation with the nationalists, in response to the RUC's failure to hold that line. In the period immediately after 1969, the British government made noises about introducing liberal reforms but made no move towards implementation of such reforms as would have given the Six Counties the elements of 'British democracy' such as the separation of powers and the impartial administration of justice. Instead, the nature of the change in British strategy at this time was simply that it took over direct responsibility for the exercise of coercion.

The powers of suppression which had been exercised through the RUC and Specials were now taken over for intensified use by the British army. The strategy of military coercion took the forms of large-scale information-gathering exercises, detention for questioning, internment and detention without trial. On the day in August 1971 when internment was introduced, 342 people were arrested; within six months, 2,357 were arrested, of whom 1,600 were released. A number of those who were interned were subjected to torture using sensory deprivation techniques. From 1972, detention without trial replaced internment.

The introduction of the Northern Ireland (Emergency Provisions) Act in August 1973 extended RUC and British army powers and set aside standard provisions of the law; it included the abolition of juries, fundamental changes in the rules of evidence, and extensive powers to detain for questioning. This provided the legal framework for the British army to conduct intensive intelligence screening, in-depth interrogation, house searches and frequent arrests for questioning including large-scale arrest operations. In 1971 there were 17,262 house searches; in 1973 the number rose to 75,000, one fifth of the number of houses in the whole of the Six Counties; almost every house searched was in a nationalist area. Further repressive powers were brought in with the Prevention of Terrorism Act in 1974 (reviewed in March 1994, and still in effect), yet even this vast armoury of powers was exceeded by many British army operations which were clearly illegal.

Other British army tactics included the use of *agents provocateurs*, assassination squads, 'counter-gangs,' undercover units, the computerization of intelligence information and new crowd control and surveillance techniques. The Six Counties became a laboratory of techniques and tactics of political suppression and counter-insurgency, all of which were directed exclusively against the nationalist population.

Much evidence has recently come to light which reveals the extent to which the British government is prepared to use covert operations and 'counter-gangs' in order to advance its political objectives in Ireland. The most alarming, and perhaps the most telling example, is the Brian Nelson case.

Brian Nelson, a native of Belfast, was a British soldier and, at the same time, was active in the loyalist Ulster Defence Association's (UDA) death squads in the 1970s. Later recruited by British intelligence, he worked undercover in Ireland from within the ranks of the UDA. In 1973, he and two other UDA members kidnapped, imprisoned and tortured a half-blind Catholic man, who subsequently died after they released him. Nelson and his accomplices were sentenced to seven years for false imprisonment (they weren't even charged with attempted murder).

On his release from prison, he left Ireland to work in Germany, but returned after he was again recruited by British intelligence to resume his role as a British agent within the UDA. The UDA, at that time a legal organization, is the largest loyalist paramilitary force, responsible for the killings of hundreds of nationalist/Catholic civilians. Nelson became Director of Intelligence for the UDA. He was directly in control of selecting targets

85

for loyalist death squads and organizing arms shipments from South Africa and other countries, and was actively assisted in this by his British Intelligence 'handlers' who directed the reorganization and rearming of the UDA.

One large shipment of arms from South Africa in 1988, organized with the collusion of British intelligence, South African embassy officials, an American arms dealer and Ulster Resistance, a group founded by Ian Paisley, has been instrumental in the increased activity of loyalist murder squads since. The AK47 rifles, Browning pistols, and RPG5 splinter grenades that were part of this shipment have been used in well over 150 killings performed by UDA and UVF hit squads.

Nelson was arrested in January 1990 as part of investigations into widespread leakage of British intelligence documents to loyalists. On 3 February 1992, a senior judge and former Attorney General for the unionist government at Stormont, Basil Kelly, handed down a minimum prison sentence to Nelson, described by Justice Kelly as a man who had shown 'the greatest courage.' During the trial, a man identified only as Colonel 'J,' the commander of a British Military Intelligence Unit in the North between 1986 and 1989, had stated that he had been responsible for handling Nelson. The Department of Public Prosecutions also received a letter sent on behalf of British cabinet minister Tom King, in support of Nelson and saying that he was a valuable agent. The sentencing of Nelson to ten years imprisonment on a series of charges related to killings in the Six Counties was the result of a deal struck between the British Attorney General's office, the North's judiciary and Nelson himself. The deal was to keep Nelson from having to disclose embarrassing information about British intelligence and its deep involvement with loyalist death squads. Fifteen of the thirty-five charges against Nelson, including two charges of murder, were dropped by the Crown Prosecution in return for guilty pleas on twenty lesser charges, five of which related to conspiracy to murder. Brian Nelson is serving his sentence in an English prison, and is expected to be released in two or three years. Meanwhile, the cover-up has still to be unravelled and the details revealed to the public.

In my view, the Brian Nelson case is the tip of the iceberg of British covert operations in Ireland. The use of agents is a long established practice and the use of 'counter-gangs' is a long standing element in British counter-insurgency strategy. Through Nelson, British intelligence controlled and directed the UDA. There is nothing to suggest that they have ceased to do this. They obviously have other agents in the UDA and other loyalist paramilitary groups which continue to threaten the entire nationalist community in the Six Counties as well as the population of the Twenty-six Counties.

British strategy up to the end of 1975 was, in summary, to conduct a war of political suppression, with the British army playing the leading role. By 1975 the British government had begun to implement its strategy of 'Ulsterization' and 'criminalization,' which, in broad terms, sought to deny the political nature of the struggle while at the same time refining and renewing the forms of suppression. The RUC was brought back again to a position from which it was intended that it should step into the front line. It was made into more of an army than a police force; its intelligence capabilities were built up, with special emphasis on the use of informers, surveillance and detention for questioning. This strategy, which aimed for 'normalization,' had been a major strand of British strategy since 1972, one which they had hoped to have fully operational by 1975. The British government has also used bilateral truces with the IRA to gain the upper hand, to cause confusion in republican ranks and to introduce new strategies. It has never engaged in a truce with the serious intention of considering or conceding the republican demands. In particular, the lengthy bilateral truce of 1974–5 was used to push ahead with the 'Ulsterization'/'normalization'/'criminalization' policy. However, the resumption of military struggle by the IRA prevented the successful implementation of this timetable.

Placing renewed emphasis on the courts, rather than internment, as a means of disposing of its nationalist opponents, the British government opened both Castlereagh and Gough Barracks interrogation centres in 1977. These were designed to supply, through the systematic application of torture techniques, the statements required to secure convictions in the courts. This has been highlighted by the *Stalker Report* and many miscarriages of justice, such as in the cases of the Guildford Four, the Birmingham Six, the Maguire Seven, Judith Ward, and others. As early as April 1977, the Association of Forensic Medical Officers made representations to the Police Authority, and, in November, Amnesty International conducted an investigation. Eighty-six percent of all defendants appearing before Diplock Courts between January and April 1979 had made confessions; fifty-six percent of prosecutions in relation to these relied solely on confessions, while another thirty percent relied primarily on confessions.

'Criminalization' aimed at isolating the republican resistance. Another form of isolation aimed at was geographical: the development of 'counter-insurgency architecture' whereby the RUC and British army were closely involved in local authority planning in the interests of counter-insurgency and the control of urban populations, with particular emphasis on confining nationalists within ghettos with a limited number of access and exit points. Powers of arrest and detention were used even more than before as a control and intimidation technique and for intelligence gathering and screening. In the ten months between 1 January and 30 October 1980, 3,868 people were arrested under the Emergency Provisions Act and the Prevention of Terrorism Act and detained for more than four hours; of these, only eleven percent were charged. The primacy of the RUC was further developed by the creation of special units which received training from the British army's SAS in the techniques that equipped them to carry out a British government-approved 'shoot-to-kill' policy against republicans.

In 1977, Roy Mason, Britain's Northern Ireland Secretary, genuinely thought he had the situation under control, that the project of pacifying the Six Counties was on the verge of completion, and that the IRA was being 'squeezed like toothpaste.' It was an appreciation of the falseness of Mason's view which led to the production of Brigadier Glover's report in late 1978 and the recognition that the element of British strategy which required the military suppression of the resistance could not be implemented. Nevertheless, the 'criminalization' policy continued to be pursued energetically, and such were the contradictions of the overall strategy that it succeeded in generating both unprecedented support for the IRA and a new political obstacle in the form of Sinn Féin's dramatic electoral successes.

The cutting edge of the British strategy of 'criminalization' was the attempt to abolish political prisoner status. But it was at this vital point that British strategy broke down. It had been delayed and frustrated in previous years by the republican resistance, but, with the hunger strikes, the mass campaign in support of the prisoners' demands and the Sinn Féin electoral achievements, it suffered a substantial reverse.

At a time when, as far as the British were concerned, the IRA had been beaten into the ground and isolated; at a time, too, when British government funds were being pumped into the De Lorean car plant on the edge of West Belfast and into leisure and community centres; at a time when the internees had been released and only a small number of 'criminals' remained in the H-Blocks, British strategy received a stunning blow. The mass campaign in support of the H-Block and Armagh prisoners, the heroic self-sacrifice of the hunger strikers, and the massive votes for Sinn Féin alerted the Dublin government, via the urging of the SDLP, that they had surrendered the high ground of nationalism and that the only people articulating the nationalist position were the 'terrorists.' Dublin saw an urgent need, which it communicated to the British government, to build an alternative to the 'terrorists' and to establish a context of credibility for establishment politics in order to undermine the substantial support that had been demonstrated for the republicans.

Since the first hunger strike in December 1980, when a 'totality of relationships' was announced, through silver tea-pot diplomacy, a short-lived 'constitutional crusade,' and the changes in governments which were as short on leadership as they were on days in office, Dublin and their northern allies, the SDLP, had been struggling to climb back to the heights of Irish nationalism which they had surrendered to the republicans. The Dublin Forum was the still-born child of that attempt and it was launched on 2 May 1984, after eleven months of deliberations and amidst unprecedented media hype.

Two months later, John Hume of the SDLP delivered a presentation of the report at a much heralded debate on this document in the British House of Commons. Only 50 out of almost 700 British members of parliament turned up to hear him. Worse was to follow. On 19 November of that year, Margaret Thatcher, in her infamous 'out, out, out' remarks, rejected the conclusions of the Forum report, humiliated the Irish establishment and stated clearly what issues would be on the agenda. Dublin's need to engage in nationalist rhetoric was of no importance to her. Charles Haughey's claims about a totality of relationships during previous talks would not be permitted to be repeated; new talks would clearly and unambiguously be about defeating 'terrorism.'

The British establishment—and in particular Sir Robert Armstrong, Secretary to the British cabinet—had been influenced by a report entitled *Britain's Undefended Frontier: A Policy for Ulster.* This report, like the Dublin Forum report, was influenced by recent developments in the Six Counties. It was produced by a right-wing group within the British establishment, the Independent Study Group, and was launched in October 1984, published by the Institute for European Defence and Strategic Studies.

It recognized the problem of what is called 'nationalist alien- ation' from British institutions in the Six Counties, and the dangers of this to Dublin. It promoted cross-border collaboration as the only alternative to a dangerous escalation of British repression which could provoke a nationalist backlash throughout Ireland. Among its proposals were included:

1. A joint London-Dublin security commission, including a military sub-committee made up of representatives of both armed forces.

2. A full-time secretariat drawn from Dublin and Whitehall civil servants.

3. London-Dublin summits at fixed intervals.

In its text the report spoke of co-operation from northern nationalists only being won if 'they are bought by political concessions.'

It outlined its view that Dublin had a crucial role to play in defeating the IRA, as had happened in the 1956–62 campaign which:

> ...was a signal failure because London and Dublin were united in wholeheartedly opposing it and in particular because internment was in operation on both sides of the border... We think it should be made clear to the Dublin government that the degree of force which must be used [by the British] in the attempt to restore order

will be in inverse proportion to the degree of effective co-operation on security which can be achieved between the two governments.

The report also advised:

We believe that British policy has suffered in the past from an excessive and misconceived regard for the sensibilities of the Irish Republic [i.e. the Dublin government].

Margaret Thatcher's 'out, out, out' rejection of the sensibilities of the Dublin government, delivered one month after this report was completed, showed that she had taken this point, at least, on board.

In addition to the impact of the hunger strikes and Sinn Féin electoral successes, the British government was also rudely awakened from complacency by the Brighton bombing. The full effects of this IRA operation will not become apparent until some British minister writes his or her memoirs. But the fact is that Óglaigh na hÉireann almost wiped out the British cabinet and that fact awakened the government to the urgent need, from their point of view, to address themselves to the issues of Ireland and the IRA.

The stage was set for the Hillsborough talks, and under the triple impacts of the hunger strike, the Sinn Féin vote and the Brighton bombing the Hillsborough Treaty was forged. Prior to 1968 the British government had basically ignored the problems of structural discrimination and sectarian power in the Six Counties; it had been happy enough to leave the unionists to get on with the business of running the place. With the failure of the unionists to keep a lid on the situation, however, Britain became involved in direct intervention, took control of state functions and began to employ its own strategies in pursuit of stability under the Crown. What the Hillsborough Treaty represented was a coming-together of the various British strategies on an all-Ireland basis, with the Dublin government acting as the new guarantor of partition.

In the final analysis, the agreement was about stabilizing British interests. It was about what the British and Dublin governments quaintly call 'security.' It addressed itself to a problem for the

British outlined in Brigadier Glover's 1978 report: British army intelligence could do nothing about the structures and organization of the IRA in the Twenty-six Counties; only 'security' harmonization with Dublin could remedy this lack. It was also, of course, about the political context of what they call the 'security problem.' It was an attempt to isolate and draw popular support away from the republican struggle while putting a diplomatic veneer on British rule, injecting a credibility into establishment 'nationalism' so that British rule and the interests it represented could be stabilized in the long term, and insulating the British from international criticism of their involvement in Irish affairs.

The duration of the republican struggle and the failure of the unionists to defeat it were major factors in the British desire to modernize her colonial arrangements. They could afford to offend the unionists; after all, there were to be no constitutional changes and the unionists, for all their protestations, had failed to subdue opposition to partition. Their blatant use of discrimination, gerrymandering and coercion, encouraged by the British government for as long as they succeeded in fulfilling the British need to neutralize opposition to their rule in Ireland, now needed to be refined. And, as Sinn Féin warned before the Hillsborough Treaty was signed, the predictable unionist reaction was needed and would be utilized to exaggerate whatever concessions might be produced by the Hillsborough process.

The major achievement for the British government was that it had succeeded in publicly tying in the Dublin government as junior partner in its strategy. Dublin thus became the guarantor of partition and the jewel in the crown of British strategy.

6

Loyalists, Unionists and Republicans

Hapless! Hapless Land!
Heap of uncementing sand!
Crumbled by a foreign weight:
And by worse, domestic hate.
William Drennan

REPUBLICANISM IS NOTHING if it is not resolutely anti-sectarian. That statement may be received with scorn by those who seek to equate republicanism with a certain tradition of Catholic nationalism. But Irish republicanism is, almost by definition, an ideology of the dispossessed seeking equality. Of course, if you seek rights of which you have been deprived, those who have deprived you of those rights and those who have appropriated those rights to themselves will appreciate that your equality can only be achieved by depriving them of their position of privilege. If the black people of South Africa achieve equality with other races, they cannot do so other than at the expense of those who have deprived them of equality and monopolized social and economic privilege—namely the whites. Is it therefore racist of the blacks to seek equality? Of course not.

Unionism and loyalism require a Protestant ascendancy—that is their *raison d'être*. Their political philosophy expresses loyalty to the union with Britain precisely and solely because that union has, to date, guaranteed them their privileges and their ascendancy. At the level of the unionist ruling class, that privilege may be substantial and real. At the level of the working class, it may be more perceived than real, and to the extent that it is real it may be marginal, but it is often marginal privilege which is most fiercely fought for.

Unionism requires a one-party state and requires the suppression of significant opposition. It has not only failed to become engaged even within the confines of the state in power-sharing, it has also failed absolutely to come to terms with the simple human proposition that the man or woman down the road has an equal right to vote, an equal right to job opportunities, and an equal right to housing.

The resolute anti-sectarianism of republicanism is not new and it is not confined to what may be termed the radical element of the tradition. This correct attitude sometimes leads republicans into ignoring loyalism as a political threat altogether and misunderstanding can arise about the exact nature of loyalism.

Colonial powers have long used the plantation of garrisons to keep down rebellious natives. These garrisons were given privileges in return for their loyalty, and these privileges usually included the lands and property of the dispossessed natives. So it was in Ireland. The garrisons were also usually in some way different from the natives. In other colonies there was a racial and often a colour difference. In Ireland the division was religious, and sectarianism was the prop or privilege by which this division was maintained.

So it is that every push against the British by the republicans and every gain won by nationalists is seen inevitably as a threat to the unionist position. The demand for 'one man, one vote' was seen by unionists as a threat. And it was a threat, a threat to unionist privilege. Once that demand was won, the unionists lost control of Derry, 'their' Maiden City.

No matter what demands one makes of the state, even trying to get a grant for a Gaelic football pitch or seeking to put up a street sign in the Irish language, these demands are seen by unionists as posing threats. No matter how non-sectarian one's intentions, the reaction by the unionist politicians is that one is encroaching on their area of privilege, that one is, in fact, threatening 'the Protestant way of life.'

This was not always the case. In the 1790s, Belfast was the centre of an Irish political movement which linked Antrim and Down with the Republics of France and America, and Belfast citizens celebrated the Fall of the Bastille, drank toasts to Mirabeau and Lafayette and studied Paine's great book, *The Rights of Man*. Presbyterians formed the Society of United Irishmen and declared for Catholic emancipation, for the abolition of Church establishments and of tithes, for resistance to rack-rents and for sweeping agrarian reforms. They gave a cordial welcome to Mary Wollstonecraft's *Vindication of the Rights of Women* and joined with their Catholic neighbours in the struggle for natural independence and political democracy.

Yet, within two generations, the majority of Presbyterians had completely abandoned their revolutionary principles, embraced the politics of the Tories and developed a deep-rooted antipathy towards their Catholic neighbours. This transformation, as the historian Andrew Boyd correctly states, is one of the most disturbing facts of Irish history. It was caused directly by the forces of reaction, supported by the wealthy landlord class who feared the union of Protestant, Catholic and Dissenter.

The Presbyterians, then as now, were the largest religious denomination apart from the Catholics. Had they remained untouched by the neo-fascism of Orangeism they would, in alliance with their Catholic countrymen, have undoubtedly transformed Irish society. They were, however, deeply divided; one faction headed by Thomas Cooke, a narrow-minded Paisley-type Tory, the other led by Henry Montgomery, a liberal whose father had been an officer in the battle of Antrim in 1798. Montgomery made no secret of his liberal political and religious principles. He campaigned for Catholic emancipation, was proud of his republican background and forthright in theological and political disputes with Cooke. Cooke, who was equally forthright in his views, was deeply anti-Catholic, and one of his ancestors had fought on the Williamite side during the wars at the end of the seventeenth century. He hated the United Irishmen and their democratic separatist principles and campaigned for control of Ireland's Presbyterians. He found support among the Tories, the landowning class and the Orange lodges, and eventually succeeded in ousting Montgomery, who left the parent Church and formed the non-subscribing Presbyterian Church.

Cooke, secure in leadership of the Presbyterian Church, built up a powerful politico-religious movement in which the Orange order, by then nearly forty years in existence, was to play a major part. The Orange order, an exclusively Protestant and bitterly anti-Catholic organization, had been formed in 1795 to protect poorer Protestant farmers and rich Protestant landlords; it was an alliance of the landed gentry and those poorer Protestants who were united in their distrust of liberalism and Irish Catholics. Until Cooke's time, the Orange order had made little impact on the Presbyterians, and the first Orangemen were descendants of the English rather than the Scottish planters. Under Cooke, this situation changed dramatically and the Presbyterians were drawn increasingly away from radicalism to Toryism and the political cult of Orangeism. Political and religious bigotry of the most extreme description were fused together and, as the power of Orangeism increased, Belfast saw the first of the riots with which we are so familiar to the present day.

Loyalism, with its bigoted and irrational hatred of Catholics and its conservative politics, has nothing to do with the Protestant religion. Due to historical circumstances, the Protestant religion has been continually dragged into association with it, and religion, and in particular Protestantism, has been brought into disrepute by this association. Loyalism as such is not based on religious considerations. Rather, it is based on power, a power which is perceived as being unsustainable without the subservience of the Catholic population. From the smooth tones of upper-class 'respectable' unionists to the virulent hate-mongering of loyalist paramilitaries, the same impression emerges of Catholics as a sub-species. But the hatred and contempt relate clearly to the question of power, and the responsibility for this rests with the British government.

It was a political crisis in Britain which led to the playing of the Orange card in Ireland and to the rekindling of sectarianism and the birth of modern loyalism. This occurred when the British Liberal Party commenced the democratization of the political system in Britain by measures aimed at reducing the authority of the House of Lords over the Commons, thus curtailing the power of the British landlords and aristocrats.

The Liberals were at this time the voice of British democracy. They represented the sensible capitalist classes who had emerged during the industrial revolution. They had no time for aristocratic superstitions, the Divine Right of Kings or the House of Lords. The Tories, on the other hand, were interested only in preserving their political power in the British parliamentary system. They had a 'born to rule' mentality and were outraged at the erosion of their power which occurred in the latter half of the nineteenth century as the Liberals extended voting rights to the ordinary British people.

At the same time the Home Rule movement, led by Parnell and aimed at breaking the constitutional link with Britain, was steadily gaining ground. The Home Rule movement was not separatist or republican; it sought a measure of Irish self-government under the British crown and it had the support of the Liberal Party from 1872.

It was the third Home Rule Bill of 1912 which was to be the test of wills between the Tories and the Liberals. The Liberals had passed the Parliament Act which curtailed the power of the Tory-dominated House of Lords. Before this the Lords had had the power to veto any act carried in the Commons. Now they could only delay a Bill or Act passed by the Commons. The Home Rule Bill became a rallying point for Tory discontent. Fearful of the consequences for the British class system if they organized against the Liberals on 'British' issues, they chose Ireland as the battlefield and Home Rule as the issue. They could not defeat democracy in Britain, so they homed in on the anti-democratic spirit of Orangeism in North-East Ulster as a means of disrupting the advance towards democracy in Britain itself.

The main leadership of the opposition to Home Rule was provided by British Tories who now championed and instigated a reactionary movement in the north of Ireland. Tories rallied to the cause to defeat the 'tyranny of the commons' and provided the training and guns for the Ulster Volunteer Force (UVF) with the help of Sir Henry Wilson, Chief of the Imperial General Staff. Weapons were stored not only in Orange Halls in Belfast but in Tory clubs in Britain as well.

Inflammatory speeches by Tory leaders led to sectarian riots in Belfast and to attacks on Catholic workmen in Belfast shipyards, and, as the temperature rose, the UVF continued to arm itself. The Liberals did nothing to suppress this Tory conspiracy because of their fear of the fledgling British Labour movement. They reasoned that, if they confronted the Tories, the Labour Party would exploit the situation and encourage a class war in Britain, in which the Liberals as well as the Tories might perish. The climax of the Tory revolt occurred in 1914, when fifty-seven British army officers resigned after being ordered to put down the revolt, and this Curragh Mutiny broke the nerve of the Liberal Party.

The Home Rule Bill was suspended with the outbreak of the First World War, but the forces of reaction which had been whipped up in the anti-Home Rule agitation commenced the process of institutionalizing the sectarianism which they had encouraged. By this time, Irish nationalist opinion had moved beyond Home Rule to the demand for an Irish Republic. When the First World War ended, the creation of the Orange State with Sir Henry Wilson as chief military adviser and Sir Edward Carson as leader was well advanced. It was established in a frenzy of pogroms and sectarian attacks.

The Tory conspiracy succeeded, not only in Ireland where it interrupted and thwarted a struggle for national independence, but, in Britain also, where reactionary notions still dominate many British working people. Although the British aristocracy is almost extinct, the ideology of the aristocracy survives and the notion that some people—usually white people—are 'born to rule' lives on in an atmosphere of jingoism and chauvinism.

In Ireland, the British partition institutionalized and provided a structure for such beliefs. Having established a Six County state, the boundaries of which were designed to secure a permanent loyal majority, and having established a 'Protestant parliament for a Protestant people,' the stability of the state and the maintenance of Protestant power required that a constant mentality of siege be maintained. This siege mentality was unconsciously described by Captain Terence O'Neill in an interview shortly after his resignation as Prime Minister:

> The basic fear of Protestants in Northern Ireland is that they will be outbred by the Roman Catholics. It is as simple as that.

Loyalism has attempted to project a conviction that certain qualities reside with 'us' and certain qualities with 'them,' and such convictions have provided inherent justification for resisting the

threat of Catholic equality. Particular Protestant qualities according
to loyalism are perceived as being cleanliness, reliability, honesty,
dedication, loyalty, respect for authority, thriftiness, respectability,
and so on. Catholics, by and large, are perceived to lack such
qualities. Thus, if Catholics are allowed to 'get in everywhere,' they
will be bound to take advantage and to respond to the privilege
afforded to them with duplicity and treachery. If they are given
decent housing they will wreck it, if they are given jobs they will
prove shiftless and work-shy, and so on. The litany would doubtless
be utterly familiar in the southern United States, in European countries with migrant workforces, in South Africa and in Britain where
the anti-Irish prejudices of the past have given way to anti-black
prejudices of the same order.

While prejudice against Catholics was firmly entrenched centuries ago and became institutionalized in the Six Counties state,
the expression of that prejudice was intensified in response to the
civil rights movement and, even before that, in response to
Unionist Prime Minister O'Neill's moves towards rapprochement
with Dublin. As loyalists mobilized to attack civil rights marches,
and as they launched pogroms to burn Catholics out of their
homes, publication of sectarian songs and stories, old and new,
flourished. Songs with lyrics such as:

> If guns were made for shooting,
> Then skulls were made to crack.
> You've never seen a better Taig
> Than with a bullet in his back.

Later, the armed struggle of the IRA would be cited as justification, almost as if it were the source of loyalist prejudice. A letter in
the February 1972 bulletin of the Ulster Defence Association
(UDA) stated:

> I have reached the stage where I no longer have any
> compassion for any nationalist, man, woman or child.
> After years of destruction, murder, intimidation, I have
> been driven against my better feelings to the
> decision—it's them or us ... Why have [loyalist
> paramilitaries] not started to hit back in the only way

these nationalist bastards understand? That is, ruthless, indiscriminate killing... If I had a flame-thrower I would roast the slimy excreta that pass for human beings.

The UDA replied: 'Without question most Protestants would agree with your sentiments. We do...'.

Most Protestants would most certainly not agree. And it must also be said that there are many Protestants who are either quite free of prejudice or who, if they are in any way prejudiced, nevertheless act in a completely non-sectarian manner. However, in the 1980s in Belfast, a loyalist local councillor enjoyed popularity with his constituents after he suggested that Catholics should be incinerated. In the wake of the signing of the Hillsborough Treaty, Catholic churches, schools and houses were attacked and ordinary Catholics were assassinated, as in the past.

Loyalist politicians and others have suggested that the IRA is engaged in a sectarian, anti-Protestant war, that it is carrying out a policy of genocide, particularly in border areas. The IRA has, over the years of its campaign, demonstrated an ability to carry out a massive bombing campaign against economic targets in the Six Counties, mortar and other attacks on RUC and British army barracks, attacks with bomb and bullet on the British army and on the state forces of the Ulster Defence Regiment (UDR), the RUC and prison warders. In the light of this demonstrated lethal ability and the experience acquired over the years, it is self-evident that if the IRA had wanted to launch attacks on the Protestant community it could have done so and inflicted unimaginable casualties. Presumably it would not be a major operation for the IRA to kill a hundred people on the Shankill Road tomorrow or to clear people off their small farms in country areas. If it is capable of mortaring heavily fortified British positions, it could presumably deliberately inflict appalling civilian casualties. But it has not done that. And if it has not done it, then it must be because it does not want to, that it has decided that it does not want to engage in a war against the Protestant people.

It is sometimes said that the attacks on the UDR are seen by Protestants as attacks on the Protestant community. The shooting of an IRA volunteer may well be considered lamentable, but it will be seen simply as an attack on an IRA person. That small community in which the volunteer lived, if it is one of those communities that are constantly harassed by the RUC and UDR, might see it as an attack on one of their own, but no one will say that the volunteer was shot because he or she was a Catholic. Despite the public assertions of unionist spokespersons, they know that if there are five UDR men lined up by the IRA there is no question of asking which of these five are Protestant and which are Catholic.

Without wishing to dehumanize—because all these people are human beings—the identification with the forces of the state by one political section of the citizens of that state derives not so much because they see those forces as their co-religionists, but because they see them as their armed forces, as the forces of unionism, and it does not matter whether an RUC man or a UDR man is Protestant or Catholic. Attacks on the forces of the state are not attacks on the Protestant religion or the Protestant community.

The major responsibility—and one can see this even in statements from the RUC and in the statements of some Protestant clergymen—for 'sectarianizing' the conflict lies with the British government. They had 22,000 British soldiers in the Six Counties twenty years ago, but their NATO commitments and the political effects of casualties in Britain caused them to 'Ulsterize' the war. In this they engaged in a similar process to the one they employed in Cyprus with the consequence that they inflamed the differences between Turkish and Greek Cypriots; they picked their side there and they built a domestic force around it and that force was used against the other side. This process in Ireland has led to a primacy of the RUC and UDR, which have been pushed into the front line while the traditional British regiments have receded into the background, and that is why there has been an increase in casualties amongst the UDR and RUC. It is not that the IRA are singling out the RUC and UDR, because it would be safe to assume that the IRA, if they had a choice, would see a greater strategic importance in actions against the Parachute Regiment than, for example, against the Cullbacky UDR platoon.

Loyalists say they have problems about their religious liberties: that 'their' Protestant tradition is one which protects the freedom to practise one's religion, while the Roman Catholic tradition does not. There is a breathtaking nerve about such an assertion.

Successive Protestant English administrations attempted to impose their faith upon the native Irish, to 'civilize the barbarians,' and they failed. In the course of that failure they used the most draconian measures to outlaw and suppress Catholicism, and in so doing they achieved a cementing of the relationship between the Catholic people and their Church.

If one wishes to understand why Irish Catholics express in action such widespread allegiance to their Church and their priests, then one must recognize the potency of the fact that people died for the right to worship, to practise their religion, to attend their own chapel.

The fact is that if one looks at the suppression of religious liberty in Ireland one finds ample and extreme evidence of it; but it is suppression by political Protestantism of Roman Catholicism and, for a period, it was the suppression by political Protestantism of Presbyterianism. Republicans have always been dedicated to guaranteeing absolutely the right to religious and civil liberties.

And it is worth noting that republicans have been, and still are, consistently condemned by a Catholic hierarchy to a far greater extent than are unionists. I have certainly been condemned more by Dr Daly, Catholic Bishop of Down and Connor—not always by name but obviously by innuendo—than has Ian Paisley. There is no way that, in terms of religious liberty, either Protestants or Catholics have anything to fear from republicans. And there is no way that republicans, in pursuit of a secular or at least pluralist society, want to see any religious hierarchy given a position as of right as part of the state. Republicans want to limit the control of the Churches to things spiritual, and to treat everyone as equal before God.

It is undeniably the case that the Twenty-six County state has been a confessional state since its inception, as has the Six County state. Separated by partition from the very substantial Protestant minority on the island of Ireland, the Twenty-six County state has contained only a relatively insignificant Protestant minority and has enacted and maintained social legislation which reflects the moral values of the Church to which the vast majority of its citizens subscribe. Defenders of this pattern of social legislation and of the intervention of the Catholic hierarchy on such infamous occasions as the Mother and Child scheme controversy, claim that

Loyalists, Unionists and Republicans

the people of the Twenty-six Counties have democratically chosen social legislation permeated by a Catholic ethos.

But neither the Twenty-six Counties nor the Six Counties constitute democratically-chosen units, and the consequences of imposed partition have been far more important than any conflict of historical perspectives. A Protestant national minority became a reactionary, sectarian majority in the Six County statelet, and the national majority found its own particular conservative religious predilections virtually unchallenged within the Twenty-six County statelet. Partition has, as Connolly foresaw, created a 'carnival of reaction' on both sides of the border.

Loyalists protest that republicans propose their absorption into the Twenty-six County state. I would not insult anyone by asking them to join a Thirty-two County state based upon the present Twenty-six County model, or by offering it, or any aspect of it, as a blueprint. But when unionist politicians condemn the Twenty-six Counties—as, for example, Bob McCartney has—for being a confessional state, I have to ask why nothing is being done about his own state.

Republicans do not propose the amalgamation of the two statelets into a Thirty-two county Free State. What republicans are talking about is political representatives of Irish people sitting down without outside interference and deciding what kind of society suits all our interests. I happen to support, although I am a Catholic, the creation of a secular society, a society which is run in the interests of all its citizens, a pluralist society which is structured in such a way as to reflect differing traditions and which is shaped by the aspirations of all its citizens. In other words, a state which 'would unite the whole people of Ireland, to abolish the memory of past dissensions and to substitute the common name of Irish person in place of the denominations of Protestant, Catholic and Dissenter...'.

What republicanism has to offer loyalists is equality. We propose deciding together what can be done about the real problems of the people, and doing so within a legislature which actually represents those people, which reflects their needs, which guarantees their liberties and which has no vested interest in disadvantaging anyone.

Republicans say these kinds of things quite often, but they are not going to be listened to while partition remains because there is no political force in the world which suddenly wakes up, perceives it has been wrong and then goes about rectifying the situation. The hard reality is that people meet new situations pragmatically, and there is plenty of history of that. The unionists were opposed to Home Rule—they accepted Home Rule; they were opposed to partition—they accepted a Six County state; they would not allow the disbanding of the 'B' Specials—they accepted the disbanding of the 'B' Specials; Stormont was to be fiercely maintained—it was prorogued.

I have had no amicable discussions with senior loyalist politicians; but I have met—in prisons and out of prisons, and even formally—a number of minor loyalist politicians and representatives of loyalist paramilitary groupings. My perception of them is that they are concerned to fight their own sectarian corner and they see no reason to stop doing that while the union with Britain still holds. Once that changes, once their corner is no longer defined by the British presence, then I think that it becomes a matter of businesslike negotiation. I have no wish to gloss over or minimize the difficulties, but it is basically a matter of Irish democrats being markedly non-sectarian but dogmatically and unapologetically democratic. Loyalists can have no significant say under British rule and they should have no veto on the British connection, but they can have and should have a very big say in the shape of an independent Irish constitution and in the shape of an independent Irish society.

Loyalism required a one-party state, and this required the exclusion of non-loyalists. Republicans desire a democratic society, and this requires the full involvement of everyone. The only way in which we can live together peacefully is in a situation where we are all equal. We cannot be equal in the Six County state: the very nature and history of the state proves that. We cannot be equal in terms of our relations with Britain because all of us, despite our political differences, are treated as second- or third-class citizens within the United Kingdom. The only context in which we can have equality is where we are in control of our own destiny.

The loyalist veto is utterly undemocratic both in the Irish and British context. If the majority of the people in the United Kingdom, of which the Six County state is supposed to be a part, decided they wanted to end the union, the veto says they could not. It is undemocratic in terms of Ireland, where clearly a majority of the people on the island would like to break the connection with Britain. The reassurance given to the Protestant ascendancy was restated once more in the Hillsborough Treaty. Indeed, it was more than restated, because now the London government could say not only that the majority of people in 'the province,' as they call it, want the union, they can also say that the Dublin government also supported the loyalist veto. And Tom King, the former British Minister for 'Northern Ireland,' could say that the agreement guaranteed that there can never be a united Ireland.

The loyalists have a desperate identity crisis. They agonize over whether they are Ulster-Scotch, Picts, English or British. When they go to England, they are Paddies. They express a massive rejection of a very rich Irish culture, despite the fact that this heritage cannot in any way reasonably be regarded as exclusive. Instead, they waste their time trying to work out some kind of obscure notion of Ulster Protestant culture. They reject Irish music, the Irish language, Irish dance, Irish history, a whole culture which should be theirs and which would be even richer for their participation in it. Yet they are not British. Loyalism is not found in Britain itself, except as an Irish export. There are no cultural or national links between the loyalists and the British, no matter how much the loyalists scream about their 'British way of life.' The British today are embarrassed by the vulgarity of loyalism and, as republicans have consistently warned over the last twenty years, would dump the loyalists if they thought they could find a more stable and internationally acceptable ally in Ireland.

The loyalists are Irish and the notion that they have of being exclusively British is a comparatively recent one. They are Irish people who wish to be subjects of the British crown for as long as that crown protects the Orange ascendancy. Before partition, all loyalists regarded themselves without question as being Irish, except that they were the loyal sort of Irish. It was only when revolutionary nationalism threatened the British Empire, upon which loyalism depended, that Ireland became repugnant as a nation because it would not co-operate passively with British interests.

This attitude was reinforced by partition when the Irish identity was allowed to become synonymous with Catholicism, disloyalty, republicanism and anything else which was imagined to be a threat to the Protestant ascendancy. In recent times, sections of the loyalist community have been promoting the idea of repartition, of 'independence' or of re-negotiating the union as a means of safeguarding their power base or as they, with unconscious irony, put it, 'safeguarding the British way of life.'

Loyalist paramilitary leaders frequently boast that I and other prominent republicans are on the top of their list for assassination, and many innocent Catholics have been murdered by organizations whose leaders have made careers out of sectarianism. I and a number of comrades were wounded in one loyalist attack, yet I feel no hatred towards those who are trying to kill us. They are doing their duty as they see it and are unfortunate dupes of salaried politicians and victims of colonialism.

While I am dogmatic and unapologetic in my opposition to the loyalist veto, one can at the same time be compassionate and understand that it is only when the British colonial prop which creates sectarian division is removed that Protestants will be able to embrace, enrich and enjoy a heritage which is in a very real sense theirs as much as it is anyone else's. God speed the day.

The Protestants of the north have been cheated for long enough. They have been cheated by being ensnared into that sectarian trap prepared for them by British imperial administrations. They can be released from that trap if peace negotiations are allowed to follow a realistic course.

Protestants need to be encouraged to recognize that the common history they share with their Catholic fellow countrymen and women in the common territory of Ireland is quite foreign to any British experience. They need to be encouraged to look at the traditions of which we can be proud, and in this regard where else need we look but to the long tradition of Protestant participation in the democratic struggle of the Irish people for self-government.

It is time again that the Protestant people heard the voice of reason and sanity from their leaders. They need a De Klerk to bring them and us into the next century. John Mitchell of the Young Ireland movement, a Protestant Ulsterman, writing an open letter to the Protestants of the north in 1848, put it like this:

> There is now no Protestant interest at all; there is
> absolutely nothing left for Protestant and Catholic to
> quarrel for: and if any man talks to you now of religious

sects, when the matter in hand relates to civil and political rights, to administration of government, or distribution of property—depend on it...he means to cheat you.

These words, if anything, are even more valid now than they were in Mitchell's time.

7

Republicanism and Socialism

The cause of Labour is the cause of Ireland.
The cause of Ireland is the cause of Labour.
James Connolly

I F YOU WANT to talk about socialism in the Irish context, you cannot divorce the socialist aspiration from the aspiration of national independence. This is the big lesson of the Connolly experience. In order to bring about a socialist society, you must have real national independence. To use Connolly's phrase, this requires the reconquest of Ireland by the Irish people, which means the expulsion of imperialism in all its forms, political, economic, military, social and cultural. It means the establishment of a real Irish republic and the organization of the economy so that all its resources are under Irish control and organized to bring maximum benefit to our people in a Thirty-two County state in which Irish culture and national identity are strong and confident.

Real national independence is the prerequisite of socialism. My understanding of socialism is that it is a definite form of society in which the main means of production, distribution and exchange are socially owned and controlled and in which production is based on human need rather than private profit. Socialism is based on the most thorough-going democratization of the economic system, side by side with the most thorough-going democratization in politics and public affairs. Socialism includes and is a stage in advance of republicanism.

You cannot have socialism in a British colony, such as exists in the Six Counties, or in a neo-colony, such as exists in the

Twenty-six Counties. You must have your own national government with the power to institute the political and economic
changes which constitute socialism. Furthermore, there cannot be
a credible movement for socialism in Ireland while the British
connection divides workers in the Six Counties and while partition prevents a unity of working-class interests. One does not
become a socialist merely by calling oneself that. Clearly socialism
is what socialism *does*. It means different things to different people and nothing to most people and is second only to republicanism as the most abused political description in Irish politics.

There is a benign imperialist attitude amongst people who profess
to be socialists when they say, 'I will support the cause for Irish
freedom if you get a socialist republic.' This is like the British
saying, 'this is the particular outcome that we want.' People have
to recognize the right of the people to national self-determination,
to develop whatever type of particular situation they want. An
internationalist position must be, to quote Connolly, 'a free federation of free people,' and the notion that nations big and small have
the right to shape their own future. It isn't a matter of supporting
the IRA, or even Sinn Féin, or any other particular model of society
in Ireland; it's a matter of supporting the right of the people here to
shape whatever type of society they want, like people in the rest of
the world. You could, of course, rail against the wrong that you see
in other countries, but that should be no excuse for direct
encroachment into those peoples' right to do what they want,
because you are dealing with different cultures, with different needs
and with different political realities.

The acid test of commitment to socialism in Ireland is to be
found in one's attitude towards Irish national self-determination.
The correct socialist attitude to Ireland must be an internationalist
one. You cannot be a socialist in Ireland without being a separatist.
You cannot be a socialist if you condone, support or ignore the
colonial stranglehold which the British government maintains over
this part of our country. There cannot be such a thing as 'Ulster
Socialism.' Those who profess to be 'Northern Ireland Socialists'
are involved in mere parochialism of the municipal gasworks and
waterworks variety. Neither does one become socialist by abandon-
ing nationalism and republicanism and replacing them with 'leftist'
slogans, or by becoming anti-national like the Irish Labour Party.

Those who seek affiliation with British socialist parties are bowing to or blinding themselves to the colonial nature of the relationship between Britain and Ireland, and they ignore the geographical, national and cultural differences between us. The relationship between socialists in Ireland and Britain should be a relationship of equals.

There are other 'international' socialists who support the legitimate rights of the people of Central America, Africa, the Middle East and elsewhere to engage in struggles for national freedom. They are hypocrites if they do not assert the same rights for the Irish people.

The Irish nationalist movement played a leading role in the development of the world-wide struggle to overthrow colonialism, and, throughout its history, republicanism has been strongly influenced by progressive movements in other countries. The ideas of the American War of Independence and the French Revolution were those which inspired the United Irishmen. Irish emigrants played a leading role in the American War of Independence and in the struggle against Portuguese and Spanish colonialism in Central and South America. In India and Africa, the Irish revolutionary tradition was one of the strongest influences in the anti-colonial movements. Even in Britain, the Chartist movement and the whole development of British trade unionism owed much to leadership from Irish radicals.

In more recent times, internationalism has been an important element in republicanism, both in terms of the tactics of guerrilla war and the development of political ideas. Republicans have learnt from struggles in other countries, and movements in many countries have acknowledged a debt to Irish republicanism. Most guerrilla movements study the IRA and its mode of struggle and see it as a major example of how to develop a people's war. In the post-colonial era, the emergence of successful struggles internationally has had a substantial effect on republicans. There is a natural affinity and there is therefore an openness to the ideas associated with these struggles.

The 'network of terror' propaganda put out by the likes of the Monday Club in Britain or in newspapers, books and magazines from the USA, by pet journalists of the CIA in particular, is a deliberate attempt to misrepresent our internationalist position.

One of the ways in which this is done is by associating the republican movement with the actions of groups such as the Red Brigade, the Red Army Faction/Baader-Meinhoff and Direct Action, despite the fact that, at successive Árd Fheiseanna, Sinn Féin has denounced the actions of such groups.

Certain liberals and self-proclaimed socialists who are implacably opposed to the struggle for independence in their own country nevertheless profess a kind of internationalism which engages in long-distance support for revolutionary movements, provided of course that their struggles are in other countries. John Hume, for example, was a sponsor of the anti-apartheid movement, as was Garret FitzGerald. The anti-apartheid movement supported the right of the African National Congress (ANC) to pursue its aims by means of armed struggle.

Irish republicans, on the other hand, have always had a natural, instinctive and deep affinity with the ANC and with the oppressed black majority in South Africa. The appearance of solidarity slogans or vividly painted murals on gable walls throughout the nationalist ghettos of the Six Counties is but one example of this identification with liberation struggles throughout the world.

All socialists must be internationalists and anti-imperialists in a meaningful way. Long-distance 'revolutionaries' will not help to free the oppressed peoples of the world if they cannot help to free their own people and class in Ireland.

A free federation of free peoples is the only conception of internationalism worth struggling for. So socialists must struggle for freedom and political power in the country in which they live, and give a lead to struggling people elsewhere.

For all these reasons, and because I am a socialist, I continue to be a republican. Republicanism is a philosophy in which the national and the radical social dimensions are the two sides of the one coin. While the national dimension has, for historical reasons, been the most dominant tendency within the republican movement, Irish republicanism has consistently been a radical political philosophy. Republicans have persistently, against great odds and often alone, struggled against imperialism. The republican movement has many inadequacies but it remains the major, many would say the only, anti-imperialist force in Ireland today. The advance from today's situation into national independence as defined by Irish republicanism places socialism on the agenda, but Irish republicanism is not a term which defines a system of society in the way that socialism does. In our case it refers to the aim of securing national independence in its broadest sense. Despite the best efforts of the Fianna Fáil, SDLP and Fine Gael leaderships to distort its meaning, republicanism is a concept easily understood by the majority of Irish people to mean national independence, unity, sovereignty and an end to foreign interference in our affairs.

You cannot be a socialist and not be a republican. Socialists will want an independent republic because it is a good thing in itself and because it is an essential step towards socialism. This will only be achieved, however, if the struggle is led by the most radical social groups and, in particular, by the working class—without whom it cannot succeed in developing the conditions for the estab-lishment of a democratic and socialist state.

Such a struggle for national independence needs to encompass all the social elements in the nation which are oppressed or held back by imperialism. Independence struggles which are led by the conservative or middle classes, as in Ireland in 1921, tend to com-promise with imperialism because their leading sections benefit from such a compromise. That is why those on the left in Ireland who regard themselves as socialists and as representing the working class should be the most uncompromising republicans.

In all of this, the question of socialist republicanism or republi-can socialism is an important one for radicals in Ireland today. The term 'republican socialism' has been used by some, for example the now defunct IRSP, but strictly speaking it is a misnomer. If you say you are a republican socialist you are implying that there is such a thing as a 'non-republican' socialist; but there is not and cannot be, at least if socialism is used in the classical sense of the term defined here. Connolly, as usual, indicated what the correct term was when he called the party he founded in 1896 the Irish Socialist Republican Party. It follows that if a republican wishes to use the term 'socialist' in defining his or her political position today, the proper term is 'socialist republican' and 'socialist republicanism,' in order to distinguish oneself from non-socialist republicans. This is perfectly valid. However, the republican struggle should not at this stage of its development style itself 'socialist-republican.' This would imply that there is no place in it for non-socialists.

There are a number of 'isms' involved in the one great 'ism' of Irish republicanism. Omit one or more and you have a different philosophy. Five related elements are separatism, secularism, anti-sectarianism, nationalism and the radical social dimension. But Irish republicanism is not and never has been a static concept; it is a living and developing ideology. The finest declaration of its principal elements is contained in the 1916 Proclamation, which has pride of place in many Irish homes. Unfortunately, it is rarely studied and its content is deliberately downgraded by the Dublin establishment whose main parties nevertheless claim to base their policies on this unique declaration of social and democratic intent.

Irish republicanism, greatly influenced by the French revolution, was first articulated by the United Irishmen and in particular by Wolfe Tone, whose writings detail the bases of republicanism in his time. These were separatism: to break the connection with England; non-sectarianism: to substitute the common name of Irish person in place of Protestant, Catholic and Dissenter; and secularism. Later, with the emergence of the Young Ireland movement, Fintan Lalor gave Irish republicanism a new base. He wrote:

> The entire ownership of Ireland, moral and material, up to the sun and down to the centre, is vested in the right of the people of Ireland. They and none but they are the landowners and law makers of this island, that all laws are null and void not made by them and all titles to land are invalid not conferred by them.

The Young Irelanders also reawakened a sense of national consciousness and national identity.

The next influence was the Irish Republican Brotherhood, or the Fenian movement, whose rise accompanied a great national revival and the foundation of national sporting and cultural organizations such as the GAA and Conradh na Gaeilge. This nationalism was not chauvinist—it was not the nationalism of imperialism—but was a progressive nationalism expressing a belief in culture and identity as well as in political independence.

Although there was a progressive social element in the writings of all the generations that have influenced Irish republicanism, and

113

although in their own time these were radical revolutionary movements, James Connolly's writings on the social and economic aspects of the struggle for Irish independence were to have the most significant effect not only in its literature but on the thoughts of the other leaders. Pádraig Pearse's *The Sovereign People* provides a sample of this:

> So that the nation's sovereignty extends not only to all men and women of the nation but to all material possessions of the nation, the nation's soil and all its resources, all wealth and all wealth producing processes within the nation. In other words, no private right to property is good against the public right to secure strictly equal rights and liberties to every man and woman within the nation.

All of these elements were crystallized in the Proclamation of the Republic in 1916 and developed further in the Democratic Programme of the First Dáil. These documents have neither been implemented nor updated to meet modern conditions, yet they are as relevant today as they were when their basic principals were conceived.

All of the movements and leaders that shaped the republican philosophy were also internationalist in outlook and considered and engaged in physical force as a means of advancing the struggle. If we compare the political positions of those politicians and political parties that pretend to be republican with all the elements of Irish republicanism, we discover how shoddy and superficial their pretence actually is.

Unless one embraces all of the 'isms' of republicanism, one cannot be a republican. That is not to say that those who may not agree with every 'ism' have no part to play in this phase of the struggle. On the contrary, agreement on one element leading to an involvement in struggle for the achievement of agreed short-term objectives is desirable, but republicans—those who embrace all the 'isms'—should always be in the vanguard and should have the ability to shape our struggle so that it draws the maximum support from all progressive and oppressed elements in Irish society today.

In Ireland, until partition is ended and a united Ireland estab-
lished, to be genuinely left-wing is to be an out-and-out republican.
This was the key lesson of James Connolly for socialists in Ireland.
That is why he was led, as a socialist, to join Pearse and the other
radical republicans and democrats in a fight to establish an Irish
Republic.

If that fight had been successful, Connolly and the socialists
would then have been in the best position to advocate the economic
and social changes which constitute socialism. They would have
proved themselves by their leadership of the independence struggle.
That is why it is a political mistake to counterpoise republicanism
and socialism in Ireland as if they were opposites or antagonistic.

The true socialist will be an active supporter of the republican
character of the national independence movement. She or he will
realize that, unless this character is maintained and unless the
most radical social forces are in the leadership of the independence
struggle, then inevitably it must fail or compromise. This classical
view of the matter contrasts with the ultra-left view, which coun-
terpoises republicanism and socialism and which breaks up the
unity of the national independence movement by putting forward
'socialist' demands that have no possibility of being achieved until
real independence is won; the result of which is that one gets neither independence nor socialism.

Partition affects all of Ireland, socially, politically and
economically, but it also affects the type of politics we have where
conservatism reigns. I have never found the Irish people to be
conservative. I don't think that we all woke up one day and elected
Mary Robinson, and suddenly started to become very liberal! I
have always found that the average Irish citizen has an attitude that
is broadly anti-imperialist, and most of the traits which we are said
to have in sexual or other matters are forced onto us by the
conservatives who are in power. You can't divorce the way we are
now from our communal past or from our communal present.

We need to differentiate between society and the Establishment.
We could get back to the free thinking and earthiness of our earlier
society if we were given a level pitch to play on and if we could say,
'yes, there's a place for the Churches, yes, there's a place for this and
there's also a place for people.' There's the Establishment depiction
of what we should be and then there's reality. Our Irishness can

only be inclusive if it takes in our diversity in all matters, and if we have a society of our own.

To ignore these lessons of history is to repeat the mistakes of the past. What is needed in Ireland, especially in the Twenty-six Counties, is the development of an anti-imperialist movement. Such a movement cannot be built around the slogan of socialism until socialism comes onto the historical agenda, until a distinctly Irish form of socialism is developed to meet our needs and conditions and until the majority class in Ireland, the working class, actually understands that this is in their interests and is what they want.

If such a mass anti-imperialist movement, with an appeal to all major sections of Irish society, could be developed—and this is the urgent task of all socialists, nationalists and republicans—it would fuse together all those whose interests are adversely affected by imperialism, and would show people the connection between their localized and special grievances and the imperialistic domination of Irish society.

The programme for such a movement would appeal to all those capable of taking a nationalist stand and would require a multi-sided campaign of national regeneration—a new Irish-Ireland movement to offset, especially in the Twenty-six Counties, the neo-colonial ethos and anti-national mentality which exists there. And such a programme would, by its very nature, be to the left of what passes for 'socialism' in Ireland today.

Politics in Ireland has been governed by a conservative ethos for some time. We're going to get a realignment of politics in Ireland in the future. I see Sinn Féin's future in that realigned group of 'normal politics.' In the meantime in Sinn Féin, we have to develop ourselves and our ability to put across our own position. The crux in Ireland, as we see it, is the question of partition and British involvement in Ireland. This has a social and an economic dimension and I think that it's up to us to inform the political agenda in Ireland about this, and hopefully to develop our party to play some significant role and to provide some alternative to the other parties' points of view. When Albert Reynold's star rises on the basis of the question of the North, one of the reasons why he has come from relative obscurity is because he's seen to be doing something.

There is a division in Ireland about the whole question of resolving the national issue. The differences in the conservative parties have become blurred at the edges. It's up to Sinn Féin to get people in the Twenty-six Counties to want to end partition on the basis of what's happening in the South. It's in people's own interests. It doesn't make economic sense to have two systems on this small island, with its population of five million. There is a range of reasons for the justice of having one economy on this island. I think if we could do anything it would be to concentrate on and move along that issue.

Connolly held that the nationalist revolution was the prerequisite of the socialist revolution. All of us who profess to be republicans or socialists would do well to study his writings. As Desmond Greaves has written, Connolly held that the political and economic aspects are the two stages of one democratic reorganization of society, each involving economic changes which it is the function of political change to promote. We who attempt to follow in his tradition must recognize that truth.

8

Culture

Mise Éire!
Is sine mé ná an Chailleach Béara!
Mór mo ghlóir!
Mé do rug Cú Chullain cróga!
Mór mo náire!
Mo chlann féin do dhíol a máthair! Mise Éire!
Is uaigní mé ná an Chailleach Béara!

I am Ireland!
I am older than the Hag of Beara!
To my great glory!
It was I who bore brave Cú Chullain!
It's to my great shame!
It was my own family who sold its mother!
I am Ireland!
I am lonelier than the Hag of Beara!

T A RECENT Sinn Féin *slógadh,* one speaker questioned the use of the term cultural to describe our political offensives on the question of language and national consciousness. This speaker held that culture is seen by many people to have something to do with ballet dancing. His point was well taken. Culture is a term with a wide variety of meanings and is understood in many different ways. Some people associate it with art, opera, classical music; others with the theatre or classical literature. In other words, it is often perceived as a highbrow commodity consisting of certain activities which are seen as the preserve of a privileged minority.

Culture is not, of course, the preserve of any one set of people or of any one class. Culture involves every aspect of our lives and is not restricted to the artistic expressions which humankind has developed. Culture consists of the ideas and attitudes of people, it is an indication of how we view things and it is our response to the environment in which we live. National culture is the reflection of the politics, economics, values, attitudes, aspirations and thoughts of a nation. It is the totality of our response to the world we live in.

Precisely because this is so, cultural colonialism formed, and forms, a major part of the conquest of Ireland. As Pearse wrote in *The Murder Machine*:

> The system has aimed at the substitution for men and women of mere things...Things have no allegiance. Like other things they are for sale...There is no education system in Ireland. The English have established the simulacrum of an educational system but its object is the precise contrary of the object of an education system. Education should foster; this education is meant to repress. Education should inspire; this education is meant to tame. Education should harden; this education is meant to enervate. The English are too wise a people to educate the Irish, in any worthy sense. As well expect them to arm us.

Pearse's observations are as relevant today as they were when they were written. An educational system which taught people to question their society, their environment, their social or economic disadvantage, an educational system which assisted people to strive for the common good, to form and voice radical opinions, to seek change, would do no service to those in control of the social and economic order in Ireland today. 'As well expect them to arm us.' Instead, our educational system instils the values of materialism, of the profit motive. It teaches the ways of colonialism, the values of imperialism and survivalism, and eradicates our sense of national culture, of independence, of individualism.

A national system of education was introduced to Ireland by the English ruling class before it was introduced in England. Its purpose was to break the national consciousness of the Irish people, to 'civilize the barbarians' by the methods later used throughout the world for the same purpose by all major powers.

There is no such thing as a neutral language, for language is the means by which culture, the totality of our response to the world we live in, is communicated; and for that reason the Irish language had to be destroyed. When a people have spoken a common language for thousands of years, that language reflects their history, sentiments, outlook and philosophy. Culture is filtered through it, and when the language is lost everything it represents is also lost. The Irish language has more than 2,000 years of unbroken history in Ireland. Apart from Greek, Irish has the oldest literature of any living European language. It is a badge of a civilization whose values were vastly different from the one which seeks to subjugate us. It is a badge of our identity and part of what we are. If we were to be made into little Englanders, that badge had to be removed, that culture destroyed and that civilization replaced by an order which accommodated and acquiesced to the interests of our new rulers.

The Gaelic social system in Ireland was communal. A substantial part of the land was common land and, although individuals could own land, they could not dispose of it as they pleased—outside the clan or sept, for example. Even cattle could not be disposed of by the individual without the consent of the clan. Chiefs were elected, usually from a single family, but there was no such concept as primogeniture. A woman could be elected as chief, and the electoral system and chieftainship often passed through the female line, as exemplified in the ancient sagas of the Ulster Cycle. The basis of early Irish law, known as the Brehon laws and first codified in the fifth century AD, was arbitration and compensation, and under the law there was a custom of ritual fasting as a method of asserting one's rights if the person who had inflicted injury was reluctant to accept arbitration.

Few of the great ancient civilizations made any provision for the poor who were sick. The Buddhists of Eastern India and the Irish were the two notable exceptions. In 300 BC, a hospital was established near Ard Macha (Armagh); each clan had its own *bruidhean* or public hostel where, free of charge, travellers were provided with shelter and hospitality. The *Senchas Mór* and the *Book of Aicill* are explicit about the rights of the sick and 'welfare state' provisions to offset the economic consequences of sickness and old age. The Gaelic educational system and the honoured position of the bards both show how emphasis was placed on improving the intellect, on creating and maintaining an ethos in which learning in its true sense flourished.

I outline the above, not because we seek to go back to those days or to that existence, but in order to sketch a brief outline of the kind of civilization which had to be destroyed to make the conquest possible. It also illustrates usefully the fact that capitalist ideas, feudalism and the concept of private property, have been imported into Ireland, not socialist ideas. That many people believe the opposite is but one example of how the revision of history has succeeded.

We do not seek to recover the past but to discover it, so that we can recover the best of our traditional values and mould them to the present. Our national culture should reflect a combination of the different influences within the nation: urban and rural, *Gaeltacht* and *Galltacht*, northern and southern, orange and green. The revival of the Irish language as the badge of identity, as a component part of our culture and as the filter through which it is expressed, is a central aspect of the reconquest.

Loyalist leaders today attack Irish culture, and particularly the language, as being non-Protestant. This is a nonsense, but the reasons for their hostility are obvious enough: for the Protestant people to embrace the Irish language today would be for them to reject loyalism.

Until 1601 and the defeat at Kinsale, our culture, shared by all our people, was dominant throughout this island and, even until the great starvation of the 1840s, Irish was the spoken language of the majority of the people. It has only ceased to be so in the last 150 to 100 years. The anglicization process was a long and cruel one and has never been totally successful. Even when the people were dispossessed and the independent aristocratic Gaelic culture destroyed with the Flight of the Earls and the great plantations, the hidden Ireland lived on as the culture of an oppressed people.

Its decline can be dated to a modernization of the relationship between England and Ireland, the Act of Union, after which the emerging middle class, unlike the Gaelic aristocracy who patronized the bards and harpers, strongly rejected the Irish language and customs. They had embraced the new order and rejected the old values. To succeed meant speaking English, rising above the herd. To be Irish was to be ignorant.

The emerging Irish establishment, including the Catholic Church, which had until that time been a source of some strength to the common people, succeeded where the *bata scóir*, the enforcement of the English language on children and the need for English in the market place, had failed. Even when they fled to 'Hell or Connaught,' the people took their culture with them. But now social and economic advancement became synonymous with the use of English language, mannerisms and culture.

This process has been refined in modern Ireland, and the native administration in the Twenty-six Counties in particular stands indicted on this score. Irish still remains the official first language, yet only two percent of state broadcasting is in the Irish language and the last bastions of the language, the *Gaeltachtaí*, are being steadily eroded as a result of a deliberate policy by the state.

Numerous reports chart the decline of the *Gaeltachtaí*, which have suffered a faster rate of depopulation in the last twenty-five years than at any time in the past century. The main reason is a particularly high rate of out-migration, accounting for two out of every three people born in the areas. In most cases, it is the better educated and younger people who go, leaving behind a population with a severe imbalance in many of its structural features. The combination of fewer young people and more old people has meant a low rate of natural increase.

The *Gaeltachtaí* are dwindling, as is the amount of Irish spoken in them. In West Donegal, which I have visited regularly since my schooldays, one now has to go further into the *Gaeltacht* than previously. The *Galltacht* is encroaching on what were once Irish-speaking areas. Many children are now being raised in English where only twenty or twenty-five years ago Irish was their first language. With the lack of economic, social and industrial infrastructure, the parents know that their children must leave home to find employment. The parents have fallen into the habit of speaking English and their children follow suit. Indeed, it is a miracle that any vestige of Irish culture or way of life remains.

Cultural colonialism demands today, as it did in the past, the lowering of national spirit, the revision of history and the destruction of our separate identity. Our cultural identity and our language would act as a counter or, in MacSwiney's words, as 'the frontier' against our submergence by a West British, shoneen ethos or by a rampant Anglo-American 'Rambo' ethos. If we are to accept our lot as a poor, partitioned off-shore island, if we are to be obedient to the dictates of the nuclear powers and the directives from Brussels, if our rulers are to be free to collaborate with the British in governing part of our country as a British possession, even if we are to accept emigration or the dangers caused by Sellafield, then we must be conditioned to become 'mere things,' because 'things have no allegiance.' In the Ireland of today our culture must not consist of our ideas and our attitudes. It must not be our view of things or our response to the environment we live in. It must instead be a reflection of the survivalism engendered by centuries of British colonialist and imperalist oppression. In other words, it must be the reflection of the politics, economics, values, attitudes, aspirations and thoughts of our rulers.

Garret FitzGerald's toadyism was a reflection of this dependency culture. Irish people cringed when he replied in English to a question in Irish at a press conference in Chequers. Later I had the opportunity to contrast his behaviour with the attitude of a foreign administration, at the extradition hearing of Gerry Kelly and Brendan MacFarlane in Amsterdam, where English is gaining primacy. The hearing was in Dutch and translated into English not, as the President of the court explained, 'because we don't understand English, but because Dutch is our language.' Irish people were to cringe even more when FitzGerald as 'their leader' left the country on St. Patrick's Day to be televised sharing a 'begorrah' with Ronald Reagan, together with a jar of green jelly-beans and a midget dressed up as a leprechaun.

This dependency culture expresses itself in both parts of Ireland today in resistance to change, in a lack of national pride, a feeling of national inferiority and in begrudgery. As Samuel Johnson observed, 'The Irish are a fair people. They never speak well of each other.' And why should they? We have been taught for 800 years not to.

Former Chief Psychiatrist of the Eastern Health Board, Dr Ivor Browne, has written:

Our past as a nation has been so crushing and so painful that we are too inclined to rush blindly ahead and leave it behind us. The fact is that we cannot go ahead in any real sense unless we identify where we are in relation to where we have been. If, as a society, we cannot take hold of ourselves so as to be effective in the running of our affairs and the management of our economy, and if we adopt a relationship of dependency to other countries and outside economic forces, then is it any wonder that the individual can find no place or room to act; that when in this country someone comes up with a creative idea, all those around him set themselves energetically to the task of denigrating that idea, of finding reasons why it could not work.

The culture being forced through most of Irish society today is a dependency culture, not only in the Twenty-six Counties but in the Six Counties as well; it affects loyalists as much as it affects citizens of the Twenty-six Counties. This dependency culture is based on escapism and plays its role in conditioning people to the acceptance of bad housing, unemployment, emigration, rising prices and falling living standards, bigotry, violence and a 'no hope' future.

Loyalist leaders who express hostility to the Irish language are actually denying their own past. Not only is this past evident in many of their names (for example McCusker and Maginnis), it is obvious also in the fact that at the time of the siege of Derry most of the population spoke Irish. Indeed, Irish Protestants in the late eighteenth century showed considerable interest in Irish music, literature and language.

In the liberal era of the 1790s the Belfast Harp Society flourished, the Belfast Reading Society (now the Linen Hall Library) was in the vanguard of the Irish revival, and the *Northern Star* published an Irish-language magazine, *Bolg an tSolar*. Belfast Academy had an Irish teacher, and pupils there, like the patrons of the Reading Society and the Harp Society and the readers of the *Northern Star*, were mainly Protestants.

Despite the sectarianism which replaced this liberal ethos, *An Cuideacht Gaedhilge Uladh* (Ulster Gaelic Society) was founded in 1830 by two wealthy Protestants, Robert MacAdam and Lord

Devonshire. MacAdam's sterling work in the promotion and recording of the Irish language is described in Brendan Ó Buachalla's *I mBéal Feirste Cois Cuin.*

While this interest amongst Protestants was to decline, the goodwill towards the language among patriotic Protestants continued. Douglas Hyde was to become one of the founders of the Gaelic League in 1893, and in the early 1900s the northern revival was led by other Protestants, such as Francis Biggar and Alice Milligan, founder of the newspaper *An Shan Van Vocht,* (The Poor Old Woman).

The struggle against cultural colonialism must be a key part of the reconquest of Ireland, of the making of a new Irish humanity. As we have seen, this does not mean going backwards. Neither does it mean merely preserving our language or our culture. Some people talk about 'preserving' the language: it is as if it was something to be kept as an archaic object to be brought out occasionally and shown to tourists. It is a notion of 'jam-jar' Irish. My own conviction is that the restoration of our culture must be a crucial part of our political struggle and that the restoration of the Irish language must be a central part of the cultural struggle. Culture is too important to be left to the cultural specialists. I agree with the late Mairtin Ó Cadháin, IRA activist, professor and writer, when he said, *'Tosóidh athghabháil na hÉireann le hathghabháil na Gaeilge.'* (The reconquest of Ireland will begin with the reconquest of the Irish language.)

Steve Biko, the murdered black Southern African leader said, 'The greatest weapon in the hands of the oppressor is the mind of the oppressed.' In this regard, I feel that many northern nationalists and republicans are much freer than their fellow Irish citizens in the Twenty-six Counties. Our minds are free: this is a truth which is understood by the imperial powers and their allies in Dublin, and it is the main reason why there has been a recent revival in Irish culture in the Six Counties and a corresponding attempt to divert this by way of petty legislation promised by the Hillsborough Treaty. As the British Minister responsible, Richard Needham, observed in a confidential letter:

> I gather that the Irish [Dublin government] place heavy significance on early progress in removing the

prohibition on the use of any language other than English in street signs. Apparently they consider that this would help to reduce the publicity and support which Sinn Féin has obtained through the use of street signs in Irish. The Irish [Dublin government] are accordingly pressing strongly for us to publish in the autumn proposals for a draft Order.

In the late 1960s, the civil rights struggle provided a broad enough appeal to bring out a substantial proportion of the anti-imperialist population. The activists of the Irish language movement had until then ploughed a lonely furrow, but the repression directed against the civil rights struggle, followed by internment, reawakened a consciousness about our language and culture. As the struggle has continued it has been accompanied by an increasing depth in the ideology of the people and a reinvigoration of our culture in all its forms.

As Padraig Ó Maolcraoibhe records:

When the men in the H-Blocks of Long Kesh and the women in Armagh prison were stripped of everything, they discovered that they could not be stripped of their language. It became a means of resistance, of asserting their dignity and identity. In the H-Blocks, with no books, no paper, no pens, no professional teachers, young men living in filthy conditions, frequently beaten, stripped naked...but unbowed, taught each other Irish by shouting lessons from cell to cell. And as one hunger strike was followed by the other the people outside learned these lessons also and they determined to carry on the cultural struggle—each one from where s/he was.

There is nothing trivial or folksy in the present interest of northern nationalists in the Irish language, and these positive attitudes do not exist only in the Six Counties but they predominate there. In Belfast there has been a considerable revival in the use of Irish, and the particular significance of this is that it is the first time it has ever happened within a working-class community.

In practice this revival is expressed in small ways, with language classes in social clubs, with all-Irish nursery schools, with the Gaelicization of street names. As a result, one finds young people with the most up-to-date fashions and hairstyles peppering their talk with Irish phrases. Rough as it may be, it represents culture in a living sense. It is 'survival' Irish, which enables people to exchange greetings and have some basic conversations. There is an all-Irish daily paper, *Lá*, today published in Belfast, the first ever daily newspaper in any Celtic language. In West Belfast there are more than sixty adult Irish classes, but the greatest hope lies in the growth of education through the medium of Irish.

In 1970 there were no schools in the Six Counties in which education was through Irish. Scoil Phobal Feirste opened in West Belfast as an all-Irish primary school with nine pupils in 1971. By 1977 it was still the only school in the Six Counties, with just thirty pupils and two teachers. By May 1986 it had 194 pupils and nine teachers, plus a nursery school with 120 pupils. There are now also four other nursery schools in Belfast and three in Derry, as well as two all-Irish streams in a County Derry primary school at Steelestown.

In 1977 there were twenty-two all-Irish nursery schools in the whole of Ireland. Today there are 150. In the 1981 census in the Twenty-six Counties, a million people said they knew some Irish. This is the highest number of people knowing Irish in the past hundred years. Modern Gaelic literature is showing a remarkable resilience and vigour, and there is now a national Sunday newspaper, *Anois*, for the first time.

There is without doubt a goodwill among the common people towards the language. And this is not confined to the North. In every survey carried out in the Twenty-six Counties, the great majority of people there have declared that they are in favour of more being done to increase the use of Irish. It is interesting to note that a recent survey commissioned by the Irish National Teachers Organization and carried out by MRBI shows that the working class and the lower middle class and the farming community as a whole are more favourable to the Irish language, and to every other aspect of Irish culture, than the middle and upper middle classes.

Culture is not a party political question or the monopoly of any one section of the people, but the destruction of our culture was a political act and its revival also requires political action. No progress can be made in any political struggle without the involvement of ordinary people, and the most pertinent point about the current modest revival is that it is happening because the ordinary people have identified with it.

Revolutionary republicans must come to understand the centrality of cultural resistance in the struggle for the reconquest of Ireland. As Pádraig Pearse said of the Gaelic League, the Easter Rising of 1916 was assured from the moment the League was founded. For their part, Irish language enthusiasts who think that the language can be fully restored without national independence must listen to the voice of Ó Cadháin when he tells us:

> *Ní hé amháin gur chóir do lucht na Gaeilge a bheith páirteach i gcogadh seo athghabhéla na hÉireann—is é an t-aon rud é ar fiú a bheith páirteach ann in Éirinn—ach is é ár ndualgas a bheith dhá chinnireacht agus dhá threorú. Bíodh an Ghaeilge ag stiúra na réabhlóide, ar an gcaoi seo bíodh an Ghaeilge ar na smaointe is forásaí in Éirinn; is ionann sin agus slánú na Gaeilge. Sí an Ghaeilge athghabháil na hÉireann, sí athghabháil na hÉireann slánú na Gaeilge. Sí teanga na muintire a shlánós an mhuintir.*

> (Not only should Irish speakers be participant in this war for the reconquest of Ireland—it is the only thing worth being part of in Ireland—but it is our duty to be its leaders and guides. If Irish is the steering force of the revolution, in this way Irish will be one of the most progressive forces in Ireland: that is the same as reviving Irish. The Irish language is the reconquest of Ireland, and the reconquest of Ireland is the Irish language. The language of the people shall revive the people.)

As with every other aspect of struggle, having agreed on our objectives the rest is a matter of agreeing on how to achieve them. This may take such small forms as deciding never again to say 'cheerio' and always say *slán*, or it may mean a total involvement in supporting the demands of the language struggle and the demands of the people of the *Gaeltachtaí* by working actively alongside them.

The media demand special attention because of their importance in influencing their audiences' opinions and values. In both the Twenty-six and Six Counties Sinn Féin calls for substantial increases in television and radio programmes in the Irish language, with special emphasis on children's programmes, and we have as a long-term aim the establishment of a Thirty-two County television and radio service entirely in Irish.

Our elected councillors in both the Twenty-six and Six Counties promote Irish culture by the erection of street signs in Irish, grant aid for *feiseanna*, bilingual council stationery, the use of Irish at formal council occasions and of Irish music at council-sponsored social events. We also want to see councils in the Twenty-six Counties supporting organizations engaged in promoting the Irish language, such as *Conradh na Gaeilge, Comhaltas Ceolteoirí Éireann* and *Cumann Lúthchleas Gael.*

In relation to the *Gaeltachtaí*, we recognize that the inferior social and economic infrastructure must be remedied if these strongholds of the language are to grow or even to avoid extinction. Hospital care is a major problem, with people having to travel long distances, and there is a special need for hospital units with Irish-speaking staff in each of the *Gaeltachtaí*. A fully elected *Údarás na Gaeltachta* should have the powers of a county council and full control of all planning in the area. They should set up a land bank and prevent land being bought by companies and individuals which will not promote the interests of the *Gaeltacht.*

A vital role in the cultural revival has been played by the republican prisoners in the prisons and concentration camps of the Six Counties, but they are denied the right to receive publications or letters in Irish or to speak Irish during visits; they are forbidden even to wear the *Fáinne*, to play Gaelic football or to have Irish musical instruments such as the *bodhrán* and tin whistle. Sinn Féin campaigns for the removal of those bans and for the prisoners' right to study Irish at formal classes up to degree level.

What is crucial is an understanding that the Irish language is the reconquest of Ireland and the reconquest of Ireland is the Irish language. A failure to grasp this, apart from a legitimate patriotic desire to restore our own language and maintain a separate Irish cultural identity, means that, as a dustbin of Anglo-American culture, we will be morally, psychologically, intellectually and materially worse off.

9

Sinn Féin Today

My business is revolution.
James Connolly

THE BASIS FOR Sinn Féin's philosophy is contained in the 1916 Proclamation, which puts forward such basic tenets as that the ownership of Ireland belongs to the people of Ireland, that all children of the nation are to be cherished equally, and universal suffrage. Essentially what we want to see is a non-sexist, economic, social and political democracy in Ireland, and either a secular society or certainly one in which no religious persuasion would have any special constitutional place in the state. We argue for the necessity of a new constitution and for a charter of human rights based on international conventions.

The situation in both states of Ireland at the moment is one where over a third of the people are living well below the poverty line, where unemployment has been chronic for generations, and where emigration is a way of life. The diaspora of Irish in the world such as in the US, where forty-one million claim Irish origin from an island with a population of five million, shows the effects of economic exile. At the same time, a very small clique at the top are making a huge amount of money, so it's not that Ireland is a poor country, in fact it ranks at sixteenth place in the world. Certainly, we live in a modern consumer society, but with all the characteristics of a developing society with people leaving the land, the build-up of a big urban centre—Dublin, where over a third of the citizens of the Twenty-six counties live—and no indigenous industry.

All of this argues for social equality and economic democracy, for, as Connolly said, 'you have to judge the quality of life by the quality of life for its lowest class.' If one looks at Ireland today, leaving aside even the tragedy of the North, it is essentially a society of 'haves' and 'have-nots,' in many ways classless, but social and economic polarization, bad infrastructure, cut-backs in the health and education sectors all need reversing. We're arguing for a just society in which there is an equality of opportunity, where people have the right to a house, the right to education, the right to a job. Discrimination of any kind will have to be eliminated.

Sinn Féin is an open political party with an elected leadership and public representatives in both states on this island. We have twelve and a half percent of the vote in the North, though much less in the Twenty-six Counties. We are a republican party, the oldest one on this island, and an unarmed manifestation of the present phase of the struggle for Irish national self-determination. Our long-term goal is for a Thirty-two County democratic socialist republic based upon the 1916 Proclamation. We would like to see a system of decentralized economic and political structures in a pluralist, bilingual, non-sexist Ireland. All of this is a matter for the Irish people to decide democratically, and our primary objective is for an Irish national democracy, for the end to partition and the restoration to the Irish people as a whole of our right to national self-determination. In other words, we are committed to a reconquest of Ireland by the Irish people.

Sinn Féin is best known, of course, for its position on the British connection and the partition of our country. We have been in the vanguard of this phase of the struggle since it began, in the 1960s, with a pacifist campaign for civil rights. Members of Sinn Féin and our families have paid a heavy price for this involvement, as have the communities from which we draw support. Eighteen Sinn Féin members have been killed in recent times, including women and councillors. The families of Sinn Féin members have also been shot at and bombed.

The death penalty is the price paid for membership of Sinn Féin (or being a member of a Sinn Féiner's family). This killing campaign cannot be divorced from the climate of demonization,

131

vilification and censorship which is the predominant ethos in Irish politics today.

Sinn Féin is the only political organization in Ireland which is substantially organized and active on a Thirty-two County basis. Despite the censorship of Section 31 of the Broadcasting Act, the combined campaigns of harassment and propaganda by the Dublin and London governments and our own organizational weaknesses, Sinn Féin is a growing force in Irish politics. That this is so is not only a tribute to our members and supporters but also proof of the validity of our political position and of the relevancy of our policies.

I am quite certain that none of the establishment parties could have survived as we have if they had had to function in similar conditions. Until 1974, Sinn Féin was banned under British law in the Six Counties and, although the late Maire Drumm and others provided a public leadership during this period, Sinn Féin lacked the organization for active political interventions and was primarily underground, thus functioning in a restricted way. While the lifting of the ban means that Sinn Féin membership is no longer an indictable offence, we continue to be subjected to a wide range of repressive legislation and petty harassment in both parts of this island.

This harassment takes many forms, from constant interference with well-known activists to intimidation of new members. In the Twenty-six Counties especially, the targeting of new members by the Special Branch is a long-established police practice. Special Branch officers visit the homes and work places—if they are fortunate enough to be in work—of new recruits, especially young ones, and question parents and employers about the political activities of their offspring or employees. Pubs and hotels which rent or lend rooms for meetings often receive similar visits and enquiries. Our members in the Six Counties are frequently victims of assassination by loyalist and British terror gangs, and, of all the political parties, Sinn Féin has suffered most in this regard.

Recruitment to Sinn Féin used to occur primarily in the wake of events such as the 1969 pogroms, internment, Bloody Sunday and the hunger strikes, so that many people became absorbed into Sinn Féin but not educated into it. Thus there was a lack of unified political consciousness and, in the absence of a relevant political education process, there was no planned development of republican politics. This vacuum was, of course, filled by other political groupings and it assisted, for example, the growth of the SDLP just as the same kind of lack had contributed to the growth of Fianna Fáil decades earlier. It also led to a certain ignoring by republicans of the need for political struggle in the Twenty-six Counties.

In the Six Counties, while Sinn Féin was more heavily involved with nationalist communities, few structured, and thus durable, links were forged from this relationship and no real advances were made. Sinn Féin was by and large perceived as, and was in reality, a poor second cousin to the IRA. This was not only how we were seen by supporters and opponents; in many ways it was also how we viewed ourselves.

Much of the change in this situation has come about because of the length of the struggle, for the struggle itself has politicized republicans. So, while there is still a spontaneous move towards Sinn Féin in the wake of some specific action like a British attack on a republican funeral, there is also, as Sinn Féin becomes more relevant on a whole range of issues and more competent on the national question, a steady and consistent flow of recruits into our ranks. New members, especially young people who have lived their entire lives in the struggle, are of a developed political calibre. They have been politicized because the political situation has been continuously developing and because the crisis has been going on for so long.

While spontaneity may be regarded as an element in the political weakness of organized republicanism, in many ways when properly harnessed it is also one of its greatest strengths, making it a living movement in struggle. Republicanism is a very potent force in Irish politics, but the vehicle of republicanism is still weak organizationally and our underdevelopment in this respect is something which we recognize and which we are constantly addressing.

Electoral success in the Six Counties and in specific areas in the Twenty-six has accelerated this process of developing a party political organization. There is nothing which concentrates the mind of a political party as much as an electoral campaign, and while we do not restrict ourselves to electoral campaigns—indeed we see it merely as one facet in a many-faceted struggle of campaigns, street agitation, cultural resistance, publicity work and education—our electoral successes have played a major role in changing the nature of Sinn Féin.

For example, prior to the 1984 local elections in the Six Counties we had no party whip and were providing no consistent, organized focus for the few local councillors that we had in the Twenty-six Counties. Suddenly we found ourselves with about 100 councillors in the Thirty-two Counties, some of them in majority positions, with two of them actually in the chair of district councils in the Six Counties. While this had occurred previously in the Twenty-six Counties, it had done so with much less public or media attention. Now we had very rapidly to apply ourselves to developing ways to service our councillors, to work out a method of accountability, to create the machinery for them to come together to discuss common problems, while at the same time making sure that these elected representatives would not become divorced from the grass roots of the party. Recognizing the reality of the Six Counties as an electoral unit, we now have a Six County Executive of Sinn Féin and we have a national chairperson with responsibility for party discipline—in effect, a party whip.

Our electoral intervention has exploded the myth that the republican movement enjoyed no support, and it has extended our relationships with our constituents. We can now get certain things done and we have access to the departments of the establishment bureaucracy that are relevant to people's everyday problems and needs.

The electoral intervention has helped to develop the party and to get rid of the novelty of politics for many of our members. There was a great feeling of euphoria after the Assembly election results. From euphoria we went into contesting other elections—we fought ten in four years (more than any other party because we are organized in both parts of Ireland)—and we began to develop a very committed group of political workers. The activists had to think and they had to apply themselves to problems, issues, structures and aspects of struggle which they had never really had to consider before. In the process of our campaign, everything was done and said by the Irish and British establishments to make it difficult for the electorate to vote for us, the London government going to great lengths to try to deprive many of our supporters of their votes; yet, despite all the pressures that were brought to bear, the people did vote for us, to the extent that in Belfast, the informal capital city of the Six Counties, Sinn Féin has become the majority nationalist party.

I find this fact particularly satisfying, not only because of the stark contrast with the situation when I joined Sinn Féin but also because of Belfast's historical ties with the conception of Irish republicanism in the 1790s. Republicanism is alive and well once more in Belfast city, the political bastion of unionism and sectarianism; republican politics and methods of struggle are debated there today as eagerly as they were in the days of Tone, Hope and Henry Joy. And no amount of manipulation or pretending it is otherwise by our opponents can disguise this fact.

I must add, that in the history of partition, Nationalists are better organized now, no matter how divided they might be between the SDLP and ourselves. Sinn Féin has obviously helped that whole process.

In Dublin, also, in the last few years Sinn Féin has gained support in the working-class areas. While this support is coming from those who are most disadvantaged by society, at the same time we have made it clear that we seek to contest some of the areas of support which are currently enjoyed by the Labour Party, Fianna Fáil and the Workers' Party. We seek to build support among the employed and the organized working class and the small-business people. In rural areas our natural constituency lies with the working farmers, small-business people and rural working class. This section of people have consistently and instinctively remained anti-imperialist and pro-republican in their outlook, and there is potential for us to convert their latent support for the reconquest of Ireland into active support for Sinn Féin.

In order to realize our potential, we have to develop our organization very considerably and we have to move into the mainstream of political relevancy. A problem we experience is that many republicans have long had a compartmentalized attitude to their republican activities, whereby they pursue republican 'politics' in isolation from their involvement in community groups, trade unions, co-operative or tenant organizations. We are seeking to change that, to break down self-isolation and to develop policy and strategy. In all of this it is important for us to act in an open, non-opportunistic and declared fashion in whatever organizations or

campaigns we are engaged in. At all times republicans need to proceed at the level of people's understanding, winning support from
that perspective, working alongside people and sharing in their
struggles, never getting too far ahead and never getting removed
from the activity of the situation.

The 'Concerned Parents' organization in Dublin offer a good
example of republicans working well in this fashion. The local
communities organized themselves against drugs and drug pushers,
and local republicans as members or these communities were
actively involved. Of course, the republicans could have intervened independently—armed IRA interventions against the main
drug suppliers or pushers would undoubtedly have enjoyed
widespread support in areas blighted by drugs—but the militant
actions of Concerned Parents, the community ostracism of the
pushers, and the humane community attitudes towards drug
addicts have had a more lasting and deeper effect, not just on the
issue of drug addiction among Dublin's youth but also in instilling
a consciousness of their own power in working-class communities.

The Gaelic revival in the Six Counties has proceeded in much
the same fashion, and in other areas of work, though with less dramatic results and with less publicity; Sinn Féin is developing along
similar lines. We have come a long way from being largely a
protest movement built around the objective of an end to British
rule and in opposition to the more obvious abuses of British rule.
We have developed into a party which has a potential for support
in the Twenty-six Counties; this potential has been exaggerated by
the establishment but the potential exists nonetheless.

In the Six Counties, our support base is well established by recent
election results and, far from being the criminal thugs, psychopaths
and isolated terrorists of British propaganda, Sinn Féin is established in a bedrock of support in nationalist areas and the SDLP
can no longer claim to be the sole representative of nationalist
opinion. In this regard, the emergence of Sinn Féin may have
unnecessarily brought out some of the class differences between
ourselves and the SDLP leadership. These differences are there, of
course, indeed they are dictated by the class nature of the struggle
and they should not be disguised.

One of the things I have discovered about career politicians is
that, Sinn Féin being a largely working-class party, the politically

organized middle class cannot cope with what they see as the audacity of people like ourselves thinking we can do things that they were put through college and university to do. They were taught their politics, methods of management, public relations work and other skills by experts. We learned ours on the streets, in prison and through a process of self-education. Working-class people who were denied the opportunity, in most cases, of advanced formal education have coped tremendously with all the problems of creating and maintaining an active political movement—not merely a political party which emerges before and retires after elections but a movement in perpetual struggle. After twenty-four years of upheaval, I feel that it is an achievement in itself to have the type of support which we do have, especially considering the opposition we face.

The way in which we work within Sinn Féin is different to the way in which any of the other parties work. We have encouraged an openness in the party by which, in a frank but comradely fashion, all issues are discussed. No subject is taboo. Our leadership actually encourages constructive criticism of itself, regular re-examination of our strategies and reviews of our policies. This is not to suggest that we are perfect; far from it. We suffer from all the weaknesses of human nature, but, by understanding the necessity for revolutionary leadership and having grasped that this involves all of our membership, we have made considerable advances in the development of a collective leadership.

You cannot take a vote on every single thing that comes up, but I think that other political leaderships expect their members to accept that their leadership should be permitted to do their thinking for them. In Sinn Féin we are striving for a situation where our membership participates in the decision-making process in the fullest way possible and to the fullest extent. They then understand and support these decisions because they have been involved in the decision-making, and thus they will be more committed and capable of implementing these decisions. This is an essential ingredient in the building of a revolutionary party. It also ensures that the right decisions are more likely to be taken.

Of importance also is a willingness to recognize, to admit and to rectify mistakes. Communication is vital, and frank and open dialogue between all levels of our organization is something we are working to create. We all have feet of clay and no revolutionary leadership can be unmindful of this very human condition. Many incompetent people pushed into leadership, or seeking leadership because of a desire for power (something I can understand in any context other than the republican movement), have possessed leadership qualities without the other necessary attributes and have thus been absolutely incapable of accepting criticism.

The cult of personality which exists in Irish public life is something which has to be overcome. As Connolly put it:

> In Ireland…we have ever seized upon mediocrities and made them leaders; invested them in our minds with all the qualities we idealized, and then when we discovered that our leaders were not heroes but only common mortals, mediocrities, we abused them, or killed them for failing to be better than God made them. Their failure dragged us down along with them because we had insisted that they were wiser than we were, and had stoned whoever declared them to be mere mortals and not all-wise geniuses. Our real geniuses and inspired apostles we never recognized, nor did we honour them. We killed them by neglect, or stoned them whilst they lived, and then went in reverent procession to their graves when they were killed.

Connolly and other writers attribute this tendency to 800 years of British colonial oppression. It is something which must be overcome, especially and first of all within the ranks of those seeking to end British colonialism.

The electoral situation in the Twenty-six Counties is far different from that in the Six Counties, and we suffer from major organizational difficulties. We have to cope with the age-old question of what part reformism plays in the building of support, and we are still constructing the foundations for an effective political party in that area. While republicans are very disciplined in terms of loyalty to the movement, we experience a lack of political acumen, which may have to do with our conspiratorial past and which certainly has to do with the confining of the struggle to the Six Counties.

The effects of Section 31 of the Broadcasting Act in the Twenty-six Counties posed a considerable problem: not so much in terms of support for Sinn Féin specifically, but in terms of disinformation—disinformation not just about the British presence in the Six Counties but also in terms of society in the Twenty-six Counties. More importantly, it denied people their right to freedom of information. The whole ethos that flows from that censorship is very pervasive and results in a failure to investigate issues fully. It is closely related to a mood of revisionism and of turning backs even on the origins of the state. The Twenty-six Counties must be unique as a state in that it did nothing to mark the seventieth anniversary of the Proclamation of the Republic, whereas in any other country such an anniversary would have been marked by pageantry and celebration. The establishment is afraid of all the skeletons in the cupboards of the state, afraid that if it scratches a Terence MacSwiney up jumps a Bobby Sands.

The most important aspect of the repeal of Section 31 in 1994 is that there's now the possibility of having a real debate through the medium from which most people receive their information. There is a problem with the management of RTE insofar as the self-censorship there has made them ultra-cautious. So now they're using Section 18, which forbids the conducting of interviews with those who might be deemed to be inciting violence. RTE has said that, in order to ensure that members of Sinn Féin are not in breach of Section 18, RTE journalists must get clearance before doing an interview with Sinn Féin members, which rules out the possibility of doing live interviews. If one looks at the record of interviews done by Sinn Féin spokespersons, then one sees that there is no question of incitement, and furthermore, if there is any question of anyone using incitement then it should be dealt with in the normal way. But one has to bear in mind that RTE has the distinction of being one of the few broadcasting networks which had to have the decision of ending censorship forced upon it. Indeed the management almost argued against this decision.

Section 31 has not only affected Sinn Féin. It affects a whole range of people, and it means that the issue of British involvement in the Six Counties is not dealt with in an informative way. The question of how partition affects people socially or economically, for example, has never received any detailed mainstream coverage. Interviews with any person of any nationalist hue, whether they be members of Sinn Féin or not, have not been broadcast, and this applies equally to people in the Twenty-Six Counties. One can only hope that, as the law against censorship is removed, the ethos of censorship will also go.

When you consider that Section 31 was in place for over twenty years, this means that anyone here under the age of thirty-three or thirty-two would never have heard a republican spokesperson. So, not only do we have the potential now to have a true debate, but there is a very strong need to reverse twenty years of misinformation, and it will take some time before we have a level playing pitch.

Sinn Féin's major problem is our failure, to date, to build an effective organization, after long periods of self-imposed isolation derived from conspiratorial politics as well as censorship, of harassment by the guards, and of a lack of political understanding. The only way I know in which this problem can be tackled is by discussing and addressing every single issue which is pertinent. If I have learned anything, I have learned that you can only proceed on the basis of people's support, and that you can only enjoy that support if you are approaching people at a level and on a ground which they understand. You have to find a common denominator between what you want to do and what people feel needs to be done. Sinn Féin became irrelevant to many people in the Twenty-six Counties, because republicans failed to examine the society in which they lived and failed to offer a political way forward. Nevertheless, in all the different walks of Irish life, there is a grudging respect for the concept of republicanism. As Conor Cruise O'Brien has pointed out, republicanism is, in a sense, the conscience of the Irish people. There is a feeling that if the Rising of 1916 was, as his generation was taught, right, then the resistance in 1969 was right and it still is. There is a tolerance and an ambivalence, because in the back of people's minds is the notion that there is some logic and rectitude to what republicans are saying.

Although Sinn Féin is a Thirty-two County organization, it has been equally subject to the uneven development of the two statelets as any other aspect of life on the island, and one way in which this unevenness expresses itself is in terms of a problem of public leadership. The organization in the Twenty-six Counties is in a relatively retarded position and lacks its own identifiable leadership. There are many very able people in the membership and in local leadership positions who are not publicly identifiable outside of their own areas. There are members with plenty of ability, talent and commitment who nevertheless would not be known outside of a Sinn Féin Árd Fheis and who might not even be known by most other Sinn Féin members. And this is a problem which has a special importance in terms of our ability to field and develop candidates for local elections.

In the last Twenty-six County local elections we received a realistic vote, which can easily be related to those places where we are well organized and have prominent individuals. We got the vote we deserved. But none of the local election seats won would work out in a general election as a Leinster House seat. The electoral intervention of the H-Block/Armagh Committee at the time of the hunger strike showed an ability to bring out more than the normal republican vote. However, when shortly after that an electoral intervention was made in the absence of a hunger strike, the figures had shrunk back to the republican vote, at about five percent. This was absolutely predictable. Electoral interventions are successful only in very special conditions. To build and consolidate electoral support, a consistent electoral strategy is required. In the hunger strike election, voters set aside the very pressing economic priorities and saddled themselves with a hung parliament, and that was significant. But once the hunger strike was over, the economic issues came to the fore again and people went back to voting for some kind of stability.

Our electoral experiences provoked a sporadic debate about abstentionism. There was some opposition within Sinn Féin to our electoral strategy because, on the electoral road, if one was serious, one would have to confront the issue of abstentionism.

There was a substantial difference between abstentionism in the Six Counties and in the Twenty-six Counties. A large part of the nationalist and republican population in the Six Counties regarded abstentionism as posing no problem in terms of giving their votes, because they did not see participation in the institutions of the state as having anything to offer them. But in the Twenty-six Counties, while people may be very scornful of the performance of the politicians and cynical about the institutions of the state, they nevertheless expect the people they elect to represent them in these institutions. In the Six Counties, people can go to an active-abstentionist representative who will work on their behalf in constituency matters. In the Twenty-six Counties, although a number of Sinn Féin TDs were elected in the 1950s, there was never a policy of active-abstentionism; if there had been abstentionism, it might not have been as significant a factor in the organization.

The subject was opened up for debate at the 1985 Árd Fheis. Despite its great emotional potential within the movement, it was argued in a logical, informative and interesting manner; there was some emotionalism and there were spontaneous outbursts of applause for rhetoric, but in the end, as has often been my experience, the vote was not in accord with the applause and was, in fact, very close. The debate took place without a lead from the platform: it was felt by the Árd Chomhairle at that time to be such a historically divisive issue that the people on the platform should have a free vote and that it would be better to arrive at positions after listening to the debate by the membership, rather than having a situation where people might be swayed by the oratory of Martin McGuinness, Danny Morrison, Gerry Adams or other leading figures.

That situation has now changed. At our 1986 Árd Fheis we dropped our abstentionist attitude to Leinster House with the aim of registering broad political gains rather than the immediate gains in terms of a seat or seats in Leinster House.

There were no real parallels between our current debate and the debate associated with the split in the republican movement in 1970 which led to the creation of the 'Stickies,' now the Workers' Party and Democratic Left. At that time the IRA leadership had decided to abandon armed struggle and then decided to drop abstentionism. The leadership brought in all its organizers and conducted and intensive indoctrination course, setting the movement on the path of constitutionality. The development can be clearly traced through the speeches and policy changes of the time—the movement from opposition to Stormont to full support for it, from shooting at the RUC to full support for them, from a call for British withdrawal to support for the British presence, from opposition to the EEC to full support. They changed their basic positions in a major ideological somersault and were involved in a new departure.

We are not engaged in any new departure. We are committed absolutely to the objective of Irish independence. And we have no illusions about Leinster House. I share and I understand the republican memory of how Leinster House was imposed on us by summary executions at Ballyseedy and other lonely spots and by the hangman's noose and firing squads in Free State prisons.

To understand the significance of this recent development within Sinn Féin, one must understand that it comes after many decades of stagnation. In the past, the republican movement was a separatist movement with radical tendencies. In its current embodiment, the radical tendency is for the first time in control, and in institutionalizing the radical tendency a very important, historic job has been done. In our thinking we have brought to light elements which were obscured in the past. The philosophers and thinkers of the 1916 Rising did not survive it, and this set the stage for counter-revolution. What we have done is take a step towards reversing the effects of the counter-revolution.

The counter-revolution of that time was followed by the abandonment by the republicans of politics in the context of a monopoly of politics by the establishment, and republicans from then on simply kept harking back. It may have been sufficient in 1918 or 1920 to merely say 'we want the 1916 Proclamation;' but with the growth of the partitionist state, which was functioning effectively, it was no longer adequate and by the thirties it was less and less so.

If we have done nothing else of significance in the 1970s, 1980s and 1990s, we have tried to do what was done in the previous high periods of republicanism. The republicans who penned the 1916 Proclamation, who wrote *The Sovereign People* and *Labour in Irish History*, sat down, discussed, thrashed out and developed their politics. They did not simply take what Wolfe Tone had said. They took the principles and they added to them and tried to develop from that basis. No matter how inadequately, we have tried to do the same thing against the background of an absence of significant critical evaluation and reassessment for about seventy years.

We have tried first of all to take the general principles of republicanism, as subscribed to in the Proclamation, and we have tried under very difficult circumstances to make these relevant. The power and strength of the establishment is massive compared to a

143

collection of working-class people such as make up the republican movement. We have tried to make the principles relevant in major ways and in what may be small, mundane ways which are reflected in how we, as opposed to the establishment parties, deal in an electoral sense with a constituent or in a broader sense with someone we are trying to win over.

To take just one example of how we have tried to implement the basic principles in practice: we have decided internally that because of the discrimination against women in Irish society we will have a policy of positive discrimination. The republican movement is not a set of abstract ideas, it is a movement of people in society and it reflects tendencies in society in general. The fact that women have historically not enjoyed a significant role in deciding policy in the movement can be related to the status of women in society as a whole. Nevertheless, the republican movement has probably had a rather better attitude to women than many institutions. There have been many leading republican women, and recognition has always been given to the fact that women provided the backbone of the conspiratorial aspect of the movement.

Now we are the only party in Ireland that has by right a quarter of the places on our Árd Chomhairle reserved for women. We have also taken measures to overcome and avoid typecasting or stereotyping of women within the party. While we have a long way to go before women comrades have full equality in Sinn Féin, rather than saying that in post-colonial Ireland women will have equality, we have taken small practical steps now, and these are measures which are more telling and more relevant than any noble aspirations.

Sinn Féin as part of society reflects, in many ways, other aspects of society. I think that our intentions may be good, that the party wants to put its resources where its mouth is. You can say that you want a woman in a leadership position, but, unless you're providing for an unmarried mother, a married mother or whatever relationship a person is in, these are empty words. You have to start providing some sort of resources. This can range from child-minding to just having meetings at a time that is better suited. We need to do a lot more than that, because a lot of the keynote positions should be held by women. The majority of people that I work with, outside of the party, are women. You go into the Lower Falls on a housing problem, it's women. You go in about children, it's women. You go in about better wages, it's women. They turn up at the meetings and, when there's an election, it'll be women on the ground who do the work. We have to try to structure the party in such a way that their involvement is reflected. For, if they can rise to leadership positions in the current situation, in a full open situation then they'd easily end up running things.

I do think that women humanize politics. I think that women are naturally more radical and, even though these are generalizations, women are more open and don't have the same tendency to be macho that men have; maybe that's because of where they come from.

While we still do not have nearly enough women candidates, women are now certainly playing a fuller role within the organization. In this context, women have started articulating their own demands and the credit for this lies with the women themselves. It is a continuing process involving conflicting views, and it doesn't by any means confine itself to women intervening on 'women's issues.' Seven of Sinn Féin's thirteen national departments are headed by women, and the General Secretary and Director of Publicity are women. The increasing participation of women is all to the good, it's all to the benefit of the party, of republicans, and I hope women would feel it was to their benefit too.

In other aspects of our philosophy and of the development of our organization, we have tried to do the same kind of thing. We hold regular internal conferences at every level of the party, and, while this may not in itself be very significant, they differ radically from party conferences/Árd Fheiseanna in other parties. The Fianna Fáil Árd Fheis, for example, is by and large a jamboree. This serves a useful political purpose, but it means that the Árd Fheis is not the place where debate takes place or where policy is formulated and agreed upon. Fine Gael suffers from the same syndrome. In the micro-groups, conferences are dominated by doctrinaire lines, splinters, splits and factions.

The Sinn Féin Árd Fheis is a developing phenomenon which perhaps twenty or twenty-five years ago was to some extent a jamboree where people came together—there was a social element to it, there was a publicity element, all the obvious advantages of being able to present the public spectacle of a party political conference.

There was, however, no meaningful debate on issues other than the obvious. But, in the late seventies, things began to change and today they are continuing to change.

Our Árd Fheis in 1994 had 192 motions on a wide variety of issues. It is actually impossible to deal with this many motions in the hours available, and it is inevitable that some interest groups have to experience the frustration of not being able to put their motion and have it discussed. And this is a real problem, because one can see that, as Sinn Féin becomes involved in more and more issues and as republicans develop their consciousness about the depth of the struggle, they naturally feel the need to put forward their particular strategies or tactics.

This process of critical self-analysis and reappraisal has led to frank and open discussion on many issues which would not otherwise have surfaced. The end result is that we have an Árd Fheis which is unique, but which presents difficulties in public presentation: an Árd Fheis which discusses a whole spectrum of issues from travellers' rights to incest and AIDS. These, I know, are minority interest subjects, but they are important nonetheless and they show that the Árd Fheis is not just being used as a jamboree but that it is actually an open democratic forum in which members dictate policy and avail of the opportunity to win support for their positions.

Another example of the realization of the importance of republican politics leading to a structured approach can be found in the production and availability of republican literature. A wide range of this literature (our opponents call it propaganda) is produced and distributed by Republican Publications and, as we have improved our political structures and our political understanding, the quality of this literature has improved.

Educational pamphlets, a number of small books, collections of poetry, policy documents, posters, an annual calendar and a republican diary are but some of the items produced and distributed by a small group of voluntary workers. They started with little previous experience and only a few hundred pounds, but with lots of common sense and commitment they have established a thoroughly professional operation. Before this structured approach, the production of republican literature was sporadic—indeed it may have amounted only to a handful of pamphlets in as many years. Now at least one new publication on some aspect of our struggle is produced every few months.

An Phoblacht, which merged with *Republican News* in 1979, is a radical weekly in as full a sense as one would wish; it can be improved, of course, but its weekly production as a centralized expression and platform of republican politics is a great achievement. If one looks at past issues of either of the two papers before the merger and seeks to analyze them as representing the politics of the movement, one may very well come to inadequate conclusions. At times, especially when many republicans were underground and unconcerned or unable to influence the content or the presentation of our newspapers, they were really a reflection of the particular politics and emphases of the few people who worked very hard to produce them. Since the merger and our re-orientation this has changed, and *An Phoblacht* has gone from strength to strength, praised even by our critics as the best political newspaper in Ireland today.

Sinn Féin also produces a large amount of bilingual material. *Saoirse*, our Irish language magazine, is the only political magazine published in Irish. Copies of *IRIS*, an occasional English language production, are now collector's items.

None of this short but slightly boastful section is an attempt to suggest that we have perfected the art of producing revolutionary literature. It is simply an effort to show that, having realized the necessity for such literature, we proceeded, with some success, to fulfil that need. It is also an unashamed and proudly proclaimed example of the fact that people in struggle can change things and, in the changing, learn how to improve and perfect their struggle.

I want now to deal with the question of violence and with the Sinn Féin attitude to it. Irish nationalists need no one to spell out the layers of violence visited upon them and the diverse forms that this takes. We have been victims of institutionalized violence, the violence of marginalization, of discrimination and of physical violence. We are familiar with, and have survived, social and economic violence. But, of course, those who inflict this violence upon us, or who act as apologists for it, project a propaganda picture which depicts violence as a nationalist or republican phenomenon. Propaganda is everything.

Thus loyalist killings are reactive. The British Crown forces are peacekeepers who 'act within the law.' This is the consensus which is promoted within the media and through the establishment, including the Churches. It is based upon semantics, propaganda and double-think.

For a republican to say that he or she supports the IRA, or for anyone to say that they understand why the IRA exists, is to be beyond the pale. Yet Church leaders can actively seek support for the RUC or the British presence in this country. Political leaders can call for greater use of British forces, for a 'shoot to kill' policy, internment, curfews and so on. Unionist politicians can collude with loyalist paramilitaries, and, of course, the British ministers posted here have a direct responsibility for the largest armed group here and for its considerable war machine.

Sinn Féin is censored and excluded, on the pretext that we are involved in violence, which effectively disenfranchises our voters. Let us be quite clear about this. The British government is attempting to defeat the republican struggle, which is why it refuses to engage meaningfully in the peace process. There is no morality involved, only expediency. The Sinn Féin position is often misrepresented. I want to outline it for the record. Sinn Féin's attitude to armed struggle is as agreed by our Árd Fheis. It is contained in our Political Report.

> Sinn Féin's position on the armed struggle is quite clear. We believe that the Irish people have the right to use armed struggle in the context of seeking Irish independence and in the conditions of British occupation in the Six Counties. Whether Irish people wish to exercise that right is a matter for them. That is our opinion. It is also a matter of political reality and a fact of life in the Six Counties. It will be so, unfortunately, until the conditions which create it are changed. Sinn Féin wishes to change these conditions. We want a total demilitarization of the situation and an end to armed struggle of all kinds in our country.
>
> Sinn Féin does not advocate violence. We understand why the conflict continues and why there is armed resistance by the IRA to British rule in our

country. The IRA has stated clearly on a number of occasions that for republicans armed struggle is a method of political struggle adopted reluctantly and as a last resort in the absence of any viable alternative.

The onus is on those who claim that there is an alternative to the IRA's armed struggle to prove that this is the case.

Sinn Féin is committed to dealing with the central issues, to challenging the causes of conflict in Ireland and by so doing to create the conditions in which real and lasting peace can be established.

It is not good enough for our opponents to hide behind the fiction that Sinn Féin is the IRA. We are not. As I have said before, Sinn Féin is an independent political party whose policy is decided by an annual Árd Fheis, representative of the party branches, and whose work is directed by the Árd Chomhairle duly elected by the party members.

Sinn Féin's peace strategy is a personal and political priority for me, and it is now the central part of Sinn Féin policy and our main function as a political party.

It is the British connection and partition which subvert democracy in Ireland. The dislocation and destabilization of Irish social, political, cultural and economic life for most of this century has come about as a direct result of the denial of Irish independence.

Sinn Féin wants stronger Irish institutions, a stronger democracy, more local democracy, a Thirty-two County parliament that embraces the entire Irish nation, structures which allow the Irish people to work out our future, and to shape our institutions in peace.

There is still a lot of work to be done before the task of building Sinn Féin into the mass organizer of the Irish people is completed. We face an uncertain future, but we can at least be confident that we face it with as much determination, more confidence and with more experience than any previous generation of Irish republicans. We know that we survived in the past and consolidated in the present, despite all our weaknesses and in spite of the strengths of our opponents. We face the future confident in that knowledge.

10

Politics in the Twenty-six Counties

A political revolution in Ireland without a coincidental economic revolution simply means a change of masters...If the Irish people do not control Irish industries, transport, money and the soil of the country, then foreign and native capitalists will. And whoever controls the wealth of a country and the process by which wealth is attained will also control its government.

Liam Mellows

THE IRISH NATIONAL parliament, Dáil Éireann—first established in 1919—was outlawed by the British because they feared its popular franchise which ratified the 1916 Proclamation of an Irish Republic. They also feared the radical intent and social commitment of its Democratic Programme.

This programme is as relevant today as it was seventy-five years ago. Its demands on behalf of the Irish people have yet to be achieved. They were lost amid the turmoil of a counter-revolution and the partition of Ireland. Since partition, Britain has retained a direct influence on Irish affairs in both parts of the island. Until the early 1970s the unionists were permitted—through a one-party state—to get on with the business of protecting British and unionist interests in the North. They did this by repressing dissent.

As we have seen, a civil rights struggle in the late 1960s was the beginning of the end of all this. The civil rights demands put the British state to the test. The state failed the test and reacted with

150

terrorism against the modest and moderate demands being put to it. In 1969 the state died. It was revived by the British government and since then it has been kept alive on a life support unit of British military forces.

The Hillsborough Treaty was supposed to end all this. So was Sunningdale, the Constitutional Conventions, round table talks, talks about talks—Rolling Devolution; all partitionist arrangements. None of them have been successful.

Is the Anglo-Irish conflict to last forever? This book says 'no.' It proposes a solution.

Critics will dismiss such a notion. They will lambast Irish republicans as being the main part of the conflict. Theirs is a partisan view, shaped by their politics. The views expressed here are partisan also; they are shaped by my politics. Yet they do not expound an exclusively republican system of government or any other system for that matter. They argue only for the right of the Irish people to national self-determination. The type of society chosen in that context is a matter for the Irish people as a whole to decide without outside interference.

Of course those with a partitionist view will try to present the Twenty-six County state as a nation. They will promote the notion that the border is a permanent boundary. They will cite the many freedoms enjoyed by citizens of that state.

In this, at least, they are partially correct. The situation in the Twenty-six Counties is much better than in the Six Counties. Citizens in the former do have the right to elect a government and at different periods such governments have advanced in terms of the restrictions placed upon the state by the Treaty arrangement of 1922. And armed insurrection, despite occasional scare-mongering, is no longer a problem.

But seventy-five years after the First Dáil, the Twenty-six County state has failed the test also. The symbols of freedom have been won but the essence of freedom is still denied us. Freedom is much more than the right to vote, though this is important. It is the right to fulfilment, the right to equality, the right to meaningful employment, the right not to be forced to emigrate, the right not to be poor.

A lot of the blame lies with successive Dublin governments and it is not my intention to try to absolve them from their share of the responsibility for the economic and social mess over which they preside. But even if a less conservative administration was elected, that administration could not correct the situation unless it was prepared to set aside the parameters enforced upon it and the people of Ireland by the British partition of our country.

The fundamental republican aim has always been to get Britain to abandon the union with Ireland and adopt instead a policy of reunifying Ireland: withdrawing from Ireland and handing over sovereignty to an all-Ireland government. That is also the stated aim of all the Dublin parties. There is a constitutional imperative upon the Dublin government to bring this about. Yet partition has endured for over seventy years and Dublin has made little progress on these matters. Why?

The term 'constitutional nationalism' is a contradiction when the constitutionalism involved is British constitutionality. Nonetheless, as it is the phrase most often used to describe the politics of the main Irish establishment parties it is so employed here.

The term constitutional nationalism, in the context of recent years, came into the political vocabulary after the 1981 hunger strikes. The Irish establishment and its political representatives realized, especially after Sinn Féin's electoral successes, that their abandonment of Irish nationalism had left the moral high ground to the republicans.

The hunger strikes had mobilized the national question and the establishment could hardly formally abandon national demands (although a right-wing split in Fianna Fáil led to the establishment of the Progressive Democrats with their formal neo-unionist position). Neither could it embrace the principles of national self-determination, independence and sovereignty. To do so would be to challenge British claims and thus threaten the common interests which the Irish and British ruling classes share.

In the debate in which all of the main parties were forced to participate, their attitudes soon became clear. The main principles of Irish nationalism were to be diluted to mere aspirations, not reasonable or just national demands, and the expectations of nationalist Ireland were to be lowered accordingly. The New Ireland Forum provides an illuminating insight into the semantic twisting and turning of political leaders caught up in the public need to do something. 'Not enough to rock the boat' appears to have been their watchwords—yet enough to thwart what they saw as the Sinn Féin electoral threat to the SDLP. So constitutional nationalism was recreated with all of its subsequent diversions—its dilution of national demands and its lowering of nationalist expectations.

In this debate, and especially since the Downing Street Declaration, the rhetoric of Irish nationalism and of verbalized republicanism is often used. This is particularly obvious following the successes of republicans in putting core issues like Irish self-determination on the public and political agenda. But an independent Ireland, one in which the Irish people would have economic and political independence as a united nation, is not in the interests of the British establishment. In this regard, elements of the Irish establishment share a common interest with the British. The ruling classes in the Twenty-six Counties have abandoned the principle of Irish national self-determination. Indeed they never really subscribed to it, but, with membership of the EU, the signing of the Hillsborough Treaty and the ratification of the Single Europe Act, they have formally accepted the British claim to, and occupation of, six Irish counties.

Thus, the energies, such as they are, of the Dublin establishment have concentrated on examining ways of reaching an accommodation with unionism. Unionism and nationalism are incompatible. Unionism is undemocratic. It is a contrived system of politics representing foreign interference in Irish affairs. It has been incapable of making any lasting accommodation with even the most accommodating tendencies of constitutional nationalism. For their part, these tendencies have completely ignored the democratic potential of a Protestant tradition free from unionism. Thus the New Ireland Forum was lacking in any vision which could distinguish between Protestantism and unionism.

Likewise, by signing the Hillsborough Treaty, the Dublin government recognized the unionist veto. This has governed all its deliberations since. It has also formally relinquished its *de jure* claim to represent all Irish people, accepting instead, in return for its recognition of the British presence, a facility whereby it could air its views of the grievances of nationalists in the Six Counties.

This illustrates precisely the weakness of the Dublin establishment, especially when it seeks new arrangements with the British about the future of Ireland. The British know that Dublin is prepared to accept the legitimacy or 'reality' of partition and of the British statelet in north-east Ireland so long as the section of the Catholic population whose interests they represent are incorporated into it. They do not envisage or aspire to a fundamental transformation of society in which the material benefits of society are shared equally by all its citizens, nor do they wish to see genuine political democracy in which the dispossessed hold real political power and control over their lives.

What constitutional nationalists and republicans really have in common at this time is a shared constituency—the nationalist community.

While it is possible to make adjustments to British rule in the Six Counties which allow for limited concessions and reforms in the interests of political stability, it is not possible for the political or social aspirations and needs of the nationalist people to be met. Nor for that matter can the needs of the majority of the people in the Twenty-six Counties be met within the context of partition. The needs of working-class northern Protestants, obscured by loyalism, cannot be advanced either in this context.

Ireland is a colony of Britain. Since partition, this has manifested itself in different forms. The history of the partition of Ireland and its effects on the north are well known, but what about the south?

The partition settlement of 1921, which was incorporated in the Free State Agreement Act and the Free State Constitution Act, gave the Twenty-six Counties a degree of independence nominally based on dominion status. There was never any suggestion that national sovereignty was involved. Under the Treaty, the British retained considerable and explicit influence in the new Free State. The Twenty-six County state was in reality a neo-colony. This was explicit in many of the new arrangements which have now been removed, for example the oath of allegiance to the English monarchy, the payment of land annuities to the English exchequer and the retention of British naval bases.

Other less explicit effects remain to this day. The new state remained tied economically to Britain. There was no partition for the banks and there was free movement of capital and labour between the two islands.

The new state was cut off from the main industrial area and the largest city, Belfast, a port which catered for over a third of national trade. Ireland lost twenty-nine percent of the population and forty percent of the taxable capacity of the country. The Democratic Programme of the 1918 all-Ireland Dáil Éireann already in abeyance, was abandoned. The whole preceding body of English law, of the civil service, the judiciary and other institutions became the basis of the new state. It was this which emerged from the horrors of the Civil War.

There was no new beginning, only a change of managers and a new scheme to control Ireland. Much of this legacy remains today so that, while maintaining the symbols of political independence, the Twenty-six Counties, though much improved from the 1920s, is still a neo-colony. In many ways and especially on the question of British interference in Ireland, it is subservient to Britain. As Lord Birkenhead described it, the Treaty arrangement was 'to protect British interests with an economy of British lives.'

The Cumann na nGael government which ruled the new Free State from 1922 to 1932, represented the most pro-imperialist elements in the state. Their economic interests in commerce, banking, trade, large farming concerns, brewing and distilling, or in sections of the higher professional groups, required free trade with Britain and close political and cultural ties. It was not that they sold out the Republic of 1916, but, as Liam Mellows said of them at that time, 'the men with a stake in the country were never for the republic.' Mellows, like Connolly, possessed great clarity of political vision, and he spelt out what was happening:

> Free State equals capitalism and industrialism equals the Empire...A political revolution in Ireland without a coincident economic revolution merely means a change of masters. Instead of British capitalism waxing rich on the political and economic enslavement of Ireland we would have Irish capitalists waxing rich on the political freedom but contrived enslavement of Ireland.

And so it came to be. The new Free State government imposed the Treaty arrangement with a terrible ferocity, greater even than the actions of the new Stormont government in the Six Counties. The new state was moulded in the image of those in control. Not only were nationalists in the Six Counties abandoned, but workers and small farmers in the Twenty-six Counties gained nothing from the new political arrangement. The Fianna Fáil party which emerged following the counter-revolution of the civil war represented the small manufacturers and distributors as opposed to the bankers, big ranchers and merchants who supported Cumann na nGael (now Fine Gael). These elements, coupled with small farmers and workers who were being starved out by Cumann na nGael's policies and denied a proper political alternative by a largely apolitical IRA, swept Fianna Fáil into power on a broadly anti-imperialist programme which was implemented to a degree in the 1930s.

The economic interests which the Fianna Fáil leadership represented were not content with the Treaty arrangement. They wanted not free trade with Britain, but a protected home market which they could exploit. They wanted home manufacture rather than imported goods from Britain. They wanted a protected Irish industry and a restriction of the freedom that British industry had enjoyed in Ireland since the union. By and large, Arthur Griffiths' old protectionist policies suited their needs.

Yet Fianna Fáil, the party of the industrial middle class and always prone to compromise with British imperialism, received support from the workers and small farmers. They, for their part, had little alternative: Labour was 'waiting,' the IRA was suspicious of 'politics.' Fianna Fáil filled the gap with republican rhetoric. But, for all this rhetoric and some moves away from dominion status, the Fianna Fáil leadership refused to tackle the partition issue in a way which could have led to independence.

Nevertheless, the rhetoric of de Valera was a potent force. Put crudely, his public attitude was that Fianna Fáil would achieve Irish reunification; the IRA was going about it the wrong way and had to be moved to one side because it constituted an obstacle. However rhetorical it may have been, it was a difficult argument for republicans to deal with when it was articulated by a national leader of de Valera's undoubted stature, and when they had failed to establish political alternatives to Fianna Fáilism.

When I first became interested in politics and read about de Valera, I was mindful of the fact that Fianna Fáil had executed republicans and that 'Dev,' in his application of the coercion acts, had been completely ruthless. Yet I was always intrigued by the meetings he had, even when he was in power, with the Army Council of the IRA. However, its history apart, Fianna Fáil hardly entered my consciousness or that of my contemporaries in West Belfast until Jack Lynch came out with his famous statement about not standing idly by. When contacts were being made between Fianna Fáil members and Six County republicans in the aftermath of the 1969 pogroms, these were seen as having to do with the Dublin government rather than with Fianna Fáil specifically.

Fianna Fáil moved rapidly under Jack Lynch from the rhetorical assertion of supporting northern nationalism to the closing of Sinn Féin's offices in Dublin and the arrests of prominent Sinn Féin members such as Daithi O'Connell and Ruairi O'Bradaigh. By 1972, most of the nationalistically-minded members of the Free State armed forces had been moved either into early retirement or by promotion sideways.

The Fianna Fáil leadership found itself in collision with elements of its own past; it could not continue with republican rhetoric in the face of an actual struggle to bring down the Six County state. In a more quiescent time it could play the 'green' card to distract attention from difficult social and economic issues, but in the face of an active movement against partition it knew where its true interests lay.

The Fianna Fáil leadership of today has nevertheless remained in touch, to some rhetorical extent, with nationalism. One sees, for example, a spontaneous nationalist response at Fianna Fáil Árd Fheiseanna.

Today the strategic concerns of British policy towards Ireland have obviously undergone many changes of emphasis and London does not act in the grand manner of its imperial heyday. But the British government, by its direct control of a part of Ireland, exerts a political influence over all of Ireland, ensuring through partition that Irish politics are neutralized and distorted, with British political influence maintained.

Economically, Ireland is subservient to the needs of imperialism. This relationship has become more complicated since the days when Ireland provided a cheap supply of food, labour and markets for British exports. This is especially so as the influence of the European Union impacts more and more on Irish affairs. Even the highly conservative Dublin Supreme Court judged, in 1988, that the limited political 'independence' of the Twenty-six County state had been eroded by the Single Europe Act.

The Treaty (Single Europe Act) marks the transformation of the European Community from an organization which has so far been essentially economic to one that is political also. The essential nature of sovereignty is the right to say Yes or to say No. In the present Treaty that right is materially qualified.

Nonetheless, the servicing of finance capital for international and multinational concerns in the EU, Britain and the USA, plus the need to curb and contest Irish economic interests and prevent them from developing into a threat to British economic interests in Ireland, remains a major concern of the British government.

Not only has partition and British domination of the economy distorted the economic potential of the country, but it has also stunted the development of class politics. The trade union movement has been subjected to this general distortion. Any Dublin-based movement immediately invokes a hostile reaction from the loyalist workforce in the Six Counties and any London-based movement has a tendency to become, at the least, benignly imperialistic. The Stormont government refused to deal with the Irish Congress of Trade Unions (ICTU) until it established a separate northern committee, thus ensuring loyalist domination of trade union affairs in the Six Counties and a major influence in British trade unions' attitudes to Ireland. Thus, the trade union movement failed to develop policies against discrimination and lost altogether the socialist republican legacy of James Connolly.

The sad truth of Connolly's perception is evident in every sphere of public life in the Twenty-six Counties. In 1897 he warned:

> If you remove the English Army tomorrow and hoist the green flag over Dublin Castle, unless you set about the organization of a Socialist Republic your efforts will have been in vain. England will still rule you. She would rule you through the whole array of commercial and individual institutions she has planted in this country and watered with the tears of our mothers and the blood of our martyrs.
>
> England would still rule you, even while your lips offered hypocritical homage at the shrine of that freedom whose cause you have betrayed.

Ordinary people throughout Ireland have absorbed the reality of their powerlessness under British domination, whether in colonial or neo-colonial form. The resources of the country lie far beyond their reach and all the decisive elements of the economy, even of society in general, are outside their control. When it comes to an industrial dispute, very often the workers cannot even get to grips with their real opponents, the foreign owners and the central decision-makers of the multinationals. The respective governments and other political and religious elements step in and warn about job losses; they complain that if the workers continue with their action the foreign company that employs them will leave the country and that Ireland's image as a place for investment will be tarnished, with the result that other jobs will not be created.

Multinationals are presented by the government with the people's money and the people's labour; then they take away the profit that is created by the people. The Dublin government is dependent on foreign and multinational capital and on the EU, despite all the evidence that this reliance has failed to generate the necessary growth and despite the immoral absurdity involved in the billions of pounds leaving the state as expatriated profits. Dublin embraces an economic strategy which means more unemployment, poverty and emigration, more borrowing and the enforced lowering of living standards. Even within the terms of domestic capitalism it is an absurd situation. Successive Dublin governments have claimed to base themselves upon the Proclamation of 1916, yet, far from the ownership of Ireland belonging to the people of Ireland, it is clear that the economy is planned in the interests of a very small clique.

The Proclamation talks about cherishing all the children of the nation equally, but the reality expressed in constant emigration is that the children of the nation not only could not be cherished equally, but were forced to leave Ireland and continue to be forced to leave.

Partition subverts the aim of an economy which can fulfil the domestic needs of the Irish people. The Twenty-six Counties has the highest proportional youth population and aged population in western Europe, and these people need a whole infrastructure of schools, houses, factories and roads; yet in all these respects the economy and the state are unable to deliver. Over a third of citizens

159

live below poverty level, 300,000 are unemployed and, in 1993, 12,000 people were forced to emigrate.

We have an agricultural country which is given over to big ranching interests exporting beef, and our horticultural imports undermine attempts to build up home-based industries. We are an island nation without any substantial marine or maritime industry. Indeed our fishing industry has never been developed to its full potential.

A precondition for creating an economy which is able to deliver on the promise of the Proclamation, or even just able to provide a living for its citizens in their own country, is independence. At present the Six Counties is administered directly in the British interest and the Twenty-six Counties is administered by Dublin governments whose economic planning is determined by British and other outside interests. The only way forward is to create an economy based on the needs of the Irish people. The key to this lies in ending partition and winning political and economic independence.

Ending partition will in itself be a massive advancement towards justice and peace. But it is not a matter of merging the colonial North into a neo-colonial Thirty-two Counties Free State. A new Ireland is needed. A new society, created by the Irish nation freed from outside interference, which will take an independent position in economic terms and put resources under democratic control.

Much of the support of ordinary nationalist people for constitutional nationalist politicians, whether in the Six Counties or the Dublin establishment, rests on the belief that the constitutional nationalist politicians do in fact represent their interests and aspirations. In the Twenty-six Counties, the failure, for historical as well as political reasons, to build an alternative has compounded this, and Sinn Féin's identification with the conflict in the Six Counties presents particular problems as we seek to redress this shortcoming.

There is an understandable aversion to the use of physical force and the consequences of physical force. This is so in both parts of Ireland, but it may be more acute in the Twenty-six Counties, not least because the political reality there is different from the Six County war zone.

The charge that Sinn Féin is out to undermine the state is often made by our opponents. It is a nonsense. Our aim is the end of partition and the establishment of a Thirty-two County state, an aim shared by most of the political parties on the island as well as the majority of Irish people, and an aim enshrined in the Irish constitution.

As a political party, Sinn Féin pursues its aims by peaceful unarmed means. Members of both government parties work alongside our representatives on local authorities throughout the Twenty-six Counties. Every time there is a Senate election they lobby our councillors for votes. They stand beside us at election counts, sit on committees with us, and, at local level, both formally and informally, they discuss with our representatives the affairs of the nation, including the question of peace.

The charge is often made that Sinn Féin is controlled by the IRA and that republicans pose an armed threat to the Twenty-six County state. This excuse is used to deny us the right to collect funds as other parties do. The same pretext is used for Special Branch harassment of our members, especially of young people who join the party.

I have stated on many occasions my firm opinion that armed struggle has no place in the Twenty-six Counties and there clearly is no IRA campaign against the Dublin government or the state.

Speaking at Bodenstown in the early 1980s, I said that 'we realize that ordinary people accept Twenty-six County institutions as legitimate' and that 'to ignore this reality is to blinker republican politics, to undermine the development of our struggle and to have a basic flaw in our analysis.'

Whatever position one takes on this issue, I have never heard any serious argument in favour of armed struggle in the Twenty-six Counties. The struggle there is and must remain an unarmed one. It is also clear that there must be a national focus to that struggle, even in its localized or regional dimensions. It is, therefore, absolutely necessary that republicans successfully convince people in the Six and Twenty-six Counties that their needs can only be met through a shift in the balance of power brought about by themselves coming positively into political activity and struggle.

They must come to understand that politics is not merely, as it is defined by the establishment parties' leaderships, politicians talking to each other in parliament, but, rather, politics is the lived experience of people, and that they as individuals and collectively can take political power into their own hands.

In this way, the establishment politicians will be persuaded to jump on (or off) the bandwagon, and opportunities for progress can be created. Thus, what is needed is a strategy to bring the greatest possible number of people into the process of struggle. Since at this stage the majority of nationalists look to establishment parties for their political leadership, this requires that they demand of these politicians that they take up and defend the interests of the people they claim to represent.

It is worth noting that, although the Twenty-six Counties is a very stable society, there is a lot of cynicism among citizens about their politicians. This may not be a uniquely Irish experience, but, given the behaviour, clientalism and opportunism of some Leinster House politicians, this scepticism is hardly surprising. It is also shared by people in the Six Counties whose historic sense of being abandoned by Dublin is shaped not only by the reality of their situation but also by the different political realities created in both parts of Ireland by partition, and by the consistent failure of Dublin politicians to deliver on their promises to redress the very substantial grievances which underpin this situation.

The northern nationalist looking at the Twenty-six Counties is not impressed. Poverty stares at you, with conditions in some working-class areas no better than the conditions in the Six Counties which the Dublin government expresses so much concern about. Dublin's inner-city poverty backs onto the contrasting world of the large stores, hotels and burger joints of O'Connell Street where beggars abound. 'Travellers' (itinerants) are harassed by reactionary mobs and by the gardai in almost every part of the state. At least in the Six Counties the nationalist people have a certain advantage in that they can become involved in the struggle which seeks to end their conditions of poverty and discrimination; they can at least, while suffering all the indignities of their position, experience the dignity of struggle. But this opportunity is, so far, basically lacking in the Twenty-six Counties.

In the Twenty-six Counties, historical revision, censorship and cultural manipulation are some of the methods used to persuade citizens of that state that the nation stops at the border and that they are residents of a branch of the European market. According to this view, Thatcherism was a progressive economic ethos, 1916 was a mistake, and any manifestation of Irishness or nationalism is seditious.

Little wonder that Irish taxpayers are duped into paying more for maintaining the British border than taxpayers in Britain itself.

However, there are many contradictions which require the political establishment to nod reverently at the notion of Irish unity. This arises mostly because it is impossible to erase national consciousness or to replace it with a projection of the Twenty-six Counties as a nation-state while the national question remains unresolved and while the continuing conflict in the North provides tragic and regular evidence that it is unresolved.

The majority of Irish nationalists retain the aspiration for a united and independent Ireland. Those who live in the Twenty-six Counties have extreme difficulty in fulfilling this aspiration. Most people are too preoccupied with trying to make a living in a punitive economic and social system. Furthermore, for over twenty years and until January 1994, they were denied their right to information by state censorship in the form of section 31 of the Broadcasting Act, and its spillover into press censorship, which ensured that they received largely the British and Irish establishment's news and other anti-republican propaganda.

Added to this are the effects of partition and the protracted nature of the Troubles which has created feelings of resignation and immobility. More importantly, they do not see the ending of British occupation as central to the development of an economic democracy which would establish, defend and enhance the prosperity of the whole country.

They are too busy resolving, mostly on a personal or individual basis, the problem of Dublin government-sponsored emigration, unemployment and cuts in health, education and the social services.

In 'their' part of Ireland, however, even in the absence of a radical political leadership and despite a failure by anti-imperialists to link partition in a relevant way with the social, economic and cultural malaise in the Twenty-six Counties, many citizens sympathize with the independent Ireland ideal, coupled with a heartfelt desire to see the conflict in the Six Counties ended in the context of Irish unity. Many of those citizens who form the grass roots membership of most of the political parties in the Twenty-six Counties are clearly supportive of Irish unity. The membership of Fianna Fáil is obviously sympathetic, even Fine Gael retains its Michael Collins tendency, and sections of the Irish Labour Party

163

have an anti-imperialist instinct. Their respective leaderships have a different view, and that is that success depends on gauging the public mood and exploiting it. Their opportunism is accurately summed up by the cliché, 'I must see where my people are going so that I can run ahead and lead them'—or divert them. Despite censorship and the massive propaganda effort to disinform and to starve of information, an instinctive republicanism remains.

I find an immense curiosity about the Six Counties amongst young people in the Twenty-six Counties. In the course of public meetings, canvassing, debates, seminars and social occasions, I find that any articulate republican spokesperson is received without the kind of heckling characteristic of so many meetings, especially those in colleges and universities. It is a strange effect of censorship that, having been projected as having two heads and cloven feet, people find a significance even in the fact of the physical presence of a prominent republican at a meeting. We find that whatever we have to say is listened to with a great amount of interest and whatever questions we are asked are, by and large, genuine questions which seek to explore what it is we stand for.

From meetings with old republicans in the Twenty-six Counties I have come away with vivid impressions and with political lessons. When I was invited to address the Kilmichael commemoration a few years ago, the response to my acceptance of the invitation was interesting in itself. The event was not organized by members of the republican movement but I met there the last survivors of those who had taken part in the famous ambush. I found that they had been put under great pressure not to attend on account of my presence. The Dublin government had objected, as had the local Catholic bishop, following in the footsteps of his predecessor who had condemned the ambush at the time; also, the customary firing party from the FCA was withdrawn on account of the fact that I would be speaking.

After the speeches, I spent the evening with the veterans, and I was struck particularly by a remark of a man in his eighties who, in words which had a ring of Liam Mellows about them, said, 'We fought the British to a standstill, and then we proceeded to hand over the politics to others, and they betrayed us.' I was also struck by a strange sense of time warp. Here were people who had been involved in the armed struggle in the Black and Tan War, and they were telling stories about ambushes and incidents which made me feel as if the Six Counties existed in some kind of time capsule along with their own experiences.

These were stories with which I could identify absolutely. Even when they were talking about identity checks, house searches, or harassment by the British forces, their stories were almost identical to the stories told amongst republicans in the Six Counties today. One old man cast an interesting light on the way in which the Tan War has been projected as a glorious period in which the Irish people were united behind the IRA against the British army. He spoke about an ambush after which they could find no place to stay as no one would let them in anywhere. In reality, it was a small number of republicans who advanced the struggle and it was only when that struggle was about to be successful that it enjoyed mass support.

But what that one evening in West Cork impressed upon me most was the great need for the republican movement to develop politically in the Twenty-six Counties, the very need that the old man had pointed to in his remark about having left the politics to others. Lack of involvement by republicans in the politics of the Twenty-six Counties in the past created a vacuum which was filled by Fianna Fáil. The traditional base of support for republicanism remains in the urban working class and amongst the small farmers, but Fianna Fáil still succeeds in gaining the electoral support of that broadly republican layer.

Because of public opinion, none of the leaders of establishment parties can erase the national aims of their respective parties. The political situation is therefore not static. British strategy for some time has been based upon an objective of marrying sections of 'pragmatic' unionists and the SDLP with some Dublin involvement in an arrangement to govern a 'reformed' Six County state. This was the core of the Hillsborough Treaty. Part of this strategy was aimed at institutionalizing an anti-republican axis of Dublin/Belfast or Dublin/SDLP/unionist. The Irish Peace Initiative started by SDLP leader John Hume and myself, which I will deal with in chapter eleven, has pointed up the potential for a new axis.

It was the emergence of this new axis which was the key factor in shattering the old anti-republican axis. It also had the effect of putting the British politically on the defensive, and of putting new, perhaps unprecedented focus on the Anglo-Irish conflict and of the core issues involved. All of this had a major effect internationally and it has opened up a new and, at this time, unquantifiable potential, particularly in the USA.

It is my view that the British do not, at this time, plan to leave Ireland. I start from this premise. However, they have moved considerably and the core issues of their involvement in Irish affairs are being exposed. If these issues are addressed properly, the arguments for their involvement and for their present policy is very hard for them to defend, especially in the international arena and particularly in the current climate. I believe that the British can be persuaded to leave Ireland, but they will do so only as a last option and when all other options have failed.

All experience to date shows that any alliance between sections of Irish nationalism and the British government in the governance of Ireland can only culminate in an unequal partnership which serves the broad British government interests. British government interests have thus been maintained to the detriment of the interests of the Irish people. What is required is an alliance of Irish political opinion, informal or otherwise, pursuing objectives which look to the interests and well-being of the Irish nation with the aim of normalizing relationships within the Irish nation and between the Irish nation and the people of Britain. The Dublin government has a central and crucial role to play in this.

It is essential that a political strategy to bring about peace and justice in Ireland is developed. The peace process will unfortunately be a protracted one and the present administration in Dublin is ideally placed to act on this opportunity. The coalition government is stable and made up of two parties which, on paper at least, share the policy objective of Irish unity.

The Dublin government has a responsibility to take the initiative and to keep taking the initiative until a lasting peace has been secured. It is now in an ideal position to set in motion with London a process with an agreed time frame, which has as its policy objective the exercise by the Irish people of our right to national self-determination and the end of British jurisdiction in Ireland, through:

1. A process of dialogue and inclusive negotiations to agree the shape of a new Ireland.
2. Structures that will allow the people of Ireland to work together to end the division of our country and to build an agreed future.
3. A process of national reconciliation which assures the cultural integrity and civil rights of all sections of the Irish people.

Such a strategy requires courage and imagination. Partition has failed, and the absence of a genuine attempt to resolve the conflict in Ireland by the British government creates a window of opportunity for the Dublin government. We are asking the Dublin government to do only what it was elected to do. Ireland remains partitioned not only because of the policy of the London government but also because of the policy of the Dublin government.

In all of this, as with the wider issues, the question of partition, of the British connection, and of peace in the North is an all-Ireland issue. Socially, culturally, politically and economically the entire nation of thirty-two counties is affected by the continuing conflict. The question of partition and how we deal with it saps our national morale. Dublin must seek to rectify this. It must seize the opportunity presented to it and it must for once fulfil its responsibilities and obligations to the people of Ireland.

The Irish constitution requires that it does so. The Irish people desire an end to conflict and a negotiated settlement. The people of the North deserve it.

11

Towards a Lasting Peace

And I shall have some peace there, for peace comes dropping slow,
Dropping from the veils of the morning to where the cricket sings;
There midnight's all a glimmer, and noon a purple glow,
And evening full of the linnet's wings
W.B. Yeats, *The Lake Isle of Innisfree*

WHEN I BEGAN this book in 1986, who could have then foreseen Nelson Mandela as the South African President, the re-unification of Germany, or the Palestinian/Israeli peace accord? Although it is a mistake to draw any direct parallels between these and the Irish situation, they prove that even a conflict that appears to be intractable can be brought to an end. Whether or not we agree with what is happening in these individual cases, there is now no doubt that the peace process in these conflicts is in the resolution stage.

One of the common threads running through all of these situations is that the central government in each case (for whatever reason: economic sanctions, domestic or international pressures) was motivated to move, while here in the Six Counties we have the British government which has not been motivated to move in the same way. Secondly, republicans have outlined a number of broad principles that we think are necessary to conflict resolution, such as inclusive dialogue; for, as the Israeli/Palestinian and South African experiences have proven absolutely, by engaging all of the parties involved and talking, some agreement can be reached.

In South Africa a white minority government apologized for apartheid and moved to dismantle it, and did so with zeal, which

168

wouldn't have been possible under other regimes. If the South African government had said 'we will move, but only when the right wing agrees,' they would still be sitting there. They decided to move regardless. This is pragmatic and sound, and is to be applauded.

The London government needs to change its policy in Ireland in a similar progressive and positive way. But at the same time republicans need to be pragmatic and flexible in our arrangements about transitional phases in order to reach a settlement.

These are some of the lessons for us in recent events in the rest of the world. They will all have an advantageous effect on Ireland and the Anglo-Irish conflict, as they enhance an international climate for conflict resolution. If people can see that durable and unjust situations in other countries can move towards democracy, then why can't it happen in Ireland?

Sinn Féin's Peace Strategy
The heartfelt aspiration of the Irish people is to see peace established. But, if this aspiration remains limited to a popular desire, it cannot become a reality. How, then, can a lasting peace be brought about?

As in South Africa, peace can only come about when the causes of a particular conflict are addressed. In the case of the Anglo/Irish situation where the conflict is political, peace must come through a political solution. The war in the Six Counties of Ireland is a legacy of the denial for centuries by the British government of the Irish people's right to national independence. The very existence of the conflict shows that the undemocratic political structures imposed on the Irish people by Britain in 1921, and maintained today, have failed and are a continuing source of division and instability.

The Irish people have a right to peace. We have a right to democratic political structures which are capable of sustaining peace, and we have a right to decide for ourselves what those political structures should be. We have an obligation to ensure that the ethos and practice of those structures guarantee equality for all our people.

For generations, the Irish people have consistently asserted our nationhood, national independence, and sovereignty, and these assertions have been expressed in many historic documents. The 1916 Proclamation and the subsequent Declaration of Independence of the first Dáil in 1919 form the foundation of the modern assertion of independence. The nation is further defined in the first three Articles of the Irish Constitution of 1937. The assertions of these three documents are reaffirmed in the Unanimous Declaration in Leinster House, Dublin, on 10 May 1949, statements to the United Nations Security Council in 1969 by Dr Patrick Hillery, Irish Minister for External Affairs, the New Ireland Forum, May 1984, and by the Irish Supreme Court in November 1985.

Ireland's right to reunification, independence and sovereignty (the right of the Irish people, as a whole, to self-determination) is furthermore supported by universally recognized principles of international law. The right to self-determination is enshrined in the two United Nations Covenants of 1966—the International Covenant on Civil and Political Rights, and the International Covenant on Economic, Social and Cultural Rights. Article 1 of each Covenant states:

> All peoples have the right to self-determination. By virtue of that right they determine their economic, social and cultural development.

The landmark Declaration on Principles of International Law Concerning Friendly Relations and Co-operation Among States in Accordance with the Charter of the United Nations declares:

> ...all people have the right freely to determine, without external influence, their political status and to pursue their economic, social and cultural development and every state has the duty to respect this right in accordance with the provisions of this Charter.

The British partition of Ireland is in clear contravention of the United Nations Declaration on the Granting of Independence to Colonial Peoples and Countries, Article 6 of which states:

> Any attempt aimed at the partial or total disruption of the national unity and the territorial integrity of a country is incompatible with the purposes and principles of the Charter of the United Nations.

That position is explicitly endorsed by the final act of the Conference on Security and Co-operation in Europe, 9 July 1975. Under Article 1(a) 'Declaration on Principles Guiding Relations Between Participating States,' Section VIII states:

> The participating States will respect the equal rights of peoples and their rights to self-determination, acting at all times in conformity with the purposes and principles of the Charter of the United Nations and with the relevant norms of international law, including those relating to territorial integrity of States.

Those in Ireland who claim to seek permanent peace, justice, democracy, equality of opportunity, and stability cannot deny that the abiding and universally accepted principle of national self-determination, in which is enshrined the principle of democracy, is the surest means through which to achieve and maintain their social and political aims. Self-determination is accepted to mean a nation's right to exercise the political freedom to determine its own development without external influence and without partial or total disruption of national unity or territorial integrity.

The refusal to allow the Irish people to exercise their right to self-determination has been British government policy. That policy is the root cause of conflict in Ireland. Furthermore, that policy and the measures taken to maintain it are the cause of the ruptures in relationships between the Irish people themselves, and between Ireland and Britain.

In 1921, the Irish national territory was physically divided by partition, with the British government assuming sovereignty over the Six Counties. The unionist political majority in the artificially created statelet has become the cornerstone of the British government's rationale for its continuing exercise of sovereignty over the Six Counties. This unionist majority is, in fact, the gerrymandering perpetrated by a British government which dictated the size and make-up of the respective populations of the Six and Twenty-six County states. The historical and contemporary purpose of that gerrymandering was, and remains, to erect a barrier against Irish reunification in perpetuity.

Today's advocates of the unionist perspective represent some twenty percent of the Irish nation. They are a national minority; a significant one, but a minority nonetheless. British government policy in Ireland arbitrarily, and by coercive force, upholds the political allegiance of the unionist community as a national minority against the national and democratic rights of the national majority. To bestow the power of veto over national independence and sovereignty on a national minority is in direct contravention of the principle of self-determination. To prescribe self-determination for a national minority as a distinct entity from the rest of the nation is a perversion of the principle of self-determination.

British rule in Ireland has rested on the twin pillars of division and coercion. Underpinning the divisions in the Irish nation, which has been central to maintenance of British rule, lies the threat and use of British force. Partition was imposed on the Irish people under the threat of 'immediate and total war.' Since its creation, the Six County statelet has relied for its existence on a system of repressive legislation enforced by military and paramilitary forces and a compliant judiciary. An abnormal state of 'permanent emergency' has been the norm.

For over twenty years repression has been the chief instrument of British rule, substituting the force of the government for the consent of the ruled. During that time, the British government has had the worst human rights record in Europe, as documented by the European Court of Human Rights.

Emergency laws, including seven-day detention without charge or trial, ill-treatment of suspects in custody, convictions on confession evidence alone, and savagely long sentences, have formed the continuing pattern of British 'justice' in Northern Ireland. Numerous travesties of justice have occurred, including the notorious cases of the Guildford Four and the Maguire family, the Birmingham Six, the Winchester Three, Judith Ward, and more.

Since 1969, the war has cost 3,290 lives. Most of the deaths have been in the Six Counties, but almost 100 have occurred in the Twenty-six Counties and 118 people have been killed in Britain. The London government and others have tried to blame all the killings on the IRA. The IRA is in fact responsible for killing over 1,000 members of the Crown forces, over 30 loyalist activists and more than 100 persons working in direct support of the British Crown forces. One hundred and one IRA volunteers have lost their lives in premature bomb explosions. A further 230 civilians have died as a result of premature explosions or in engagements between the Crown forces and the IRA.

The British themselves are known to be directly responsible for 370 deaths, and loyalist groups, with or without the assistance of Crown forces, have killed 915 people. At least eighty percent of these have been uninvolved Catholic civilians, including 18 members of Sinn Féin as well as 43 civilians in the Twenty-six Counties. Thirty-three of these were killed with the assistance of British intelligence in the Dublin/Monaghan bombings, the worst day of atrocities in all of the past twenty-five years. Loyalists have killed 12 members of the Crown forces and four times that number of their own membership have died in loyalist feuds. Of the British killings, more than fifty-four percent of the victims have been civilians. One hundred and twenty-one IRA volunteers have been killed by Crown forces.

In the Six Counties, the economy is heavily geared to the war. Military occupation, policing and prisons directly employ over 35,000. This is equivalent to more than a third of those employed in what is left of the North's manufacturing industry. There is now one member of the Crown forces for every 3.5 nationalist males aged sixteen to forty-four. Every year the British spend £9,500 policing each and every one of these.

The war-related costs of British intelligence, the British army, the RUC, the juryless courts and the prisons now stand at £1.2 billion a year. This is about the same as the North's education budget, two-and-a-half times what is spent on industry and employment, and five times the amount spent on housing. Fifty thousand jobs in manufacturing may have been lost in the Six Counties because of the war. In many other smaller ways the financial burden of the war is felt in compensation costs, financing British propaganda abroad, for example in the fight against the MacBride lobby in the States, the extra resources put into promoting tourism and securing inward investment, delays at border and other checkpoints, private security costs, health service costs, payments for informers, and the money used to contest extraditions and cases brought under the European Convention of Human Rights. In the North alone, the British have spent nearly £18 billion on this war since 1969.

The costs of the war are increasing in Britain itself: the Prevention of Terrorism Act, other policing costs such as security for politicians, damage to property, higher insurance premiums, proliferation of closed-circuit television and the disruption of commuter traffic. These costs now run into billions each year. Sealing off the city of London has been priced at £100 million, with recurring costs of £25 million a year.

The war has cost Irish governments an estimated £2.5 billion over the years. The North costs the Twenty-six Counties £200 million a year now. It is a sad and expensive irony that taxpayers in Ireland pay two to three times more to maintain the border than their counterparts in Britain.

The British government needs 30,000 armed men and women to maintain its presence in the North. The nationalist people bear the brunt of this military occupation with harassment on the streets and in their homes, confiscation of their land, and destruction of their property. The British government holds over 700 political prisoners in its jails. None of these men and women would be behind bars if it were not for the political conflict, and the British government has instituted a rigid censorship policy in Britain and the North in order to hide the facts from the people.

Apart from the political conflict and sectarian divisions which partition reinforced, the social and economic consequences have been disastrous for ordinary people, north and south. Partition has led to job discrimination (as unionists tried to perpetuate their majority) and the waste of millions of pounds on 'security' every year. The separation of the two economies has also contributed to the external dependency of both states, which has resulted in levels of industrial underdevelopment, unemployment, emigration, and poverty which are significantly higher than European norms.

Partition has allowed social backwardness to prevail throughout Ireland. The creation of two states, both of which were dominated by the most conservative elements on the island, set back social progress for decades. The position of women in the two states, the ban on divorce in the Twenty-six Counties, and the degree of clerical control or influence in both states in the areas of education, health and other public policy are further signs of the stagnation which partition helps to sustain.

The recognition of the undemocratic reality of the partition of Ireland is the starting-point of the resolution of the conflict. Above all else, the pursuit of a democratic solution capable of making a self-sustaining peace is dependent on the recognition of those facts by a British government. Britain must accept that partition has failed and the only realistic option is to finally recognize the right of the Irish people as a whole to self-determination.

The search for peace in Ireland is everyone's responsibility. In particular, it is the responsibility of the representatives of organized society—the political parties, the Churches, trade unions, leaders of industry, the women's movement, cultural organizations, and the media. Specifically, it is the responsibility of the two 'sovereign' powers in London and Dublin. They have the power to effect the necessary change. And in today's 'global village' it is also an international responsibility.

Peace as an aspiration, or expressed only in terms of popular desire, is of itself of limited use only. The achievement of peace requires a peace process. To be achievable and sustainable, peace must have self-determination as its foundation and democracy as its aim. The criteria by which any initiative which claims peace as its end is to be judged is the degree to which it promotes the conditions in which the right to national self-determination can be exercised.

Britain claims that, while 'preferring' to keep the Six County statelet within the 'United Kingdom,' it has 'no selfish strategic or economic' reasons for doing so. British preference in relation to matters internal to Ireland holds no validity against the preference of the clear majority of the Irish people for national independence as expressed for generations. And, since they have 'no selfish or economic' reasons for maintaining partition, then it is logical that their best interests lie in ending partition.

Britain created the problem in Ireland. Britain has the major responsibility in initiating a strategy which will bring a democratic resolution and lasting peace. That must involve, within the context of accepting the national rights of the majority of the Irish people, a British government joining the ranks of the persuaders in seeking to obtain the consent of a majority of the people in the North to the constitutional, political and financial arrangements needed for a united Ireland.

Without the explicit expression of a desire on the British government's part to end partition, unionists are not likely to be influenced and will remain intransigent, in the confidence that the

British government will continue to underwrite their contrived majority with force and finance.

Notwithstanding the overall responsibility of successive British governments for the creation of conditions which have sustained the past twenty years of continuous conflict, Dublin has a clear responsibility and a major role to play in providing the democratic resolution which will bring about a lasting peace. It possesses the resources, and has political and diplomatic access to the world centres of power.

For the greater part of the Twenty-six County state's existence, successive Dublin governments have adopted a negative attitude in regard to the issue of national democracy. For most of that period, the issue of the British-imposed border has been addressed largely for the purposes of electoral gain. From Hillsborough until recently, Dublin's approach has supported partition of our country.

I would argue that, if there is to be peace in Ireland, the Dublin government will have to assume its national responsibility and develop a strategy aimed at:

1. Persuading the British government that the partition of Ireland has been a disastrous failure.

2. Persuading the unionists of the benefits of Irish reunification and seeking their consent on the constitutional, political and financial arrangements needed for a united Ireland.

3. Persuading the international community through the use of international forums and institutions to support Irish national rights.

4. In the interim, promoting and defending the democratic rights of the population of the Six Counties.

5. Resisting further erosion of the national integrity by opposing the deletion or dilution of that claim as contained in Articles 2 and 3 of the Irish Constitution of 1937.

Those parties in Ireland which describe themselves as nationalist, including Fianna Fáil and the SDLP, wield considerable influence, be it in Dublin, London, Brussels, or Washington. This, of itself, places on them a responsibility to forcefully and continuously represent the interests of the nationalist people. If these parties believe that Britain has 'no selfish interest' in remaining in Ireland, they should seek to get Britain to actually carry this to its logical conclusion and formally accept the right of the Irish people to self-determination.

Peace in Ireland requires a settlement of the long-standing conflict between Irish nationalism and Irish unionism. I would like to see that conflict, often bloody, replaced by a process of national reconciliation through constructive dialogue and debate.

If there is to be a movement towards conditions in which the debate about national reconciliation can take place, the British-bestowed unionist veto needs to be removed. While nationalists recognize the obstacles to dialogue with the unionists, we believe that it is necessary to break out of the present conception of politics prevalent in Ireland, where one side's gain is automatically conceived of as another side's loss.

The Protestant people of the Six Counties who are presently committed to a pro-British unionism have nothing to fear from a democratic and secular Ireland. Irish republicans realize that, to achieve national reconciliation, the deep fears held by people must be addressed honestly, going beyond political rhetoric to the real underlying issues. While democratic debate will be difficult to achieve in present circumstances, it is not impossible. We all lose from the continuation of the current impasse.

Demilitarization is a necessary step in the process towards a lasting peace. But this process must consider the cessation of violence by all sides in the conflict in light of the history of the current crisis.

The British army was introduced by the British government in 1969, not as a response to the IRA—which was then virtually non-existent as a military organization—but to shore up a political and security crisis brought about by the violent unionist reaction to the civil rights campaign. In the period from 1969 to 1971 (the IRA killed the first British soldier in this period of the war), the nationalist community was subjected to repeated attacks from the RUC, loyalist paramilitaries, and the British army. It was in that context that the present phase of the armed struggle by the IRA began.

The obvious response in Ireland to the continuing division of our country and our people by the British government should be the development of the maximum degree of political unity and action possible in the peaceful pursuit of democracy. I will continue to argue in the national and international arena for a British withdrawal and a solution based on the creation of an Irish national democracy.

I believe that such a scenario is achievable based on the following:

1. The recognition by the British government that the Irish people have the right to national self-determination.

2. That the British government change its current policy to one of ending partition and handing over sovereignty to an all-Ireland government whose selection would be a democratic matter for the Irish people.

3. That the future of the unionists lies in this context and that the British government has a responsibility to influence unionist attitudes.

4. The London and Dublin governments should consult together to seek agreement on the policy objective of ending partition.

These four propositions, if enacted by the British and Irish governments, would secure for the peace process the maximum national, international, political and popular support. Both governments would then be in a position to publicly outline the steps they intend taking to bring about a peaceful and orderly British political and military withdrawal from Ireland within a specified period.

In the event of the British refusing to agree to the above scenario, the Dublin government should take the initiative. Dublin should strive to mobilize international support for a viable peace process in Ireland and utilize every avenue available in international forums, including the UN, in support of a programme to achieve democracy and peace in Ireland. The assistance of British public opinion should be sought through a diplomatic offensive, and a debate leading to a dialogue with Northern unionists should be initiated. Dublin should reassure the unionist community of a total commitment to their civil and religious rights and persuade them of the need for their participation in building an Irish society based on equality and national reconciliation. A concerted national campaign to mobilize popular support for a process of national reconciliation in every aspect of Irish life should be launched, and a democratic structure by which the peace process can be agreed upon, implemented, and overseen, should be established.

By any objective international standards, the conflict in the North represents a failure of the normal political process. In view of the intolerable consequences which flow from such a failure, a peaceful resolution may entail international co-operation through the agencies of the European Union and the United Nations.

The political and economic transformation of Europe provides a golden opportunity for Ireland to finally resolve its British problem and embark on a process of economic and political reunification to the benefit of all its people. Within Europe, there is a popular consensus, reflected even by some governments, that Irish reunification is not only inevitable, but a prerequisite on the road to a durable peace. It is essential that the Irish government galvanize that opinion and translate it through the political mechanisms of the European Union into practical proposals.

International law, and the United Nations Charter, accords the right of self-determination to peoples rather than governments. If the governments concerned fail to recognize this inalienable right, the people may seek to implement the right directly. The UN Secretary-General and the Decolonization Committee share a duty with the member states (through the Friendly Resolutions Declaration) to create conditions in which the 'freely expressed will of the peoples concerned' can be reliably ascertained.

A necessary precondition for such free expression of the people's will is the removal of all forms of repression by the state apparatus of the administrating power. In the context of Ireland, this would require not only the abolition of emergency laws and special courts, but also the removal of every barrier created to enforce and maintain the partition of the national territory of Ireland.

As the process of withdrawal is underway, any deadlocks encountered could be dealt with through an application to the UN for assistance by one or both governments. In that context, the United Nations could be requested to convene an international conference on the democratic resolution of the conflict in Ireland.

This bid to break the deadlock would involve representatives of all political views in Ireland meeting together, along with international experts on decolonization and conflict resolution. The UN would examine these issues and the need for constitutional guarantees for the economic and political rights of all the people of Ireland, with express protection for the rights of a minority in a united Ireland. As a body with the experience and expertise necessary to assist all parties to resolve their differences, the UN has an indispensable role to play in creating a democratic and peaceful future for the whole of Ireland.

The Irish Peace Initiative

In the 1990s, Sinn Féin has continued to engage in dialogue with a wide range of groups and individuals in Ireland, Britain and the United States, including our political opponents and enemies, at both public and private levels, to encourage the development of an overall peace process. But my talks with John Hume of the SDLP were the most significant element of all in formulating a new peace initiative. John Hume and I met in 1988 and have continued to meet on and off since then. After some lengthy discussion, we moved on to delegation discussions, where representatives of Sinn Féin and the SDLP exchanged papers and views. This was very useful, for while we did not come to any conclusive agreement, we were able to isolate areas of agreement and disagreement.

From his comments since then it is clear that Hume accepted that the marginalization and attempted exclusion of Sinn Féin couldn't work. Against all predictions and the background of censorship, and a very serious effort to undermine us, local government election results for Sinn Féin had remained high. He could also form the opinion, during the course of our discussions, that republicans were sincere in trying to develop the struggle towards a peace process and a democratic settlement.

There was no movement from the unionists, with all their talks about talks, such as two-and-a-half years of Brooke talks and Mayhew talks, for example, which just didn't go anywhere. Nobody in Ireland, whether a very informed person or a casual observer, had any confidence in those talks and they were seen as a sham. It was in this context that Hume and I agreed on a new initiative and one that wasn't set just in the Six County context. Thus, after initial discussion on the matter, we were able to issue a joint statement which said that internal settlement is not a solution.

The culmination of these ongoing talks was the Irish Peace Initiative. We both reached an understanding of the principles that were involved, or at least which we felt were involved, quite quickly. Amongst the important things discussed were a series of broad principles, and the need for a time frame for coming up with definite policy objectives and moving towards them. We were able to agree on a set of proposals which, we believed, could form the basis of a viable peace process.

The proposals outlined a number of basic principles:

1. That the Irish people as a whole have the right to national self-determination.

2. That an internal settlement is not a solution.

3. That the unionists cannot have a veto over British policy, but that the consent and allegiance of the unionists, expressed through an accommodation with the rest of the Irish people, are essential ingredients if a lasting peace is to be established.

4. That the British government must join the persuaders.

5. That the Irish and British governments have the major responsibility to secure political progress.

A process to realize these principles was agreed, containing the political dynamic which could create the conditions for a lasting peace and a total demilitarization of the situation.

It is obvious that the Irish Peace Initiative—and particularly the agreement between Mr Hume and myself—acted as a major catalyst, not only on Irish nationalist opinion, north and south, but also in focusing the two governments on the issue of peace in Ireland in an unprecedented manner.

For me, the major and most significant aspect of the talks with John Hume is that we have what could be called a Northern Nationalist Consensus, that for the first time ever we have the nationalist electorate, through their leaders, saying 'this is what we would like done.' It is also a time when we could determine the end product and present it as a matter for negotiation for the Irish people themselves to work out. This consensus precipitated change by uplifting the people in Ireland, and it prevented any attempt by the British to marginalize those core issues, placing them on the political agenda. For, regardless of how they are addressed, they are on the agenda, as is obvious given the words that have been on everybody's lips recently—'self-determination.' The talks have acted as a catalyst for nationalist Ireland as a whole, put the British government on the defensive, and, as Hume and I have been relaying to the world, our talks are, we still believe, going to bring about peace.

Sinn Féin and the British government

A line of communications has existed between Sinn Féin and the British government for over twenty years, although it has not been in constant use. It has been used in an intensive way during such periods as the bilateral truce of 1974–5, and the Long Kesh hunger strikes of 1980–1. It was reactivated most recently by the British government in 1990, leading to a period of protracted contact and dialogue.

At all times, republicans have avoided the disclosure of this line of communication, even when such revelations would have been to our advantage. Despite the fact that the British government has shown little interest in seeking a real settlement, we regard the contact as a potentially important element in the development of a peace process. For this reason we have endeavoured at all times to protect this contact, believing that the objective of peace was far more important than the short-lived political effects of disclosure.

However, we also made it clear to the British government that, if the contacts did become public, we would not tell lies by denying their existence. The onus was on both sides to ensure confidentiality. For some time, and going back to the beginning of the latest round of communications in 1990, we have been concerned about leaks, whether initiated by elements of the British establishment or the unionists, and consequent speculation in the press. On each occasion that this happened, we formally protested to the British government and expressed our concern.

It is right that there is contact between the British government and Sinn Féin, and we have always sought to protect this process. However, the British government has recently abused it. It has acted in bad faith, and official British statements have been aimed at sowing confusion and distracting attention from the real issues. John Major's statement that the prospect of having talks with me would 'turn his stomach' was followed by an abrupt about-face when a document to the contrary was leaked to the press by Democratic Unionist Party MP William McCrea. Mr McCrea claimed to have received this from a British official. The matter came to a head when the British government subsequently admitted contact with Sinn Féin, but stated that the contact was in response to a message sent by the IRA that the conflict was over. This is absolutely false and for this reason I reluctantly was forced to go public to correct the lies which were being told. In November 1993, we therefore published the communication documents to prove that the British government was telling lies.

These documents show that, in the early part of 1993, the British government proposed a series of meetings with Sinn Féin, arguing that an intensive round of such meetings would result in Irish republicans being convinced that armed struggle was no longer necessary. Written position papers were exchanged and venues and timetables for delegation meetings were discussed.

The British requested that Sinn Féin seek a two or three week undeclared suspension of IRA operations to facilitate these discussions. Given the importance of all of this, we sought, and were given a commitment from the leadership of the IRA that it would suspend operations for two weeks to enable us to explore the potential of the British government's assertions. We conveyed this undertaking to the British government on 10 May 1993.

Although we were informed that the positive response by republicans to the British proposal was the subject of high level meetings by British ministers and officials, including John Major, there was no positive response from them. In fact, the British moved away from their proposal and refused to follow through. This was brought about in part by political difficulties which overtook the Tory party leadership at the time, and other difficulties in the House of Commons which led them to depend on unionist votes at Westminster.

It then became clear, from early summer 1993, that the British government had reneged on its proposal and the previous indications that it was actively seeking a way out of the conflict. Despite the fact that my talks with SDLP leader John Hume had reached a point of significant progress, and the resulting Irish Peace Initiative provided the best opportunity and framework for peace if they had the political will to move forward, communications from the British continued to avoid the main issues. Simultaneously, the volume of leaks and rumours increased quite noticeably. The British government was now trying to sow confusion and division among republicans, and soon resorted to blatant lies and falsifying of documents, as the records show.

The behaviour of the British government, the lies, omissions, falsifications, forgeries, diversions and distractions are all proof of its opposition to peace in our country, which arises from its dogged refusal to concede to the people of Ireland, all of us, our right to determine our own future—our right to govern ourselves, free of division and conflict.

But there are positive aspects to this situation. For example, no government on these islands can ever again claim that there is any popular support for a policy of excluding Sinn Féin. The pompous, self-righteous rhetoric of British government officials, and of John Major saying that he will not talk to us, is nothing more than cheap political manoeuvering. People support inclusive dialogue, as it is the only way forward.

The main issue, to paraphrase the words of John Hume, is that the British government 'holds the key' to peace in our country, and between the people of Britain and Ireland. John Major has refused to turn this key. All of us, Dublin, London, republicans and nationalists, must work together to seek the support of the unionist section of our people, and must strive to build upon the peace process.

The challenge facing all political leaders in Ireland and Britain continues to be the necessity to establish a basis for a lasting peace that brings to an end all conflict in our country. Sinn Féin is totally committed to this, and it remains a personal and political priority for me. My hope continues to be for the creation of a process that leads to a new united Ireland which would, of necessity, be democratic and pluralist, and would allow for the development of a tolerant and open society which would respect freedom of conscience and freedom of choice for the individual.

12

Peace in Ireland?

As to any union between the two islands, believe us when we assert that our union rests upon mutual independence. We shall love each other if we are left to ourselves. It is the union of mind which ought to bind these nations together.

United Irishmen

I N DECEMBER 1993, the leaders of the British and Irish governments were moved to address republicans directly through the Downing Street Declaration. This effort is a fundamental shift in policy and is in contrast to strategies which aimed to ignore republicanism as part of a policy of marginalizing and isolating us, and it marks the failure of every strategy which preceded it. It is also, specifically, a direct response to the developing, and increasingly effective, peace strategy which Sinn Féin publicly launched in 1987.

Sinn Féin's peace strategy is now the central plank of party policy. As well as the public promotion of this strategy, there has been protracted internal discussion, and discussions with a wide spectrum of political and religious opinion in Irish society. The inter-party talks with the SDLP in 1988 were part of that, as were all subsequent discussions and exchanges between myself and SDLP party leader John Hume. Likewise, we approached the recent protracted contact and dialogue with the British government, in the context of our peace strategy. To the degree that our resources have permitted, we have made an effort to relay our peace strategy to the international community, particularly within the United States and Britain. We have also taken some limited first steps to do this in the EU.

Sinn Féin believes that a lasting peace can be achieved by the eradication of the causes of conflict. We have held up the democratic and universally accepted principle of national self-determination as the route through which that can come about. We have argued that both the London and Dublin governments should adopt this as their policy objective, to be achieved within an agreed timescale—in other words, as part of a process. We have argued that this be accomplished in consultation with all the parties involved, and the consent of the unionists must be actively sought during this process, a process during which national reconciliation can begin; a process culminating in a negotiated settlement. In all of this we have identified the British government as the major player. It has the power and responsibility to move things on. Its policy in Ireland casts it either in the role of keeper of the status quo or as key persuader in movement towards a lasting peace, founded on democratic principles.

We have also recognized that a united Irish nationalist/republican voice is a potent political force, not just in Ireland itself but in Britain and internationally. Irish republicans, by ourselves, simply do not possess the political strength to bring about these aims. However, we do possess the ability to create conditions which can move the situation towards these aims and we have the power to prevent another settlement on British government terms which would subvert Irish national and democratic rights.

We would never have moved the British to engage with us in the first place if we had been the isolated, non-representative group depicted by its propaganda machine. It is my confident prediction that we will be in dialogue again, either with John Majors' administration or with his successors. For our part, we are ready to recommence talks at any time. There cannot be peace without dialogue.

At the beginning of 1993, the British government proposed delegation meetings between Sinn Féin and its representatives. We negotiated the preliminary procedures for these discussions. In order to assist this process, the IRA responded positively to a British request for a temporary suspension of operations. However, on receiving this principled, flexible, but positive response from both Sinn Féin and the IRA, the British government backed down.

Why does the British government behave in this way? Why the exclusion order against me? Why, more recently, its hysterical opposition to an inclusive peace conference in New York? Why the lies, omissions, falsifications, forgeries, diversions and distractions? And remember, London did not confine itself to dealing only with Sinn Féin in this way. Our dialogue with London was conducted against the background of the developing Irish Peace Initiative and both governments were kept fully informed of all developments at every stage of my discussions with John Hume, before and after these discussions became public.

The British government knew that the Irish Peace Initiative represented a real opportunity for peace. Both John Hume and the Dublin government told them this privately and publicly. Yet John Major denied any knowledge of the Irish Peace Initiative's contents and denied being in contact with us.

This phase of our history, when the opportunity for peace was so near, is one of the most shameful in twenty-five years of conflict, or perhaps since the partition of this country. The British government's attitude to peace proposals from nationalist Ireland, whether represented by Albert Reynolds or John Hume or Sinn Féin, has been despicable. It has been marked by stalling tactics, refusals to engage meaningfully in the peace process, diversions, lies and petty manipulations. At all times in its dealings with nationalist Ireland, the British government sought to insist on its position, tried to apply pressure, to create and win a contest of wills, to mislead and to demand concessions and one-sided gains. It sought victory on its own terms, not peace on democratic terms, and it aimed at all times to fragment the consensus around the Irish Peace Initiative.

Observers and apologists for the London government may seek to discount these allegations. But let us not forget that, in the battle of the documents, Sinn Féin's version of the exchanges with the London government was proven to be the correct one. So when we witness the stalling tactics of the British since the Downing Street Declaration, remember this stance goes back beyond 15 December 1993, and remember the distractions, the diversions and the lies which marked British attempts to sideline the Irish Peace Initiative at all times since its conception.

It is not my intention to examine here all the significant words and phrases in the Downing Street Declaration. Readers should do this themselves, even if only by way of mine-sweeping. That is an exercise which must be done, for nobody in this world is so adept as the British civil service in the laying of documentary booby-traps! But, because it is the most important single issue the document raises for republicans, I feel I must deal with the way the issue of self-determination and, allied to it, the question of a veto for unionists, is treated.

The fact that the declaration addresses the issue of Irish national self-determination at all is a significant departure from the attitude of the British towards Ireland which has endured for centuries. However, having declared that the Irish are entitled to exercise the right to self-determination, there can be no justification for trying to instruct the people, whose right to self-determination you have just conceded, how they are to use it.

How Irish national self-determination is exercised is a matter for the Irish people to decide. It is not the business of the British.

In my discussions with John Hume we accepted 'that the Irish people as a whole have a right to self-determination.' We went on to say:

> ...this is a view shared by a majority of people on this island, though not by all its people. The exercise of self-determination is a matter for agreement between the people of Ireland. It is the search for that agreement, and the means of achieving it, on which we will be concentrating. We are mindful that not all the people of Ireland share that view or agree on how to give meaningful expression to it. Indeed we cannot disguise the different views held by our different parties. As leaders of our respective parties, we have told each other that we see the task of reaching agreement on a peaceful and democratic accord for all on this island as our primary challenge.

This remains the challenge. The British government appears to be prepared to accept our right to national self-determination only in the context of its claim to sovereignty over all 'persons, matters and things in Northern Ireland' (Section 75 of the Government of Ireland Act).

There is no suggestion by the British prime minister of the need for British constitutional change. We must remember that, in British constitutionality, the parliament is sovereign, therefore the British parliament has the authority to change any Act of that parliament without reference to anyone outside the parliament. Yet there is not even a hint of any proposed change in the Government of Ireland Act. It is not even mentioned. On the other hand, the Taoiseach pledges changes in the Irish Constitution in the context of an overall settlement.

Furthermore, northern nationalists are not even explicitly mentioned in the declaration, though there are numerous references to the unionists. John Major tells us why this is so saying:

> I have gone to great trouble to ensure that the constitutional guarantee is firmly enshrined in the Joint Declaration, so that there can be no doubt that those people who care about the union—and we are primarily concerned about the people in Northern Ireland who care about the union—shall have it within their own hands, with the full support of the government, to remain within the union for so long as that is their wish.

Are nationalists invisible, Mr Major?

There is much unnecessary confusion, as well as deliberate misrepresentation of the republican position on this principle of unionist consent. We subscribe to the classical, democratic position of Irish nationalism. It was Britain that partitioned Ireland, turning the Irish unionist minority into an artificial majority in the Six-County area. Unionists are not—and do not claim to be—a nation with a right to national self-determination, as this is universally recognized in international law. Unionists are an Irish national minority, a religious/political minority, with minority rights not majority ones. Unionists can have no veto of British government policy or Irish government policy either.

The unionist position is, in fact, logically and politically an absurd one, for they in effect claim to possess a unilateral right to union with the British state, the majority of whose people do not want them, when there can only be unilateral rights of separation, never of union.

189

At the same time, while nationalists deny that unionists have any right of veto over British or Irish policy directed at seeking to dissolve the Union, most nationalists and republicans recognize as a matter of pragmatism that it is desirable in practice that the consent, or assent, of as many unionists as possible should be obtained to the steps that would be practically required to bring about the ending of partition and establishing a united Ireland.

These steps relate, of course, to the complex financial, constitutional and legal aspects of a final all-Ireland settlement, as well as other details and the time-scale involved. Republicans recognize that the national interest demands that the consent, or assent, of as many of our unionist fellow countrymen and fellow countrywomen as possible should be obtained to these steps. We believe that the consent of the majority of present-day unionists could, in fact, be won, over time, to these steps to reunification, provided that the two governments, and primarily the British government, made that the basis of their policy. That is why nationalists want Britain to 'join the ranks of the persuaders,' to base their policy on encouraging the coming together of Protestants and Catholics, not underwriting our continued separation; as up to now.

My joint statements with John Hume have made very clear that the ultimate objective of the peace process in which we are involved seeks agreement among the divided peoples of Ireland, an agreement that must earn the allegiance, and agreement, of all traditions and that both governments and all parties must be involved in this process. The underlying assumption of these joint statements is that the only interest to be accommodated and the only problem to be resolved would be the division between the two main sections of the people who inhabit this island and that there would be no selfish British interests involved. But the view of republicans and nationalists is that British imperialism created the problem in the first place and has maintained it ever since.

At the heart of Irish nationalist concerns are fears about loyalist violence and unionist bigotry, the intimidation of nationalist communities by the British army, and social deprivation and job discrimination. Also, there is the denial of full and equal recognition of Irish cultural rights within the Six Counties.

Many nationalists are concerned that Britain remains unwilling 'to join the ranks of the persuaders.' Major says no and refuses to embark on a policy of working to undo the wrong of the partition of Ireland. Why? There is an assertion of British 'neutrality' between the nationalist Irish majority and the unionist Irish minority but the British Minister for Northern Ireland, Sir Patrick Mayhew, now says that the British government will be 'persuaders for an agreement,' without it necessarily being Irish unity, as if Britain has no independent, self-interested views of its own about the Irish boundaries of the United Kingdom state. Is that credible? It can only be tested in practice, and that is one of the challenges ahead.

On the positive side, Major says that Britain no longer has any 'selfish, economic or strategic interest' in staying in Ireland. In a general sense that may be true as a result of the ending of the Cold War and the unlikelihood of a war in the North Atlantic. He fails to say that they have no political interest. Indeed, the British government certainly has a political interest in remaining, at least for the present. They remain politically committed to the union. They may see the weakening of the union as the first stage in the disintegration of the United Kingdom. John Major has said that he does not wish to oversee the disintegration of the United Kingdom. However, the Downing Street Declaration marks a stage in the slow and painful process of England's disengagement from her first and last colony, Ireland. It may be a small step, as was the Hillsborough Agreement of 1985, which—leaving aside justifiable republican criticisms—gave Dublin, for the first time, a 'foot inside the door' in the Six Counties. That door, which is now slightly ajar as a result of the struggle and sacrifices of the past twenty-five years, culminating in the advances made possible by the Irish Peace Initiative, needs now to be pushed wide open to let the clean, fresh and invigorating air of Irish democracy blow through the politically stagnant atmosphere of the Six Counties which so many of us have to endure and which we are so anxious to be rid of.

Neither Hillsborough nor the Downing Street Declaration have brought the northern nationalist nightmare to an end. The pointers to how that nightmare can in reality be ended can only come in the process of clarification of the Downing Street Declaration's contents, which republicans and nationalists require if they are to be confident that the way ahead will improve our position, not make it worse. Clarification of the declaration is necessary, not just because republicans are asking for it but because there are valid questions which need to be answered.

What are Britain's long-term intentions regarding Ireland? What guarantees are there or will there be that there will be no return to bigoted Orange supremacy in northern nationalist communities pending final British disengagement? What about security issues? What about collusion? What about equality and parity of esteem for nationalists in all areas? What about an end to electoral gerrymandering to keep nationalists down? What about the prisoners? The devil is in the details, as the phrase goes. But the details must be provided if republicans are to take British protestations of goodwill and good intentions seriously.

The British government refuses to admit that our call for clarification of the provisions of the declaration is a reasonable one. Yet all other parties receive clarification on request and there appears to be no end to clarifications of a provocative and negative nature, about 'decontamination' periods, about 'no amnesty for political prisoners, and about an 'IRA surrender of weapons.'

Why does the London government demand an IRA surrender, as a precondition to dialogue with Sinn Féin? For over three years, the British government was involved in contact and dialogue with Sinn Féin without such preconditions. The declared purpose of that contact was to explore the possibility of developing a real peace process. Now when it claims to have the basis of a peace settlement it refuses to do this.

Also, does anyone really expect the IRA to cease its activities so that British civil servants can discuss with Sinn Féin the surrender of IRA weapons after we have been 'decontaminated'? Yet this is what John Major is demanding of me and he is threatening dire consequences if I do not acquiesce. Why?

Sinn Féin is not the IRA and there isn't any organic relationship between Sinn Féin and the IRA. Sinn Féin cannot be held responsible for IRA actions nor can Sinn Féin voters be held responsible for IRA actions.

No matter about the shared history of Sinn Féin and the IRA, Sinn Féin is quite clearly a completely separate organization that stands on its own feet, makes its own judgements and decisions, and moves forward with its own unarmed and democratic agenda.

I want to see an end to the IRA. I want to take the gun out of Irish politics. I am confident, not about how long it will take, but that we will actually take the gun out of Irish politics once the cause of the conflict is addressed.

Last year, in response to questions from journalists, I made it clear that, if a viable peace package is produced, I am quite prepared to take this to the IRA. I am confident that the IRA would respond positively to a package containing the principles, process and dynamic which were presented to the British government as a result of the Hume/Adams Irish Peace Initiative.

To the best of my knowledge the IRA's door remains open and the IRA leadership has outlined its positive attitude to these proposals in a series of public statements. Why does London say no? If a formula of words was all that was required one has to presume that we would have had peace two decades ago. The British are in no doubt, I am sure, about the capacity and commitment of the IRA. If this is the case then it appears to me that the utterances of British ministers, including Mr Major, especially since 15 December, 1993, are deliberately provocative.

The two governments cannot argue that they have a basis for peace unless they can produce it and explain what it is. The Dublin government has been concerned to explain its position, but both governments need to do this because, while Sinn Féin remains committed to building a real peace process, as I have said many times before, we cannot do so without the co-operation of the British government. Given the historic and current stance of that government, this will not be an easy task. Why can London not go the extra mile to accept the proposals put to it in the Irish Peace Initiative and to which the IRA gave a positive response?

The onus is clearly on John Major to clarify his position. He should be mindful of the advice of one of his own: the original man in a grey suit?

> There is a tide in the affairs of men, which taken at the flood, leads on to fortune; omitted, all the voyages of their life is bound in shallows and in miseries.
>
> On such a full sea are we now afloat, and we must take the current when it serves, or lose our ventures.
>
> Brutus, Act IV, Scene 3, *Julius Caesar*

It is against this background that Sinn Féin is being asked to judge the Downing Street Declaration. Sinn Féin remains committed to a lasting peace and to developing and promoting the peace process until this is achieved. Mr Major may hope that his refusal to provide clarification and his efforts to stall the momentum will have the effect of defusing the peace process and thus let his government off the hook. I can assure him that this will not happen. The search for peace and the need for peace in Ireland is too serious an issue to be sidelined in this way.

What is required is an approach which creates political conditions in which, for the first time, the Irish people can reach a democratic accommodation, in which the consent and agreement of both nationalists and unionists can be achieved, in which a process of national reconciliation and healing can begin. Unionist participation in this is essential.

Sinn Féin is willing to set aside all that has occurred up to now. The British government should do likewise. I have frequently said that a new beginning is needed. I call upon all who are concerned to end conflict, to redouble their efforts to move this situation on in a manner which takes account not only of all the sensitivities and difficulties involved, but more importantly, of the prize of peace which must be the basis for our commitment to this process.

The atmosphere of suspicion and doubt in Ireland and between Ireland and Britain, must be filtered out so that rational and pragmatic discussions can replace the old animosities. Each side must accept that clinging to intransigent positions will not, and cannot, advance the situation.

Sadly, the British government, whether because of its cynical and short-sighted 'arrangement' with the unionists in the British House of Commons, or because of some anachronistic belief in its own imperial standing, has as yet proved unwilling to take the measures that would transform an understandable desire for peace into a genuine peace process.

Despite this hard-line posturing from British politicians, realism and accommodation are not impossible. After the political upheaval that accompanied the signing of the Anglo-Irish Agreement in November 1985, it was accepted by both the Irish and British governments that, if a different formula or a better, more practical Accord were necessary, or could be reached in any new accommodation, it would be incumbent upon all the participants to facilitate, and agree to, such change. The British saw no difficulty in agreeing to alter or modify an internationally ratified Accord, and yet they are currently unwilling to even discuss the Downing Street Declaration with Sinn Féin, despite the fact that a real and lasting peace in Ireland might be achieved as a result.

Should there be a general consensus that the Irish Peace Initiative and/or the Downing Street Declaration are, or are perceived to be flawed, incomplete, or incapable of producing movement, they too can and should be changed, especially if the end result will produce the peace that all parties are theoretically committed to achieving.

The Irish and British governments, their respective parliamentary oppositional parties, republicans, the SDLP, the unionists, the political and community representatives of all the people on this island, the Church, the cultural and social bodies, are all pieces in the Anglo-Irish jigsaw. They must all be involved, and they must all be part of the negotiating process that will, hopefully, slot the pieces together.

Sinn Féin has the authority and the electoral mandate to represent a very important section of the Irish people. Our mandate is as valid as any other party, and the people who voted for Sinn Féin have an inalienable right to be represented in any genuine peace dialogue. The British government should recognize our rights as a political party, the validity of our mandate and the rights of our electorate. Clarification of the British position is necessary so that we may properly explore how the peace process can be moved forward. It should be provided on that basis. Clarification has been provided to all other parties on request. Sinn Féin and our electorate have the right to equality of treatment.

Is it unreasonable for democrats to seek the British government, given not only its responsibility for its legacy of the past but its authority in the present situation, to commit all its resources to heal divisions and to promote agreement among our people?

Is it unreasonable to ask the British government what process, time-frame and framework it proposes for reaching such agreement?

Is it unreasonable to ask in advance what would be its reaction if any section of the people who inhabit our island refused to seek such agreement, given the cost of disagreement not only to the Irish people but to the British people as well?

And are these not reasonable requests, given that unionist politicians have never faced up to the central problem of reaching agreement with the rest of the people of this island and, in fact, have acted in collusion with the loyalist death squads to prevent such agreement?

This generation of republicans seeks an end to Anglo-Irish conflict forever. If the British government commits itself to embracing and promoting the policy I have outlined here, then we republicans will commit all our energies and resources to reaching such an agreement. And, when such an agreement is reached, we will continue to use all our resources to promote the healing process that will be necessary to unite the Irish people and to protect the democratic dignity, civil rights and heritage of all our people. The compelling logic of our situation and the climate of international opinion demands a democratic and negotiated settlement of the Anglo-Irish conflict. The alternative locks all of us into a perpetuation of conflict. Is this what the British government wants?

Since 1969, the war has cost 3,280 lives and 33,500 people have sustained injuries. Two-thirds of the injured are civilians. This is the reality of the conflict in human terms. It needs to be ended. Unconditional inclusive dialogue is required, leading to a durable settlement, a total demilitarization of the conflict and a healing programme of national reconciliation.

Ireland and Britain have much to gain from peace. A lasting peace in Ireland is as much in the interests of the British people as it is in Irish interests. The billions now spent on war can become investments in peace; investments in jobs, in housing, childcare, transport, health and education. Britain's subvention to the Six Counties has now reached £4 billion a year. But most, if not all, of this could be saved within the North and in Britain if a lasting peace could be agreed. With no other changes in economic policy, the unification of the economies will generate tens of thousands of jobs. Peace will release a tide of new economic activity and investment.

A proper peace process will involve a plan for economic transition and reconstruction, including an international aid package. The logic of economic and social development lies with Irish unity, not in union with a declining British economy, nor with the escalating costs of war. This is now recognized by even the most conservative elements of Irish society, by the bankers and business community, as the 1983 Report of the New Ireland Forum put it:

> The division of the island has been a source of continuing costs, especially for trade and development in border areas, but in general also to the two separate administrations which have been pursuing separate economic policies on a small island with shared problems and resources.
>
> We conclude that partition and its failure to provide political stability have resulted in extra costs in many sectors and have inhibited the socio-economic development of Ireland, especially in the North. Division has had an adverse effect on the general ethos of society and has contributed to a limiting of perspective, north and south. Had the division not taken place, or had the unionist and nationalist traditions in Ireland been encouraged to bring it to an end by reaching a mutual accommodation, the people of the whole island would be in a much better position to benefit from its resources and to meet the common challenges that face Irish society, north and south, towards the end of the 20th century.

Thus the full benefits of integrating the two economies can only be realized by ending partition.

Today the debate about Irish self-determination and the fight to end partition takes place within a political, social and economic context that has been fundamentally altered by the creation of the European Union. The fight against the Single European Act and the Maastricht Treaty has been lost, and the reality is that Ireland will remain in the European Union for the foreseeable future. We face new challenges as a result, but the fight for national self-determination is, if anything, more urgent, and more relevant, than it has been at any time since partition.

The catalyst effect of the Irish Peace Initiative and the effect of the strategies employed by the various parties, will all bring their own influence to bear. There is a high risk for all involved, but

Sinn Féin is taking a greater risk than any of the others. But what is clear is that we need to bring all-Ireland nationalist opinion with us. In all of this, we in Sinn Féin have a responsibility to build on the progress which has been made.

So where do we go from here?

Sinn Féin has accepted that the Irish Peace Initiative could form the basis for a lasting peace. Nevertheless, we are politically and morally bound to consider the Downing Street Declaration in the context of our own peace strategy and with a view to determining what contribution it has to make to the development of a peace process aimed at delivering a lasting peace.

Again, we have publicly committed ourselves to a process of internal and external consultations on our own peace strategy, the broader peace process and on the declaration, and we have established a commission for that purpose. As has also been shown, Sinn Féin has a clear view of what is required to achieve a lasting peace founded on democratic principles. We have a clear peace strategy aimed at moving the situation in that direction.

Sinn Féin should attempt to keep building on the conditions created by our peace strategy and the Irish Peace Initiative and to seek to ascertain what role there is for the Downing Street Declaration in advancing the peace process. This would involve Sinn Féin in bringing into play, in a very direct way, our electoral mandate, our total commitment to establishing a lasting peace in our country, and whatever political influence we have to secure a political package so that the IRA can make judgements in relation to future conduct of its armed campaign.

The reality is, however, that the IRA will make its own decisions on this. We are not the IRA. Sinn Féin is not engaged in armed struggle, but we have helped to formulate proposals which have moved the IRA to say publicly that the acceptance of these proposals by the British government could provide the basis for peace. The rejection by the British government of this offer has made our task more difficult. Nonetheless, we must seek to move the situation forward and we must do so in conjunction with those who formed the Irish Peace Initiative.

And indeed, we must do this regardless of the outcome of our assessment as to whether or not the Downing Street Declaration represents a first step in the direction of peace for the British government. In essence, Sinn Féin would be attempting to reconstruct an Irish political consensus on the basis of the principles, dynamic and process contained in the Irish Peace Initiative, to politically reinforce commitment to such a consensus and to sustain political action based on it.

What is additionally required are narrower, more specific short-term and intermediate objectives to advance the possibilities which our established peace objectives have provided.

The political reality of all this is that there can only be advance, continued advance, if we grasp the opportunities of the times. This means working together, even though we are rivals with other parties. It means winning and maintaining the backing of the Dublin government for the long neglected northern nationalist people and co-operating together to obtain the powerful international allies the Irish nationalist cause needs.

In the short to medium term, we need to advance the position of northern nationalists in every conceivable way. This means strengthening the nationalist agenda.

It means no return to unionist domination over local nationalist communities in the Six Counties. What is abundantly clear, and the political representatives of unionism must inform themselves and their supporters of this, is that there is no going back to the days of Stormont and unionist rule.

It means local republican activists being able to represent and speak for our communities in conditions of peace, not being interfered with by the British military or the RUC, free of personal harassment and free from the threat of the death squads.

It means the real ending of job discrimination against Catholics, who are up to three times more likely to be unemployed than Protestants.

It means full recognition of the rights of *Gaelgeoiri* and an equality of status for the Irish language including proper funding.

It means the speedy release of all long-term political prisoners pending a full amnesty for all political prisoners.

It means an end to all repressive legislation.

It means an end to collusion.

Political concessions of this kind from Britain will not be won without a hard and disciplined struggle. It will require unity between republicans and nationalists in the North, such as the Hume/Adams initiative presaged. It will require the support of the government in Dublin. And it will require the support of the powerful allies abroad, within the EU, in Britain itself, internationally, and especially in the USA.

To ensure that the demands and interests of northern nationalism are given maximum weight and brought to bear fully on the British government in the period ahead, it is essential that public opinion all over Ireland, but particularly in the Twenty-six Counties, pressures the government in Dublin to give wholehearted support to the democratic cause, and helps to obtain allies for this cause all over the world.

This is the main political task for republicans in the south in the period ahead. There are powerful reactionary interests in this part of the country which resent deeply the efforts on the northern issue made by Mr Albert Reynolds' government in response to the Hume/Adams initiative. The neo-unionist and anti-nationalist people on the opposition benches in the Irish Dáil are all deeply dismayed at the success so far of the Irish Peace Initiative. They are biding their time and will do everything to turn Dublin again in an anti-national and anti-republican direction, reverting to a position of bolstering the British government's failed strategy for victory.

That is why all republicans and nationalists need now to consider how best to advance the basic national demands in the light of the new conditions and possibilities opening up before us. We need particularly to consider how we can appeal to the national sentiment that is strong particularly at the grassroots of Fianna Fáil, among the ordinary members of and voters for that party, but also among many Labour Party people, and more widely among those disenchanted with, or uninvolved in, party politics.

They need a political focus for their aspirations and activity. They need something around which they can build political unity and concrete common action that will appeal to all true Irish patriots. That is why I suggest the need for nationally-minded people to consider the launching of an Irish Freedom Charter—A Charter for Justice and Peace in Ireland—around which the broadest sections of the Irish people can rally and unite. This would consist of the most fundamental national demands and aspirations relating to Irish politics, the Irish economy and our society as a whole, which the widest range of nationally-minded Irish people can support and which can provide not only a focusing point but a rallying point as well.

The demands of this Freedom Charter should be directed at the British and Irish governments and appeal to international support. I suggest that the first proposition of such a charter should be an adaptation of the first principle of the Freedom Charter of the South African National Congress, which guided their long and inspiring freedom struggle that is now coming to fruition in a free South Africa. It would read: 'Ireland belongs to all who live in it,' just as South Africa belongs to all who live in it.

For the first time in twenty years, there is tangible evidence throughout Ireland of increasing self-confidence and awareness among nationalists. Every effort must be made to harness this energy, to build upon it, and to direct it in a way which will advance the peace process and secure a negotiated settlement based on democratic principles.

An editorial in the Dublin *Sunday Business Post* commenting on my recent visit to New York asked, '…what might be achieved if the Irish Government made a coherent attempt to galvanize Irish America in support of national policy?'

This is something that Irish republicans and nationalists need to think about. For the outcome of the visa controversy showed that, for the first time ever in Anglo-American relations, Washington, faced with a choice between Ireland and Britain, chose Ireland. And it would not have happened either but for the extraordinary effort of lobbying and campaigning by leading members of the Irish-American community, including political leaders, business leaders, trade unionists and media people, or without the support of people in Ireland. Full credit to everyone involved.

Of course this could only have happened in the new international political context where, with the Cold War over, Britain's value as America's principal ally against Russia is no longer relevant.

What the coming together of progressive political forces over the visa issue demonstrated was the potential and possibilities of what can happen if Irish nationalism unites and wins powerful allies. It might seem a relatively minor matter—obtaining a visa for one Irish republican. But what was achieved was of enormous symbolic and political importance. It also illustrated that international interest and concern can play an important and constructive part in the development of a viable peace process. There has been a consistent need for the international community to exercise its good will and influence to help end conflicts worldwide. This is generally recognized and, at times, acted upon. It has not, however, been a factor in the Anglo-Irish conflict. This situation needs to be rectified.

There is a widespread interest in, and concern about Ireland within public opinion in the United States. This stems from the historical links between our two countries and the large Irish-American community in the USA. The potential has, therefore, always existed for the US to play a part in the construction of an effective response to human rights abuses and this has been done particularly in the MacBride Campaign for Fair Employment. It is only proper that this potential is realized in the wider search for a lasting settlement, and while I acknowledge and applaud the efforts that have been made, I would appeal to all those in civic, political and industrial leadership in the USA to apply their energy in this direction.

The US government can play a significant and positive role in encouraging the peace process by helping to create a climate which moves the situation on. It can do this by facilitating free exchange of information and in this context I commend President Clinton for the waiver on visa denial which allowed me to address the National Committee on American Foreign Policy. I welcome the committee's concrete contribution to the search for peace in Ireland and the substantial and significant support which has been generated on these matters recently in the USA.

The British have been bent on damage limitation since. But don't believe anything they say in this regard. They have a difficulty you see. London still believes that it rules the world. It doesn't. One thing is clear, however, we must apply ourselves to finding ways to enable wider allies to be won, and won more firmly and solidly in the US, in Europe, in Britain and internationally.

This year marks twenty-five years of British Crown forces being redeployed on Irish soil. They have been traumatic, mind-bending years of human tragedy for all caught up in the conflict. Patrick Galvin, the poet, had this to say:

When you came to this land
You said you came to understand.
Soldier, we are tired of your understanding,
Tired of British troops on Irish soil
Tired of your knock on the door
Tired of the rifle butt on the head

Soldier,
We are tired of the peace you bring
To Irish bones.
Tired of the bombs, exploding in our homes
Tired of the rubble, growing in the streets
Tired of the death of old friends
Tired of the tears and funerals—
Those endless, endless funerals.

In other parts of the world, conflicts which were formerly deemed intractable are moving towards resolution. These struggles may be more politically developed than ours, but what is at the core of all our effort is our will to be free. This makes the impossible possible. We are into a new and final phase of struggle which will allow us to put the legacy of conflict behind us. It is that time in our history.

We dream here.
We dream that this land
Is our land.
That one day
Catholic and Protestant
Believer and non-believer
Will stand here
And dream as Irish men and women.

We dream
Of a green land
Without death
A new silence descending
A silence of peace.

Chapter Twelve

The republican struggle is strong, confident and will continue for as long as it needs to. We have come through the years of vilification and marginalization. We are never going back to that. We are moving forward. There are no backward steps, no standing still—there is only one way—and that is forward to a free Ireland and a lasting peace.

Poblacht na hÉireann

The Provincial Government
of the

IRISH REPUBLIC

To the people of Ireland

Irishmen and Irishwomen: In the name of God and of the dead generations from which she receives her old tradition of nationhood, Ireland, through us, summons her children to her flag and strikes for her freedom.

Having organised and trained her manhood through her secret revolutionary organisation, the Irish Republican Brotherhood, and through her open military organisations, the Irish Volunteers and the Irish Citizen Army, having patiently perfected her discipline, having resolutely waited for the right moment to reveal itself, she now seizes that moment and, supported by her exiled children in America and by gallant allies in Europe, but relying in the first on her own strength, she strikes in full confidence of victory.

We declare the right of the people of Ireland to the ownership of Ireland and to the unfettered control of Irish destinies, to be sovereign and indefeasible. The long usurpation of that right by a foreign people and government has not extinguished the right, nor can it ever be extinguished except by the destruction of the Irish people. In every generation the Irish people have asserted their right to national freedom and sovereignty: six times during the past three hundred years they have asserted it in arms. Standing on that fundamental right and again asserting it in arms in the face of the world, we hereby proclaim the Irish Republic as a Sovereign Independent State, and we pledge our lives and the lives of our comrades-in-arms to the cause of its freedom, of its welfare and of its exaltation among the nations.

The Irish Republic is entitled to, and hereby claims, the allegiance of every Irishman and Irishwoman. The Republic guarantees religious and civil liberty, equal rights and equal opportunities to all its citizens, and declares its resolve to pursue the happiness and prosperity of the whole nation and of all its parts, cherishing all the children of the nation equally, and oblivious of the differences, carefully fostered by an alien government, which have divided a minority from the majority in the past.

Until our arms have brought the opportune moment for the establishing of a permanent national Government, representative of the whole people of Ireland, and elected by the suffrages of all her men and women, the Provisional Government, hereby constituted, will administer the civil and military affairs of the Republic in trust for the people. We place the cause of the Irish Republic under the protection of the Most High God, Whose blessing we invoke upon our arms, and we pray that no one who serves that cause will dishonour it by cowardice, inhumanity or rapine. In this supreme hour the Irish nation must, by its valour and discipline, and by the readiness of its children to sacrifice themselves for the common good, prove itself worthy of the august destiny to which it is called.

Signed on Behalf of the Provisional Government,

Thomas J. Clarke

Sean MacDiarmada	Thomas MacDonagh
P. H. Pearse	Eamonn Ceannt
James Connolly	Joseph Plunkett

Democratic Programme
of Dáil Éireann

WE DECLARE in the words of the Irish Republican Proclamation the right of the people of Ireland to the ownership of Ireland, and to the unfettered control of Irish destinies to be indefeasible, and in the language of our first President, Padraig Mac Phiarais, we declare that the Nation's sovereignty extends not only to all men and women of the Nation, but to all its material possessions, the Nation's soil and all its resources, all the wealth and all the wealth-producing processes within the Nation, and with him we reaffirm that all right to private property must be subordinated to the public right and welfare.

We declare that we desire our country to be ruled in accordance with the principles of Liberty, Equality, and Justice for all, which alone can secure a permanence of Government in the willing adhesion of the people.

We affirm the duty of every man and woman to give allegiance and service to the Commonwealth, and declare it is the duty of the Nation to assure that every citizen shall have the opportunity to spend his or her strength and faculties in the services of the people. In return for willing service, we, in the name of the Republic, declare the right of every citizen to an adequate share of the produce of the Nation's labour.

It shall be the first duty of the Government of the Republic to make provision for the physical, mental and spiritual well-being of the children, to secure that no child shall suffer hunger or cold from lack of food, clothing, or shelter, but that all shall be provided with the means and facilities requisite for their proper education and training as Citizens of a Free and Gaelic Ireland.

The Irish Republic fully realises the necessity of abolishing the present odious, degrading and foreign Poor Law System, substituting therefor a sympathetic native scheme for the care of the Nation's aged and infirm, who shall not be regarded as a burden, but rather entitled to the Nation's gratitude and consideration. Likewise it shall be the duty of the Republic to make such measures as will safeguard the health of the people and ensure the physical as well as the moral well-being of the Nation.

It shall be our duty to promote the development of the Nation's resources, to increase the productivity of its soil, to exploit its mineral deposits, peat bogs, and fisheries, its waterways and harbours, in the interests and for the benefit of the Irish people.

It shall be the duty of the Republic to adopt all measures necessary for the recreation and invigoration of our Industries, and to ensure their being developed on the most beneficial and progressive co-operative and industrial lines. With the adoption of an extensive Irish Consular Service, trade with foreign Nations shall be revived on terms of mutual advantage and goodwill, and while undertaking the organisation of the Nation's trade, import and export, it shall be the duty of the Republic to prevent the shipment from Ireland of food and other necessaries until the wants of the Irish people are fully satisfied and the future provided for.

It shall also devolve upon the National Government to seek co-operation of the Governments of other countries in determining a standard of Social and Industrial Legislation with a view to a general and lasting improvement in the conditions under which the working classes live and labour.

Glossary

Arms Trial In 1970, Neil Blaney and Charles Haughey (both members of the Fianna Fáil Cabinet of Jack Lynch), Haughey's brother Captain Kelly (a Free State army intelligence officer), John Kelly of the IRA, and Albert Luykx (a Belgian businessman) were charged with illegally importing arms. The defence maintained that the arms importation was sanctioned by the Dublin government. The charges were dismissed.

Ballyseedy Scene of one of the worst atrocities of the Civil War, when Free State forces killed several republicans in cold blood.

Bata scóir A stick marked to record the times a schoolchild spoke Irish. Each additional notch incurred a beating.

Birmingham Six One of many cases of miscarriage of British justice (*see also* 'Guildford Four' and 'Maguire Seven'). Six Irish people arrested in the wake of a bombing in Birmingham, in 1974, on very insubstantial evidence, and sentenced for life. Their 'confessions' were given involuntarily. Despite asserting their innocence and having many campaigns on their behalf, leave to appeal was refused in 1973. They were freed in 1991, but the British judiciary has still not admitted their innocence.

Black and Tan War (or Tan War) The War of Independence. Took its name from khaki uniform and black caps of reinforcements, recruited from unemployed ex-servicemen, known as the Black and Tans, sent from Britain to aid the police force. They are remembered for their brutality and indiscipline.

Bloody Sunday January 30, 1972. Thirteen people attending a demonstration in Derry against internment were killed by British soldiers.

'B' Specials A Protestant military force formed in 1920 to supplement the police in ensuring that the Protestant ascendancy would remain.

Comhaltas Ceoltoiri Éireann Association of Irish Musicians.

Conradh na Gaelige Gaelic League which encourages the speaking of Irish.

Croppy A derogatory term for Irish nationalists originating from the rebellion of 1798 when the Irish sympathizers were referred to as 'croppies' because of their cropped hairstyle.

Cumann Lúthchleas Gael Gaelic Athletic Association for the promotion of Irish sports.

Cumann na Gaedhael Forerunner of the political party Fine Gael.

Cumman Local political party branch.

Easter Lily A badge in the form of a lily worn to honour the 1916 Easter Rising.

Fáinne A ring or badge worn to denote an Irish speaker.

FCA *Fórsa Cosanta Aitiúl,* the local defence force of the Twenty-six Counties.

Feiseanna, fleadhanna Festivals of Irish music and dance.

Fenian Now a derogatory term for an Irish person, taking its name from the Fenian nationalists of the nineteenth century.

Free State The Twenty-six Counties from 1922 to 1937 when the name changed to *Éire.*

GAA *see Cumann Lúthchleas Gael*

Gaelic League Founded in 1893, organized Irish lessons and promoted the language, music and games, becoming a major element in the nationalist movement.

Gaeltacht Irish-speaking area.

Galltacht English-speaking area.

GPO General Post Office, in Dublin, occupied by the revolutionary forces as a focal point of the 1916 Rising.

Guildford Four Sentenced to life imprisonment in 1974 for their alleged part in the Guildford/Woolwich bombings. Wrongfully accused, on no hard evidence and despite claims by another group that they had set the bomb, they were not released until 1989 after fifteen years in prison.

Internment The holding of suspected terrorists without trial in Northern Ireland. Used in 1922, 1939, 1956 and 1971–5, internment has only ever been used against republicans, never against unionist extremists.

Irish Republican Brotherhood (IRB) A revolutionary secret society dedicated to establishing an Irish Republic by force. It was first known as the Fenians and organized a rising in 1867. It was reorganized as the IRB in 1873, planned the 1916 Rising and reorganized the Volunteers into the IRA in 1918 to 1919. Under Michael Collins' influence it supported the Treaty and ceased to have much influence after his death.

Maguire Seven Again on shaky evidence, the Maguire Seven, an Irish family living in England, were found guilty of possessing nitroglycerine and were linked to the Guildford bombings. Like the Birmingham Six and the Guildford Four, they continually asserted their innocence, but were not released until 1985.

Mother and Child Scheme A scheme for free medical treatment for pregnant women and children up to the age of sixteen, proposed by the then Minister for Health Dr. Noel Browne, in 1950–1 in the Republic. The Catholic hierarchy was outraged, stating that it was contrary to Church teaching for the state to provide for the healthcare of individuals, and called for Browne's resignation. The controversy provided an insight into Church–State relations at the time and fuelled unionist fears of 'Home rule being Rome rule.'

NICRA Northern Ireland Civil Rights Association. Established in January 1968, it spearheaded the early years of the civil rights campaign.

Orange Order Founded in 1795 during Protestant–Catholic clashes over land, it was dedicated to maintaining Protestant supremacy and the link with Britain. No Catholic and no-one whose close relatives are Catholic may be a member. It played an important part in defeating Home Rule. After partition, the Unionist Party developed from the order, while the 'B' Specials were almost exclusively 'orangemen.' As well as being effective in mobilizing the Protestant masses, it has had close links with the British Conservative Party.

Republican Congress Initiated by Peadar O'Donnell, George Gilmore and Michael Price, the Republican Congress of 1934 was an attempt to unite republicans, socialists and trade unionists in an anti-imperialist front. Many later fought with the International Brigade in Spain.

RUC Royal Ulster Constabulary. The Six County police force.

SAS Special Air Services. Elite undercover unit of the British army, trained to shoot to kill. Best remembered for their killing of three unarmed IRA members in Gibraltar in 1988.

Section 31 of the Broadcasting Act, 1960 Renewable every year. Forbade the media from transmitting interviews with Sinn Féin spokespersons. Not renewed in 1994.

Shoneen, Seoinín toady.

Slógadh Gathering.

Taig Derogatory term for nationalist.

Three Fs Fair rent, fixity of tenure and freedom for tenants to sell their holdings. Aims of agrarian reformers in the latter half of the nineteenth century, beginning with the Tenant League and then the National Land League, organized by Michael Davitt and C. S. Parnell, and also the Ladies Land League.

Twelfth of July Commemoration of the Battle of the Boyne every year by the Orange Order, the 'marching' or 'silly season.' More than parades and pageants, this is a time when unionist fervour is at its height and clashes occur regularly with Catholics.

UDA Ulster Defence Association. The Protestant paramilitary organization.

Údarás na Gaeltachta Authority for the economic, industrial and cultural development of the *Gaeltachta* (Irish-speaking areas).

UDR Ulster Defence Regiment. A part-time reserve force, its membership drawn initially from disbanded 'B' Specials.

UVF Ulster Volunteer Force founded in 1912 as a private army to resist Home Rule and armed with 25,000 German rifles. Many members of the UVF enlisted in the British army and served in a separate unit, the 36th (Ulster Division). In the late 1920s, the UVF was involved in pogroms and other attacks on Catholics. The name was revived in 1966 by a loyalist sectarian paramilitary group which murdered two Catholics in that year and later planted the bombs that led to the fall of O'Neill. It remains in existence as a loyalist paramilitary organization.

Glossary of names

Ashe, Thomas Writer, musician, teacher and republican. Leader of the IRB after the 1916 Rising in which he commanded a successful action in Co. Meath. In 1917, his death on hunger strike in pursuit of political status rallied mass support for national independence.

Casement, Roger Knighted in 1911 for his service to the British Crown. Joined the Volunteers in 1913 and organized arms for the Rising. Hanged by the British in 1916.

Collins, Michael Member of the Volunteers in the 1916 Rising, Minister of Home Affairs and later Minister of Finance in the First Dáil, and director of organization and intelligence for the IRA. One of the signatories of the Anglo-Irish Treaty of 1921 and subsequently Commander-in-Chief of the government forces in the Civil War. Killed in an ambush in 1922.

Connolly, James Founded the Irish Socialist Republican Party in 1896. Worked in the US as an organizer for the Industrial Workers of the World (IWW) and Belfast organizer of the Irish Transport and General Workers' Union (ITGWU) from 1911 to 1913. Involved in the Dublin lock-out of 1913 and in the formation of the Irish Citizen Army, a workers' defence force. He was in the vanguard of the struggle against imperialism and joined with revolutionary nationalists in the 1916 Rising, being one of the signatories of the Proclamation. Wounded in the Rising, he was executed by the British authorities.

Craig, William Minister of Home Affairs in the Six Counties 1963–4, Minister of Health and Local Government 1964, Minister of Development 1965, and Minister of Home Affairs again in 1966–8. Established the Ulster Vanguard Party in 1972 with strong support from paramilitaries.

De Valera, Eamon Commandant in the Irish Volunteers in the 1916 Rising, he was sentenced to death but was reprieved, becoming President of Sinn Féin in 1917 and President of the Dáil in 1919. Opposed the Treaty and was the political leader of the anti-Treaty forces in the Civil War of 1922–3. Founded Fianna Fáil in 1926 and was Prime Minister 1932–48, 1951–4, 1957–9 and President of the Twenty-six Counties 1959–73.

Drumm, Maire Acting President of Provisional Sinn Féin 1971–2 and Vice-President 1972–6.

Faulkner, Brian Unionist MP for East Down at Stormont 1949–73, Minister of Home Affairs 1959–63, Minister of Commerce 1963–9, Minister of Development 1969–71, Prime Minister 1971–2. Set up breakaway Unionist Party of Northern Ireland in 1974. Chief Executive of Northern Ireland Executive in 1974.

Hyde, Douglas Scholar, professor of modern languages, collector of folklore, poetry and song, translator. First President of the Gaelic League 1893 and first Professor of Modern Irish, University College Dublin. Free State Senator 1925–6, and first President of the Twenty-six Counties 1937–45.

Kitson, General Frank Served in Kenya, Malaya and Cyprus before commanding the 39th Infantry Brigade in the Six Counties 1970–2. Developed British army strategy of psychological warfare and counter subversion. Author of *Low-Intensity Operations*.

Lalor, James Fintan Fighter in the cause of agrarian reform, Lalor later edited the *Irish Felon*, newspaper of the Young Irelanders.

Larkin, James Great syndicalist and agitator, founder of the Irish Transport and General Workers' Union (ITGWU) and leader of the Dublin workers in the 1913 lock-out. His absence and later imprisonment in America removed him from the scene of Irish working-class politics at a crucial stage and after his return in 1923 he was never again the same towering force.

Lemass, Sean Member of the Volunteers in the 1916 Rising, founder member of Fianna Fáil, Minister for Industry and Commerce 1932–9, 1941–8, 1951–4, Minister for Supplies 1939–45, Deputy Prime Minister 1945–8, 1951–4, 1957–9, and Prime Minister 1959–66.

Mac Donagh, Thomas Poet and teacher, he helped found Pearse's bilingual school in 1908. Member of the IRB military council set up to plan the Rising, signed the 1916 Proclamation and was executed by the British.

Mac Swiney, Terence Author of plays, poetry and political journalism and of *Principals of Freedom*, and full-time organizer of the Irish Volunteers. Elected to first Dáil for West Cork, and then Lord Mayor of Cork. He was arrested in Cork City Hall in 1920 and his subsequent hunger strike focused world attention on Ireland. He died on the seventy-fourth day of his hunger strike in Brixton Prison.

Mellows, Liam Leader of the Galway Volunteers in the 1916 Rising and a member of the First Dáil, he was shot without trial while a prisoner of the Free State forces in 1922.

O'Neill, Terence Six County Minister for Finance 1956–63, and Prime Minister 1963–9.

Paisley, Ian (Revd) Loyalist demagogue who, in 1951, set up a 'Free Presbyterian Church.' From this base he attacked the civil rights campaign, the so-called 'Romeward trend' of the Presbyterian Church and the 'treachery' of the unionist leaders who met with many Twenty-six County politicians. MP for North Antrim since 1970, he founded the Democratic Unionist Party in 1971.

Pearse, Patrick Educationalist, writer and revolutionary, founder of a bilingual school, member of the IRB, he was Commander-in-Chief of the forces of the Irish Republic in the 1916 Rising. One of the signatories of the Proclamation, he was President of the Provisional Government and was executed by the British.

Glossary of place names

Catholic areas of West Belfast:
Andersonstown, Ardoyne, Ballymurphy, Divis Flats, Falls Road, Longstone Road, Turf Lodge, Unity Flats, Woodvale

Protestant area of Belfast:
Shankill Road

Catholic area of Derry:
Bogside

Chronology

12th Century Norman conquest of Ireland.

1541 Henry VIII declared King of Ireland.

1601 The Irish and their Spanish reinforcements defeated by the English at the Battle of Kinsale, which marked the end of the old Irish world.

1607 'Flight of the Earls'. Voluntary exile of leading lords of Ulster.

1608–10 Plantation of confiscated lands in Ulster by mainly Scottish settlers.

1690 Protestant William of Orange defeats Catholic King James II at the Battle of the Boyne.

1720 Act of Parliament allowing for Westminster to legislate for Ireland.

1791 The publication of *Argument on Behalf of the Catholics* by Protestant Wolfe Tone, seeking Catholic emancipation.

Society of United Irishmen founded. Its members strove to change public opinion and argued for electoral and parliamentary reform and swore to obtain Catholic emancipation.

1795 Foundation of the Orange Society (later, Order).

1798 Rising by the United Irishmen, aided by French soldiers. Wolfe Tone arrested and sentenced to death for his part in the organization of the rebellion.

1801 Act of Union whereby Ireland becomes part of England.

1823 Catholic Association founded.

1829 Catholic Emancipation. Restrictions on Catholics from taking their place in parliament removed.

1840 Repeal Association founded for the repeal of the Act of Union.

1842 First issue of the *Nation* by Young Irelanders.

1845–9 Famine following blight of potato. In this period the population of Ireland is depleted by over two million through starvation, disease or emigration.

1848 Young Ireland rising in attempt to win self-government for the Irish.

1850 Founding of Irish Tenant League with the aim of achieving fair rent, fixity of tenure and freedom for tenant to sell their holding (the 'Three Fs').

1858 The Irish Republican Brotherhood, the Fenians, founded by former Young Ireland members. This revolutionary movement's aim was to be independent of Britain, using physical force to achieve this aim.

1867 Failed rising of the Fenians. Overhaul of the movement.

1867 Disestablishment of the Protestant Church of Ireland.

1870 Home Rule movement formed, seeking to achieve control for the Irish over their own local government affairs.

1873 Home Rule League formed. Won more than half the Irish seats in the 1874 election.

1875 Charles Stewart Parnell returned to parliament as a member of the Irish Parliamentary Party.

1876 *Clan na Gael*, an Irish-American group raising funding and support for Irish independence, joins with IRB.

1879 Irish National Land League founded. Parnell elected president of League whose principal aim was agrarian land reform based on the Three Fs.

1879–82 The 'Land War'.

1881 Land Act lessening power of the landlords, in effect the granting of the 'Three F's.'

1884 Gaelic Athletic Association formed to revive Irish games.

1886 Gladstone's Home Rule Bill defeated in the House of Commons.

1890 Split in Irish Party over Parnell's leadership.

1891 Death of Parnell.

1892 Ulster Unionist Convention in Belfast, attended by 12,000 unionists opposing Home Rule.

National Literary Society formed in Dublin by Yeats and Hyde.

First socialist party founded in Ireland, the Belfast Labour party.

1893 Introduction of second Home Rule Bill.

Conradh na Gaelige, the Gaelic League, set up by Douglas Hyde and Eoin MacNeill, taking its place in the Anglo-Irish literary revival. Primary aim of the League is to restore Irish as the primary spoken language in Ireland.

1896 James Connolly forms Irish Republican Socialist Party.

1900 *Cumann na nGaedhael* formed by Arthur Griffith.

1905 Republican Dungannon Clubs founded in Belfast.

1906 Arthur Griffith founds and edits the first issue of *Sinn Féin.*

1907 Dock Strike in Belfast, led by James Larkin, turns into lock-out and lasts four months.

Sinn Féin League formed from *Cumann na nGaedhael* and Dungannon Clubs. The league proposed a dual monarchy for Ireland and Britain, declaring the Act of Union to be illegal.

1908 Sinn Féin organization contests its first by-election.

1912 January—Home Rule Bill passed by the House of Commons.

September—Over 450,000 people sign the Ulster Covenant to pledge their resistance to the introduction of Home Rule.

1913 Ulster Volunteer Force set up to protest Home Rule; arms running from Germany and a provisional government formed for the day that Home Rule would be introduced.

Great lock-out in Dublin organized by James Larkin and the Irish Transport and General Workers' Union. Citizen Army formed to protect strikers.

1914 Home Rule Act suspended for duration of First World War.

1916 Easter Rising and Declaration of the Irish Republic by the Provisional Government.

Leaders of Rising executed.

1918 Sinn Féin wins seventy-three seats in election.

1919–21 War of Independence (or Black and Tan War) between the Irish Volunteers and the British 'black and tans' and Auxiliaries.

1919 Sinn Féin calls first Dáil Éireann.

Irish Volunteers become known as the IRA, Sinn Féin outlawed.

1920 Government of Ireland Act allowing for two parliaments in Ireland, one in Dublin and one in Belfast.

1921 Anglo-Irish Treaty granting dominion status to Twenty-six Counties.

1921–3 Irish Civil War between those accepting and those against the 1921 Treaty.

1922 IRA declared illegal by Northern Irish parliament.

Saorstát Éireann (Irish Free State) comes into being.

1925 An agreement between the parliaments of the Irish Free State, Britain and Northern Ireland to keep the border with Northern Ireland.

1927 Fianna Fáil party founded in Dublin.

1936 IRA declared illegal in the Irish Free State.

1937 New Constitution of *Éire*. Articles 2 and 3 lay claim to the Six Counties.

1939 IRA begins bombing campaign in England.

1939–45 *Éire* remains neutral in the Second World War.

1949 *Éire* becomes a republic. UK Act recognizes the Republic of Ireland but declares that Northern Ireland will remain part of the UK unless N.I. parliament decides otherwise.

1954 Flags and Emblems Act of Northern Ireland forbidding the display of flags other than the Union Jack.

1956–62 IRA bombing campaign in Northern Ireland.

1966 UVF outlawed.

1967 Northern Ireland Civil Rights Association (NICRA) formed.

1968 Marches and demonstrations all over Northern Ireland to protest at injustices by the state against Catholics. Clashes between marchers and police.

1969 Ulster Defence Force (UDF) formed.

British troops arrived in Northern Ireland.

1970 Sinn Féin and IRA split into Official and Provisional IRA.

'B' Specials disbanded, Social Democratic and Labour Party (SDLP) founded in Northern Ireland.

1971 Internment (the holding of suspected IRA members without trial) introduced.

Democratic Unionist Party formed by Ian Paisley.

Section 31 of Broadcasting Act, 1960, implemented in the Republic.

1972 'Bloody Sunday.' Thirteen demonstrators at a banned civil rights march shot dead by British army soldiers in Derry.

Fall of Stormont, the Northern Irish parliament. Northern Ireland now ruled directly by Westminster.

IRA resumed bombing campaign in Britain.

1973 Ireland and UK joined EEC.

1974 In Birmingham, six Irish people protesting their innocence were jailed for bombs which killed twenty-one people, and were finally released in 1991.

1975 Ending of internment.

1976 NICRA called off Rent and Rate strike.

Peace People formed in Northern Ireland.

1980 Internment law repealed. Republican prisoners started hunger strike in H Block in the Maze prison (Long Kesh) as part of protest over right to recognition as political prisoners, and, thus, the right to wear their own clothes.

1981 Ten republican prisoners died on hunger strike in the Maze prison, including Bobby Sands M.P.

1985 Anglo-Irish Agreement, reiterating that, as long as the majority in Northern Ireland so wish it, Northern Ireland shall remain part of the UK.

Also available from Roberts Rinehart Publishers

Falls Memories: A Belfast Life
Gerry Adams $10.95 paperback

This nostalgic and very personal account of a working-class Irish community abounds with light-hearted humour.

'An interesting and indeed important addition to the understanding of the ingredients that coalesced to lead to the long years of violence in this part of the world.' *The Derry Journal*

The IRA: A History
Tim Pat Coogan $27.95 hardcover

'...the standard reference work on the subject...' *The New York Times*

'No student of Irish history can afford to ignore this book. No scholar is likely to improve upon it...A fascinating book, of the greatest possible value to us all.' *The Times Literary Supplement*

The Man Who Made Ireland: The Life and Death of Michael Collins
Tim Pat Coogan $24.95 hardcover, $14.95 paperback

'Superb...this will be a hard Life to beat.' *The Times Literary Supplement*

'Thanks to *The Man Who Made Ireland*, readers here can get the full story of this good-humoured patriot...[a] heroic account.' *The New York Times Book Review*

To order any of the above please call the toll free number or order from the address below. Send payment with order (check, VISA, Mastercard) and include $3 for postage and handling for each order.

Roberts Rinehart publishes a number of titles of Irish interest. To receive further information and to be put on our mailing list, please write to us or telephone the toll free number below.

Roberts Rinehart Publishers
P. O. Box 666
Niwot, Colorado 80544   1 800 352 1985